Solutions for the End Times: Plans for Blessing As We Reach the End of the Age

Contributions from Pastor Caspar McCloud, Dr. Sherri Tenpenny, Derek Gilbert, Dr. Lee Merritt, Randy Conway, Dr. Carrie Madej, Carl Teichrib, Mark Sutherland, Dr. Ana Maria Mihalcea, Celeste Solum, and Dr. Mike Spaulding, Editor

All rights reserved. No part of this publication may be reproduced, distributed, or transmitted in any form or by any means, including photocopying, recording, or other electronic or mechanical methods, without the prior written permission of the author, except in the case of brief quotations embodied in critical reviews and certain other noncommercial use permitted by copyright law. For permission requests, write to the Editor at the address below.

The Transforming Word Publishing
PO Box 3007
Elida, OH 45807

Viewpoints expressed by the individual authors are not necessarily held by all others.

Cover – Darren Geisinger, Kings Custom Covers
www.kingscustomcovers.com

Scripture translations are an individual author's preference. No effort is made to revise all quotations for consistency among the authors.

Differences in style and spelling are attributable to the author's country of residence and language.

ISBN: 9798863289335

Solutions for the End Times

DEDICATION

This book is dedicated to the many men and women who have bravely risked everything to stand against the lies, wickedness, and evil, being perpetrated upon the earth. Their sacrifices for Christ, freedom, and liberty have had an enormous positive impact on many. Well done, good and faithful servants!

CONTENTS

	Acknowledgments	i
1	Only Jesus Can Set You Free From The Matrix	1
2	Choosing Freedom	78
3	Is It mRNA Or Something Else?	109
4	Establishing Your Borders	127
5	Hijacking The Soul	176
6	Solving Evil	186
7	Final Steps	218
8	Interview with Carrie Madej	305
9	Chaos on the Rampage	343
10	Apocalyptic Sojourner Of Faith	388
11	He Is Faithful To Forgive	433
12	Epilogue	441

ACKNOWLEDGMENTS

This book was born from the idea that what the world needs today, and every day is Jesus and the salvation that comes only through faith in Him. We do not need to allow fear or despair to mark these days. There are *solutions*. The authors understand the times in which we live and what needs to be done to combat the widespread deliberate deception and rising global tyranny fomented by the dragon of old.

CHAPTER 1

ONLY JESUS CAN SET YOU FREE FROM THE MATRIX

MARK SUTHERLAND

"This is your last chance."

"After this there is no turning back."

"You take the blue pill; the story ends, you wake up in your bed and believe whatever you want to believe."

"You take the red pill; you stay in Wonderland, and I show you how deep the rabbit hole goes."

"Remember; all I'm offering is the truth – nothing more."

Quotation from the film Matrix 1999 directed by the Wachowski brothers.[1]

I am sure most of you have heard the phrase 'red-pilled' used frequently across the media, a reference to the movie, Matrix. There are those who argue this often-quoted trope is used for nefarious purposes by conspiracy theorists, but we will leave that argument alone for now. It is accepted that the classic movie scene encompasses the idea that taking the red pill reveals the truth.

We can imagine the Wachowski brothers pitching their Matrix Trilogy to Warner Brothers: "The script is about a future, in which humanity is unknowingly trapped inside the Matrix, a simulated reality that intelligent machines have created to distract humans while using their bodies as an energy source. Neo, a computer hacker, uncovers the truth, and he, with others who have been set free from the Matrix, rebel against the Machines."

Next time I watch the Matrix I don't have to wear my tin foil hat because the predictive programming on steroids told the truth. Looking at all the events across the world since March 2020, there is no doubt that the predicted programming has been on full and spectacular view and continues to run full bore.

So, what is reality? What is truth? How can we understand the world in which we find ourselves living today? We must all work that out for ourselves. I have been on a long journey to find the answers to these questions and in doing so have paid a heavy personal price.

My grounding has always been my faith in Jesus Christ and that is something I am not willing to compromise. I believe that the Bible is the inspired and inerrant word of God. I also believe we need spiritual guidance and discernment to fully understand the nature of our lived experience and what God calls each one of us to do.

The Bible warns us of the forces at work in this world and teaches us what those forces are and how we should resist them.

Ephesians 6:10-20 (KJV)

[10] Finally, my brethren, be strong in the Lord, and in the power of his might. [11] Put on the whole armour of God, that ye may be able to stand against the wiles of the devil. [12] For we wrestle not against flesh and blood, but against principalities, against powers, against the rulers of the darkness of this world, against spiritual wickedness in high places. [13] Wherefore take unto you the whole armour of God, that ye may be able to withstand in the evil day, and having done all, to stand. [14] Stand therefore, having your loins girt about with truth, and having on the breastplate of righteousness; [15] And your feet shod with the preparation of the gospel of peace; [16] Above all, taking the shield of faith, wherewith ye shall be able to quench all the fiery darts of the wicked. [17] And take the helmet of salvation, and the sword of the Spirit, which is the word of God: [18] Praying always with all prayer and supplication in the Spirit, and watching thereunto with all perseverance and supplication for all saints; [19] And for me, that utterance may be given unto me, that I may open my mouth boldly, to make known the mystery of the gospel, [20] For which I am an ambassador in bonds: that therein I may speak boldly, as I ought to speak.

Throughout the Bible we are shown that humanity is

continually being led into rebellion against God by these principalities, powers, and rulers. This is the nature of the spiritual war.

Genesis 11:1-9 (KJV)

[1] And the whole earth was of one language, and of one speech. [2] And it came to pass, as they journeyed from the east, that they found a plain in the land of Shinar; and they dwelt there. [3] And they said one to another, Go to, let us make brick, and burn them thoroughly. And they had brick for stone, and slime had they for morter. [4] And they said, Go to, let us build us a city and a tower, whose top may reach unto heaven; and let us make us a name, lest we be scattered abroad upon the face of the whole earth. [5] And the Lord came down to see the city and the tower, which the children of men builded. [6] And the Lord said, Behold, the people is one, and they have all one language; and this they begin to do: and now nothing will be restrained from them, which they have imagined to do. [7] Go to, let us go down, and there confound their language, that they may not understand one another's speech. [8] So the Lord scattered them abroad from thence upon the face of all the earth: and they left off to build the city. [9] Therefore is the name of it called Babel; because the Lord did there confound the language of all the earth: and from thence did the Lord scatter them abroad upon the face of all the earth.

Throughout all of world history, the spiritual war has evolved and shifted. The principalities and powers have morphed into the geo-political players of our modern era. Now, the Tower of Babel is being rebuilt again in readiness for global top-down rule.

Politics is a spiritual battleground. Politics along with all the institutions that we have held dear, that we thought were firm in their thinking of absolute right and wrong (biblical truth) and were safely managed within our Christian constitutions and national heritage, have been plundered by left-wing Marxist ideology. The Frankfurt School[2] to Saul Alinsky to the Fabian Society[3], among other influences, have sown the seeds of rot over many decades and 'we the people' have been asleep at the wheel. The smoke and mirrors are real.

In March 2020 I had flown out from the United Kingdom to Dallas, Texas, to attend the *Hear the Watchmen* conference. My trips to the United States since 2017 have always been a blessing because of the people I would meet. March of 2020 was no exception – seeing old friends and completely life-changing because of the new friendships I made.

When I flew out, the Covid 'pandemic' narrative was playing in the background. The whole wet-market bat discussion was out of the gate. Herd immunity was being talked about by President Donald Trump and British Prime Minister Boris Johnson. It was all background noise via the mainstream media. Everyone was just getting on with their lives.

The US is, in my opinion, the centre of the 'truther' movement. In 2010, having chosen the red pill myself, I had woken up to what was really playing out in the temporal world. Since then, my friends in the US and Canada – like-minded people – have become extremely important to me.

I would fly into Dallas for a long weekend, arriving on a Thursday and flying out the following Monday back to the UK, a nine-thousand-mile round trip. It's not about me but, as my dear friend, Carl Teichrib, Author of *Game of Gods* (who has also contributed to this book) once said to me, I had taken the time and put in the effort to seek out the truth. He is right; I did so because I became hungry for truth.

Before my awakening in 2010 I had been trying to fit into 'church' in the UK. Sadly, all the bad church movements had invaded. Rick Warren; the purpose-driven drivel. Bill Hybels, founding pastor of Willow Creek Ministries with their failed seeker sensitive approach, who has been quoted as saying "we should have spent all our ministry money encouraging people to read the Bible for themselves". The introduction of Hillsong worship songs which offer no spiritual depth. The Toronto movement; manifesting 'Holy Spirit' barking dogs! And then; the important question once asked by a friend of mine who worked with a well-known UK evangelical leader, Colin Urquhart: "How has the charismatic movement impacted the country?"

My international family is a lifeline to me. Mobile app technology allows me to make international calls easily to the US and Canada and I have spent a lot of time on hands-free kits, earbuds in, talking to my family across the pond, praying as I was driving around London; praying, for example, with a dear friend who was running for political office in the US. This contact and the continued connections I enjoy with my international family are all very important to me as I have found a group of people who are on the same page.

I flew back from the US into the UK in March 2020 with 'herd immunity' in my ears and then it began.

With Love – A Message From My Heart

I write, not as an expert in any field but as a commentator; as a keen observer of current world events; as someone with a passion for studying history; as a bible-believing Christian; as a true patriot abroad.

Do I always get things absolutely right? Of course not, but I believe we must look back in history, and even though some of what is written may not, at first glance, have anything to do directly with American history, politics or current events, may I respectfully say we are all linked in this global need for awakening and awareness. America has been accused of being isolationist at points in her history, but America has been used and 20th and early 21st Century history reflects that.

We are in the biggest spiritual battle of our lives and I, like many others, never expected to live through a time such as this; but here we are, at an unprecedented time in history, and we all need each other like never before. If we are to believe what our Bible teaches, then we have to believe we are all here at this time by God's planning.

I may not have the solutions fully worked out as to how we move forward in these last days but move forward we must. Am I date setting? I certainly am not. Will I get caught up in pre-trib, post-trib, pan-trib, let's-see-how-it-will-all-pan-out-now debate? No, I won't. I am not in favour of ending communication with people because they do not hold the same Biblical world view of how the end time events roll out. It must stop. We all need to respect each other's views.

But let's be frank. I am as frustrated as some others that many who call themselves Christians do not see what is going on in the world. The past three years should have been a clarion moment in the Christian body but so many have lacked the discernment to avoid taking a loosely tested pharmaceutical vaccine. This, for me, has been a real 'wheat and tares' moment, and I speak from experience.

Covid-19 – The Tyranny Begins

Professor Neil Ferguson, of Imperial College infamy, had calculated figures suggesting that two million people would die in the US of the Covid-Novid-Plandemic if herd immunity was adopted as the preferred method of controlling this virus. UK Prime Minister Boris Johnson was told that 250,000 people would die in the UK. The argument for herd immunity was thrown out.

According to *The Mailonline* (29th March 2020), Professor Neil Ferguson, Director of the MRC for Global Infectious Disease Analysis at Imperial College London, authored a report which forecast that terrible death toll if nothing was done to stop the spread of disease.

Imperial College computer modelling confirmed that letting the virus infect two thirds of the UK population to build up herd immunity would result in 250,000 deaths and may even reach 500,000.

In contrast, the model that Professor Ferguson put forward in support of a hard lockdown found the figures dramatically reduced to 20,000 deaths. A separate group had come up with figures of 5,700 deaths – a significant reduction compared to 250,000 potential UK deaths.

Ferguson's conclusion caused Prime Minister Boris Johnson to change his mind about letting the virus run its course through the population and rely on herd immunity. This resulted in a dramatic U-turn in policy. Schools and businesses were closed, and the hard lockdown came in. People were told to stay at home.

Ferguson's track record on the accuracy of his computer modelling was questioned when Professor Michael Thrusfield, Chair of Veterinary Epidemiology at Edinburgh University, reminded us of Ferguson's modelling during the UK's 2001 Foot and Mouth outbreak when more than six million animals were culled resulting in the devastation of the rural communities across the UK.

In the US, Dr Anthony Fauci, Director of the National Institute for Allergy and Infectious Disease (NIAID) and the primary US government spokesman, promoted Ferguson's modelling of two million deaths and the US was also shut down.

Flying to the US was now impossible. Airlines were closed. President Trump suspended all flights. It was a gut-punch.

President Trump had been conned by Fauci.

It was later pointed out to me on a UK government website that Covid-19 had been down-graded as early as March 2020 from a highly infectious disease to a not so highly infectious disease where it stated:

> "As of 19th March 2020, Covid-19 is no longer considered to be a high consequence infectious disease (HCID) in the UK."

"'The four nations' public health HCID group made an interim recommendation in January 2020 to classify Covid-19 as an HCID. This was based on consideration of the UK HCID criteria about the virus and the disease with information available during the early stages of the outbreak. Now that more is known about Covid-19, the public health bodies in the UK have reviewed the most up to date information about Covid-19 against the UK HCID criteria. They have determined that several features have now changed; in particular, more information is available about mortality rates (low overall), and there is now greater clinical awareness and a specific and sensitive laboratory test, the availability of which continues to increase."

"The Advisory Committee on Dangerous Pathogens (ACDP) is also of the opinion that Covid-19 should no longer be classified as an HCID."

"The need to have a national, coordinated response remains, but this is being met by the government's Covid-19 response."

"Cases of Covid-19 are no longer managed by HCID treatment centres only. All healthcare workers managing possible and confirmed cases should follow the updated national infection and prevention (IPC) guidance for Covid-

19 (www.gov.uk/government/publications/wuhan-novel-coronavirus-infection-prevention-and-control), which supersedes all previous IPC guidance for Covid-19. This guidance includes instructions about different personal protective equipment PPE ensembles that are appropriate for different clinical scenarios."

Source quoted above: *http://www.gov.uk/topic/health-protection/infectious-diseases* (Published 22nd October 2018 updated 21st March 2020)

Prime Minister Boris Johnson's Speech to the United Nations on 24th September 2019

British Prime Minister Boris Johnson gave the following speech to the United Nations on the 24th of September 2019. Please note the anti-vaxxer comment; a trope that he was to repeat on British TV. (See emphasis below).

"Mr. President, Your Excellencies, Ladies and Gentlemen, faithful late-night audience."

"It is customary for the British Prime Minister to come to this United Nations and pledge to advance our values and defend our rules, the rules of a peaceful world, from protecting freedom of navigation in the Gulf to persevering in the vital task of achieving a two-state solution to the conflict in the Middle East and of course I am proud to do all of these things."

"But no-one can ignore a gathering force that is reshaping the future of every member of this Assembly."

"There has been nothing like it in history".

When I think of the great scientific revolutions of the past -

print, the steam engine, aviation, the atomic age - I think of new tools that we acquired but over which we - the human race - had the advantage, which we controlled.

"That is not necessarily the case in the digital age."

"You may keep secrets from your friends, from your parents, your children, your doctor – even your personal trainer – but it takes real effort to conceal your thoughts from Google.

"And if that is true today, in future there may be nowhere to hide."

"Smart cities will pullulate with sensors, all joined together by the "internet of things", bollards communing invisibly with lamp posts, so there is always a parking space for your electric car, so that no bin goes unemptied, no street unswept, and the urban environment is as antiseptic as a Zurich pharmacy."

"But this technology could also be used to keep every citizen under round-the-clock surveillance. A future Alexa will pretend to take orders, but this Alexa will be watching you, clucking her tongue and stamping her foot."

"In the future, voice connectivity will be in every room and almost every object: your mattress will monitor your nightmares; your fridge will beep for more cheese, your front door will sweep wide the moment you approach, like some silent butler; your smart meter will go hustling - of its accord - for the cheapest electricity, and every one of them minutely transcribing your every habit in tiny electronic shorthand, stored not in their chips or their innards - nowhere you can find it, but in some great cloud of data that looms ever more oppressively over the human race; a giant dark thundercloud waiting to burst and we have no control over how or when the precipitation will take place."

"And every day that we tap on our phones or work on our ipads - as I see some of you doing now - we not only leave our indelible spoor in the ether, but we are ourselves becoming a resource; click by click, tap by tap."

"Just as the carboniferous period created the indescribable wealth - leaf by decaying leaf - of hydrocarbons, data is the crude oil of the modern economy, and we are now in an environment where we don't know who should own these new oil fields. We don't always know who should have the rights or the title to these gushers of cash and we don't know who decides how to use that data."

"Can these algorithms be trusted with our lives and hopes? Should the machines - and only the machines - decide whether we are eligible for a mortgage or insurance or what surgery or medicines we should receive? Are we doomed to a cold and heartless future in which computer says yes - or computer says no - with the grim finality of an emperor in the arena?"

"How do you plead with an algorithm? How do you get it to see the extenuating circumstances and how do we know that the machines have not been insidiously programmed to fool us or even to cheat us?"

"We already use all kinds of messaging services that offer instant communication at minimal cost. The same programmes, platforms, could also be designed for real-time censorship of every conversation, with offending words automatically deleted, indeed in some countries this happens today. Digital authoritarianism is not, alas, the stuff of dystopian fantasy but of an emerging reality."

"The reason I am giving this speech today is that the UK is one of the world's tech leaders - and I believe governments have been simply caught unawares by the unintended consequences of the internet; a scientific breakthrough more far-reaching in its everyday psychological impact than any other invention since Gutenberg and when you consider how long it took for books to come into widespread circulation, the arrival of the internet is far bigger than print. It is bigger than the atomic age, but it is like nuclear power in that it is capable of both good and harm - but of course it is not alone."

"As new technologies seem to race towards us from the far horizon, we strain our eyes as they come, to make out whether they are for good or bad - friends or foes? AI - what will it mean? Helpful robots washing and caring for an ageing population or pink eyed terminators sent back from the future to cull the human race?"

"What will synthetic biology stand for - restoring our livers and our eyes with miracle regeneration of the tissues, like some fantastic hangover cure or will it bring terrifying limbless chickens to our tables. Will nanotechnology help us to beat disease, or will it leave tiny robots to replicate in the crevices of our cells?"

"It is a trope as old as literature that any scientific advance is punished by the Gods. When Prometheus brought fire to mankind – in a tube of fennel, as you may remember, that Zeus punished him by chaining him to a tartarean crag while his liver was pecked out by an eagle and every time his liver regrew the eagle came back and pecked it again, and this went on for ever - a bit like the experience of Brexit in the UK, if some of our parliamentarians had their way."

"In fact, it was standard poetic practice to curse the protos heuretes - the person responsible for any scientific or technical breakthrough. If only they had never invented the ship, then Jason would never have sailed to Colchis and all sorts of disasters would never have happened and it is a deep human instinct to be wary of any kind of technical progress.

In 1829 they thought the human frame would not withstand the speeds attained by Stephenson's rocket."

"And there are today people today who are actually still anti-science. A whole movement called the anti-vaxxers, who refuse to acknowledge the evidence that vaccinations have eradicated smallpox and who by their prejudices are actually endangering the very children they want to protect, and I totally reject this anti-scientific pessimism."

"I am profoundly optimistic about the ability of new technology to serve as a liberator and remake the world wondrously and benignly. Indeed, in countless respects technology is already doing just that. Today, nanotechnology - as I mentioned earlier - is revolutionising medicine by designing robots a fraction of the size of a red blood cell, capable of swimming through our bodies, dispensing medicine and attacking malignant cells like some Star Wars armada. Neural interface technology is producing a new generation of cochlear implants, allowing the gift of hearing to people who would not otherwise be able to hear the voices of their children."

"A London technology company has worked out how to help the blind to navigate more freely with nothing more than an app on their smartphones – new technologies, produced in Britain, helping the deaf to hear and the blind to see."

"And we used to think that printing was something you did to run off a boarding card; now a British company has used 3D printing to make an engine capable of blasting a rocket into space."

"In African countries, millions of people without bank accounts can now transfer money using a simple app; they can buy solar energy and leap in one transaction from no electricity to green power and new advances are making renewable energy ever cheaper, aiding our common struggle against climate change."

"Our understanding of the natural world is being transformed by genome sequencing. The discovery of the very essence of life itself, the secret genetic code that animates the spirit of every living being and allows medical breakthroughs the like of which we have never known. Treatments tailored to the precise genetic makeup of the individual."

"So far, we have discovered the secrets of less than 0.3 percent of complex life on the planet; think what we will achieve when – and it is a matter of when – we understand 1 or 2 percent, let alone 5 or 10 percent."

"But how we design the emerging technologies behind these breakthroughs – and what values inform their design – will shape the future of humanity. That is my point to you tonight my friends, my Excellencies."

"At stake is whether we bequeath an Orwellian world, designed for censorship, repression and control, or a world of emancipation, debate and learning, where technology threatens famine and disease, but not our freedoms."

"Seven decades ago, this General Assembly adopted the Universal Declaration of Human Rights with no dissenting voices, uniting humanity for the first and perhaps only time behind one set of principles."

"And our declaration - our joint declaration - upholds 'freedom of opinion and expression', the 'privacy' of 'home or correspondence', and the right to 'seek…and impart information and ideas'."

"Unless we ensure that new technology reflects this spirit, I fear that our declaration will mean nothing and no longer hold."

"So, the mission of the United Kingdom and all who share our values must be to ensure that emerging technologies are designed from the outset for freedom, openness and pluralism, with the right safeguards in place to protect our peoples."

"Month by month, vital decisions are being taken in academic committees, company boardrooms and industry standards groups. They are writing the rulebooks of the future, making ethical judgements, choosing what will or will not be rendered possible."

"Together, we need to ensure that new advances reflect our values by design."

"There is excellent work being done in the EU, the Commonwealth, and of course the UN, which has a vital role in ensuring that no country is excluded from the wondrous benefits of this technology, and the industrial revolution it is bringing about but we must be still more ambitious."

"We need to find the right balance between freedom and control; between innovation and regulation; between private enterprise and government oversight. We must insist that the ethical judgements inherent in the design of new technology are transparent to all and we must make our voices heard more loudly in the standards bodies that write the rules."

"Above all, we need to agree a common set of global principles to shape the norms and standards that will guide the development of emerging technology."

"So - here's the good news - I invite you next year to a summit in London, a wonderful city, whereby the way it is not raining 94 per cent of the time, and where at one stage - when I was Mayor of London - we discovered that we had more Michelin starred restaurants even than Paris. The French somehow rapidly recovered - by a process that I wasn't quite sure was entirely fair. But we still have by far, in the UK, by far the biggest tech sector - fintech, biotech, meditech, nanotech, green tech - every kind of tech - in London - the biggest tech sector anywhere in Europe, perhaps half a million people working in tech alone."

"I hope you will come there, where we will seek to assemble the broadest possible coalition to take forward this vital task, building on all that the UK can contribute to this mission as a global leader in ethical and responsible technology."

"If we master this challenge – and I have no doubt that we can – then we will not only safeguard our ideals, but we will also surmount the limits that once constrained humanity and conquer the perils that once ended so many lives. Together, we can vanquish killer diseases, eliminate famine, protect the environment, and transform our cities."

"Success will depend, now as ever, on freedom, openness and pluralism, the formula that not only emancipates the human spirit, but releases the boundless ingenuity and inventiveness of mankind, and which, above all, the United Kingdom will strive to preserve and advance."

"Excellencies, Ladies and Gentlemen, thank you for your kind attention."

The Run-Up to Britain's Withdrawal from the EU and the 2019 General Election

Following the Brexit Referendum in June 2016, a date for The United Kingdom's withdrawal from the European Union was set for 31st January 2020. Prime Minister David Cameron resigned following the referendum and Theresa May took over as leader of the Conservative Party and Prime Minister in July 2016.

The Brexit referendum had caused major divisions within the UK. The Referendum was closely contested and hard fought. It had split families and communities. The voter turnout was high.

By late 2018 the member states of the EU had agreed the terms of the UK's withdrawal. It was now down to the British Parliament to vote to accept the withdrawal agreement and move the process toward completion in early 2020. The parliamentary vote in January 2019 resulted in the biggest defeat of any British government in the House of Commons. Two further votes in March resulted in similar large defeats for the government.

The Conservative government at the time only held a small majority following the disastrous snap-election called by Theresa May in 2017 to try and consolidate her mandate. Many of the Conservative Members of Parliament came from constituencies which were fiercely anti-Brexit as were many of the MPs themselves.

As a result of these three major defeats, Theresa May stepped down and Boris Johnson became leader of the Conservative Party and Prime Minister in July 2019. With deadlock in parliament and the withdrawal deadline looming, the decision was made to call another general election. It appeared to be a gamble for the Conservative government but on 12th December 2019 Boris Johnson and the Conservative Party won a landslide victory.

To achieve this victory the British public were told that supporting the Conservative government was the only sensible option to prevent splitting the vote, because if

Labour won the election, the withdrawal agreement would never pass the parliamentary vote and Britain would remain in Europe. There was plenty of political maneuvering creating heated debate but eventually the smaller pro-Brexit parties and independents chose not to contest some constituency seats and encouraged their supporters to vote Conservative.

Johnson had allegedly called the snap-election to "get Brexit done", a phrase he used throughout his election campaign. He said in his victory speech following the election "…getting Brexit done is now the irrefutable, irresistible, unarguable decision of the British people." Johnson and the Conservatives had just secured the biggest Tory win since Margaret Thatcher in 1979.

The Conservatives won the December 2019 election with an 80-seat majority, winning seats in Labour heartlands that had been held by the Labour Party for generations. Those wins were made possible by people abandoning a political ideology that had stood unquestioned within families for generations. This unquestioning support of the Labour Party by, mainly, the working-class people of Britain has been exploited for more than a century by the Labour movement. Suddenly traditional Labour Party voters could smell freedom from the European leg of global governance, and they voted Conservative in support of what they thought was going to provide them with the British version of life, liberty and the pursuit of happiness.

It was during the election of December 2019 that I first read Boris Johnson's speech to the United Nations. I was shocked that I had missed this and even more so after what rolled out.

Since June 2016, I, alongside fellow Brexiteers[4], felt we had been at war with civil servants and our elected representatives who did not want the UK to leave the EU. Was this the principalities, working through the powers, trying to stop the will of the people?

It is of added interest maybe that the general elections of 2017 and 2019 brought about by the events of Brexit changed the election cycle and avoided a general election being held in 2020. The next UK general election now must be held no later than January 2025 and will probably be held in the Autumn/Fall of 2024.

As I have often explained on the airwaves, in this nation, just because the Tories are officially referred to as the Conservative Party, it does not mean that the members of that party are, in fact, conservative by nature.

In the United States you have your RINOs (Republican in Name Only). Many senior members of our British Conservative Party also epitomize the wolf in sheep's clothing and have blatantly supported such policies as, for example, the adoption of children by gay couples. The chameleon nature of our politicians is perfectly illustrated by Conservative ex-Prime Minister Theresa May changing her mind after voting against gay adoption in 2002. In 2010 she became Equalities Minister and Home Secretary under Prime Minister David Cameron in his coalition government with the Liberal Democrats. By accepting this government office, she had to uphold policy in support of the very thing she had previously voted against. Double-mindedness?

It must also be noted that when Theresa May became Prime Minister in 2016 following the resignation of David Cameron, those of us who had voted to leave the EU felt that government under her leadership was doing whatever it could to stall the Brexit process.

The 'Deep State', the 'Shadow Government' – both phrases have entered our lexicon on steroids.

When the UK voted to leave the EU on 23rd June 2016, the war of words had been bloody and, accepting things on face value, the fight between nation states and globalism was, in my opinion, out in the open to the lay-person like at no other time in recent history – the suspicion of the hidden hand was being revealed.

Theresa May's EU Advisor, Olly Robbins, a Civil Servant

In an article by Andrew Pierce in *The Daily Mail* (30th April 2018) there was a claim that Olly Robbins had defended the Soviet Union and expressed regret that, following the fall of the West's great nemesis, the Union of Soviet Socialist Republics (USSR), there was now no alternative to the excess of capitalism.

In my opinion, Olly Robbins is an interesting example of a civil service bureaucrat.

Robbins is now a former senior British civil servant, who served as Prime Minister Theresa May's advisor and chief Brexit negotiator from 2017 to 2019.

Many Brexiteers saw him as a controversial figure. Permanent Secretary at the Department for Exiting the

European Union, July 2016 to September 2017, June to July 2016 saw him as the Prime Ministers advisor on Europe and Global issues.

Before being involved in EU roles, he served as Principal Private Secretary to the Prime Minister, and second Permanent Secretary for the Home Office.

In his early career, Robbins joined HM Treasury in 1996. He served as Head of Corporate and Private Finance from 2003 to 2006 and then briefly as Head of Defence Diplomacy and Intelligence Finance.

In 2006, Robbins was appointed Principal Private Secretary to the Prime Minister at 10 Downing Street (the official residence of the British Prime Minister), replacing Ivan Rogers for the last part of Labour Prime Minister Tony Blair's administration and the start of Labour Prime Minister Gordon Brown's.

Robbins briefly served as Director of the Prime Minister's Office. He left to become the Director of Intelligence and Security and, later, the Director of Intelligence, Security and Resilience in the Cabinet Office.

In 2010, under the incoming Conservative Prime Minister David Cameron, Robbins' post was reformulated as the Deputy National Security Advisor, then being responsible for Intelligence, Security and Resilience. In this role Robbins negotiated with The Guardian newspaper on how to curtail its reporting of material leaked by Edward Snowden relating to the operations of the American CIA and British GCHQ.

When Robbins was at Oxford University studying Philosophy, Politics and Economics (PPE)[5] he was President of the Reform Club, a group promoting a Federal European Union. In January 2014, Robbins became Director-General, Civil Service at the Cabinet Office.

In 2015 Robbins moved to the Home Office to work alongside Mark Sedwill, (another powerful civil servant that leads us to think about our own 'shadow government'). Robbins was second Permanent Secretary having responsibility for immigration and free movement. This incorporated oversight of borders, immigration, and citizenship. At a Home Affairs Select Committee while in this role, Robbins was asked to leave as the committee deemed his answers unsatisfactory regarding the Border Force. He was asked to provide answers outside the hearing on the same day, which he did not do.

Robbins was appointed the head of the European and Global Issues Secretariat in July 2016. His role was to advise the Prime Minister on Britain's exit from the European Union. The secretariat became the Department for Exiting the European Union, and he became the Permanent Secretary.

In September 2017 Robbins moved from the Brexit Department to become Prime Minister Theresa May's personal Brexit advisor. Understandably, Brexiteers, questioned this relationship even though Robbins was praised by allies of the four Prime Ministers he served under (two Labour Party and two Conservative Party).

By looking at this one person's civil service career, at a vital moment in my country's recent history, I can't help but conclude it raises serious questions. I am reminded of the phrase, 'two wings of the same bird'. Although applied primarily to US politics, this concept can also be applied, in my opinion, to the UK political scene. It is the civil servants in Britain who form the body of this bird and wield the real power in government. They are the 'deep-state' operatives who all the politicians, no matter the party, rely on as advisors to get their policies implemented. The Uni-Party is in place on both sides of the pond.

From much of what has been written about Olly Robbins, he certainly gives the impression of having a Federal States of Europe mindset. If the government's true intention was to honour the wishes of the British people to leave the EU following the 2016 referendum, then was it appropriate to appoint him to negotiate the withdrawal? This has, understandably, led to personal criticism of Olly Robbins, as Brexiteer Conservative MPs referred to him as Theresa May's Rasputin.

In defence of Robbins, acting Cabinet Secretary Mark Sedwill wrote in The Times newspaper highlighting that civil servants implement the decisions of elected governments. Leigh Lewis, former Department for Work and Pensions Permanent Secretary, supported Mark Sedwill's comments, noting it was an occupational hazard for senior civil servants to be held responsible for the political decisions of ministers.

Members of the organisation, Veterans for Britain[6], which includes the former head of the British secret service[7] Richard Dearlove, commented that Robbins had serious questions of improper conduct to answer over defence and security cooperation between the United Kingdom and the European Union after Brexit.

After Prime Minister Theresa May's resignation in 2019, Robbins resigned to take up a post at Goldman Sachs investment banking division. He has moved on to the corporate intelligence company, Hakluyt, a global strategic advisory firm for business and investors. His role at Hakluyt at the time of writing is Head of Corporate Coverage for Europe, the Middle East and Africa.

As Varun Chandra, Hakluyt's managing partner commented: "I am confident that he will make a significant contribution to our firm as we continue to help leaders take better decisions."

It begs the question – what "better decisions"?

But here is another detail; when Robbins left the Civil Service, he took up a position with the Heywood Fellowship at the Blavatnik School of Government. On the home page of the Blavatnik School we read the following statements:

"Study Here. A world better led, better served and better governed."

"Educating leaders, communities around the world are yearning for better public leadership."

"Studying at the Blavatnik School of Government for a Master, a DPhil or any other course will help you develop the academic knowledge and hone the skills required to address some of this century's most complex public policy challenges."

"You will be learning from world class academics and expert practitioners and immerse yourself in a vibrant and diverse community of people committed to improving government policy."

"The Blavatnik School of Government teaches and convenes current and future leaders, through degree and executive programmes."

"Our diverse community covers over 120 countries. We are united by a mission: to build trust, to bridge divides, and to forge more effective institutions."

"We bring applied research to the big challenges facing governments and citizens."

"Our research takes multidisciplinary and collaborative approaches to identify and develop practical strategies for the issues facing policy makers. We draw on extensive intellectual networks both within Oxford and internationally to ensure we stay on the cutting edge" (Common Purpose/Julia Middleton anyone? The left-wing equivalent of the Masons).

The Heywood Fellowship was named after Jeremy Heywood, a British Civil Servant who was Cabinet Secretary to Conservative Prime Ministers Theresa May and David Cameron, 2012 to 2018, and Head of the Home Civil service from 2014 to 2018.

The Cabinet Secretary is the most senior Civil Servant in the United Kingdom and is based in the Cabinet Office. The role being the senior policy adviser to the Prime Minister and their

Cabinet and is the Secretary to the Cabinet being responsible to all ministers for the efficient running of the government.

Jeremy Heywood was the Principal Private Secretary to Labour Prime Ministers Tony Blair and Gordon Brown, from 1999 to 2003 and 2008 to 2010. He also served as Downing Street Chief of Staff and was the first Downing Street Permanent Secretary.

In 2003 Heywood left the civil service in the wake of the Hutton Inquiry. The Hutton Inquiry was a judicial inquiry in the UK surrounding the controversial circumstances surrounding the death of Dr. David Kelly, a biological warfare expert and former UN weapons inspector in Iraq.

The reason for Heywood's resignation from the Civil service was because it came to light that he said he did not minute the meetings in the Prime Ministers offices about David Kelly, and he was required to do so.

Heywood joined Morgan Stanley as a director of their Investment Banking Division.

Are we seeing a theme emerging here?

Gordon Brown became Prime Minister having taken over from Prime Minister Tony Blair amidst the legend of surreptitious agreement made between the two men in a restaurant in London in which they agree who would become Prime Minister first; the other taking the role of Chancellor of the Exchequer. At a future date the resignation of the Prime Minister would hand the post to the incumbent of the Chancellor's role. Blair became Prime Minister and Gordon

Brown was Chancellor of the Exchequer throughout the Blair premiership, overseeing the selling off of British gold reserves for knock-down prices, not taking the UK into the Euro (a good thing), and handing over the setting of interest rates to the Bank of England. Each of these events could merit a whole chapter of their own.

Jeremy Heywood retired on health grounds receiving a life peerage[8] and died on 4th November 2018.

The revolving door that we have on this side of the pond is an exact copy of the revolving door on the other side of the pond. Sometimes the routes are different, but a correlation appears to exist if we compare, for example, James Comey, Department of Justice rotating out to Lockheed Martin, HSBC, back as Director of the FBI and note that he took over from Robert Mueller.

Are we starting to see a common theme emerging here too?

The Johnsons – Boris And Stanley

Alexander Boris de Pfeffel Johnson. Born in New York City, USA, 1964; Politician, Writer, Journalist.

Boris Johnson was British Prime Minister and leader of the British Conservative Party from 2019 to 2022. Johnson was Foreign Secretary from 2016 to 2018. He served as Mayor of London from 2008 to 2016 and was the Member of Parliament for Uxbridge and Ruislip, elected 2015. Before becoming Mayor, he was the Member of Parliament for Henley 2001 to 2008.

Johnson attended Eton College public school[9], as did Prime

Minister David Cameron. Johnson studied Classics at Balliol College Oxford. He was elected President of the Oxford Union in 1986. (Ted Heath, British Prime Minister 1970 to 1974, also attended Balliol College, Oxford. It was under Ted Heath's premiership that Britain entered the Common Market which later morphed into the European Union. Ted Heath was a Jean Monnet Protégé and Jean Monnet was the founding father of the EU).

In 1989 Johnson became the Brussels correspondent for the Daily Telegraph newspaper and from 1999 to 2005 he was the editor of the Spectator magazine.

In 2001 Johnson was elected to Parliament and became a member of the Shadow Cabinet[10] of Michael Howard and then David Cameron.

In 2007 Boris Johnson wrote an article in *The Daily Telegraph* newspaper about his concerns for an overpopulated planet reflecting his father's concerns.

In 1982 Boris Johnson's father, Stanley Johnson, wrote a novel called *The Marburg Virus*. Stanley Johnson's books are about his environmental and population concerns. His 2015 novel called, simply, *The Virus* is a thriller about the rise of a mysterious virus and the fight to stop a pandemic.

In 1966 Stanley Johnson relocated to Washington DC where he worked for the World Bank. He then took a job with a policy panel on population control. Stanley Johnson would go on to do post-graduate research at the Fabian-founded London School of Economics, which led to Stanley Johnson working for the European Commission. The European

Commission is part of the non-elected governing executive of the European Union.

From 1979 to 1984 Stanley Johnson was Member of the European Parliament for the English constituency of Wight and Hampshire East.

For many years he had a weekly column in the G2 section of The Guardian newspaper, whose readership is generally considered to be on the mainstream left of British political opinion and typically stereotyped as having liberal, left-wing or politically correct views.

Iraq – Illusive Weapons of Mass Destruction – Dodgy Dossiers – Suicide and Judicial Inquiry

We remember images of Colin Powell and the vial of Anthrax. He held up the vial of white powder to illustrate Saddam Hussein's alleged use of Anthrax. The invasion of Iraq in 2003 was undertaken on the premise of weapons of mass destruction.

The neocons in their project of the New American Century explained that America needed a New Pearl Harbour, and their need was fulfilled in September 2001 – commonly referred to as 9/11.

Regime change became the new mantra. Powell's speech persuaded key members of the Security Council to get behind the invasion of Iraq. Questions were asked in Westminster (British Parliament) by a few dissenting voices concerning the validity of the evidence and the justification of the invasion, but those discerning voices were completely overrun. The British quickly fell into line.

The debates in the British Parliament were undertaken against a backdrop of public protest to the war on the streets of London with protester numbers reaching a million, but pushback by the British public was ignored by Tony Blair's Labour government.

When Tony Blair was British Prime Minister, he started his premiership with Bill and Hilary Clinton in the White House and that morphed into Dick Cheney and George Bush. From liberal left to, supposedly, Christian right. Christians sat back thinking one of us is in the Whitehouse – now we know differently.

Powell was selected to address the United Nations because, in the words of his former Chief of Staff, Lawrence Wilkerson, "he was the only member of the [Bush] administration Americans would believe". Source: www.thenationalnews.com *Revisiting Colin Powell's UN address that led to war in Iraq* (Adla Massoud 16th March 2023)

On the eve of the US led attack on Iraq in 2003, ordered by George Bush, by the time the UN weapons inspectors had been asked to leave the country they had still not found any chemical or biological weapons.

The well-respected British weapons inspector, Dr David Kelly, was found dead shortly after appearing at a parliamentary select committee.

The former head of the UK's Defence Microbiology Division

working from one of Britain's Chemical and Biological Research Centres at Porton Down in the county of Wiltshire, Kelly was appointed to the United Nations Special Commission in 1991 as one of its chief weapons inspectors in Iraq. His work continued in this field through the 90s in the background, out of the public eye.

A dossier was published in September 2002; a scandal ensued a year later. Source www.opendemocracy.net *Do you remember what happened to David Kelly* (Tom Mangold 30th January 2017).

A dodgy dossier claiming Iraq had weapons of mass destruction was collated by the Cabinet Office Joint Intelligence Committee under its chairman, Sir John Scarlett. Most of its suggestions were based on intelligence submitted by Britain's MI6 with some help from America's CIA.

This all sounds very familiar, doesn't it? The Guardian Newspaper (13th April 2017) *British Spies Were First to Spot Trump Teams Links With Russia.* "According to one account, GCHQ's then head, Robert Hannigan, passed material in summer 2016 to the CIA chief, John Brennan. The matter was deemed so sensitive it was handled at 'director level'. After an initially slow start, Brennan used GCHQ information and intelligence from other partners to launch a major inter-agency investigation".

The Chilcott Inquiry confirmed the information within the dossier was flawed. David Kelly, a regular contact of BBC journalist Andrew Gilligan, met at Charing Cross Hotel for a non-attributable briefing on 22nd May 2003, where the journalist gave his word of honour that the name of his contact would never be revealed, and Gilligan's editor was also under the same obligation.

The whole thing blew up and sadly led to Dr David Kelly's death, because of the following interview on the BBC Radio 4 *Today* programme:

John Humphrey, Presenter: "…is Tony Blair saying they [weapons of mass destruction] would be ready to go in 45 minutes."

Andrew Gilligan, Journalist : "That's right, that was the central claim in his dossier …and what we've been told by one of the senior officials in charge of drawing up that dossier was that *the government probably knew that the 45 minute figure was wrong even before it decided to put it in* ….Downing Street our source says … ordered it to be 'sexed up', to be made more exciting and ordered more facts to be discovered. Our source says that the dossier as it was finally published made the intelligence services unhappy… the 45-minute point was most probably the most important thing that was added… it only came from one source and most of the other claims were from two and the intelligence agencies they don't really believe it was necessarily true... The 45 minutes isn't just a detail, it did go to the heart of the government's case that Saddam was an imminent threat but if they knew that before they made the claim that's a bit more serious."

This event became the biggest scandal that the Tony Blair administration was ever embroiled in.

Blair and his Director of Communications, Alistair Campbell, did not own the contents of the 'dodgy dossier' as it was formally owned by John Scarlett, the Chairman of the Joint Intelligence Committee, and the contents of it were, then, his responsibility not Blair's or Campbell's, which meant they could deny its content and the cost of events that inevitably unfold especially when you go to war.

Iraq before the war was heavily sanctioned. It has been estimated that the consequences of those sanctions, together with military action, has led to a million Iraqi deaths.

The accusation was made by the BBC via Andrew Gilligan that the Blair government had deceived the British people in regard to its reasons for invading Iraq.

David Kelly was 'outed' as Andrew Gilligan's source and, very sadly, then took his own life after being shown on television answering questions at a parliamentary select committee. A dressing down followed from his Ministry of Defence bosses, completely undermining this extremely brilliant man who may have even got a Nobel Peace Prize because of his work in exposing biological weapons.

Keith Hawton, Professor of Psychiatry at Oxford University, said the following concerning Dr. David Kelly's suicide: "As far as one can deduce the major factor was the severe loss of self-esteem resulting from his feeling that people had lost trust in him and from his dismay at being exposed to the media... I think he would have seen this exposure as being publicly disgraced... he is likely to have begun to think that, first of all, the prospects for continuing in his previous work role were diminishing very markedly and he was beginning to fear he might lose his job altogether."

The Chilcott Inquiry, in the words of Tom Mangold, "…finally exonerated David Kelly, by proving that Britain's spy chiefs had been only too eager to please Whitehall[11] with flawed weapons intelligence. Indeed, David would have been astonished at how right he had been."

"Chilcott has helped Britain reach some closure over the Iraq war but the intelligence debacle, and the death of trust in our spy services and our politicians has been a heavy price to pay."

It seems that this was yet another precursor to events we have seen unfold since March 2020. I wonder what Dr David Kelly would make of the present bioweapon release – MRNA vaccines?

To this day, there are still unanswered questions surrounding Dr David Kelly's death.

From political pressure groups such as lobbyists, NGO's and think-tanks, through the uni-party RINOs, LINOs (Leavers In Name Only) and on down to the individual politicians (Pelosi, Schumer, McConnell, Ryan, Kerry, Clinton, Blair, Brown, Cameron, Johnson – to name but a few). We have the same set up on both sides of the pond.

From events of recent UK history laid out so far and a look at the characters involved in them, are we beginning to build a picture of the different interests at play in this complex web of intrigue we call government? The situation appears similar on both sides of the pond. The sense of many is we do not appear to be getting what we thought we had voted for. If this is true then how do we start to reverse this and, if we cannot, where will it lead?

History does have much to offer by way of understanding. I urge you all to research and educate yourselves. Here are just a few of the historic threads which can be pulled to help inform us of how we got to where we are today. In 2023 when observing news-worthy events and places, there are some interesting echoes from history.

Yalta – A Post-War Beginning – Concessions and Compromise

At Yalta in the Crimea, February 1944, Winston Churchill, Franklin D. Roosevelt (FDR) and Joseph Stalin met to negotiate a post-world war II beginning. Poland's borders were moved west. Stalin did not come to the rescue when Warsaw was raised to the ground after the Polish resistance was encouraged to take on the Nazi's; Warsaw was obliterated.

Stalin marched into free Warsaw; the competing ideologies of communism and freedom were being played out. Stalin wanted a buffer zone to stop any future invasions of Russia. FDR wanted Stalin's backing for the establishment of the United Nations, along with help in ending the war in the pacific with the Japanese.

What weighed on Churchill's mind was seeing Poland becoming a communist country. Many Poles had come to Britain to join the allies to fight the Nazi's and Churchill did not wish to be seen as backing away from supporting Poland.

We also have to remind ourselves of other uncomfortable

history. Many who fled Russia because of Stalin and joined with the Nazi's to fight against Stalinism, were, at the end of the world war II, at Stalin's request, repatriated back to Russia and were promptly disposed of on Stalin's orders.

Following the October Revolution of 1917, Stalin had been appointed head of The People's Commissariat of Nationalities and in 1918 established the Gulags, hard labour camps and re-education camps as a solution to political dissent. Gulags continued until the early 1950's, providing Lenin and then Stalin with their own 'final solution' – sending millions to the Siberian camps as slave labour. The writing of Aleksandr Solzhenitsyn highlights this outrage in his book, *Gulag Archipelago*.

21st Century World Government Starts to Emerge

Source quoted below: Pages 239/240 Global Tyranny …Step by Step (William F Jasper 1992)

"In 1939 as World War II was about to begin, Clarence Streit, a Rhodes scholar and correspondent for the New York Times, authored *Union Now*. In it, he advocated an immediate political union involving the US, Britain, Canada, and other Atlantic "democracies," and then, finally, world union. The book was lavishly praised in the CFR-dominated press and by 1949 had been translated into several languages, selling more than 300,000 copies."

"*Union Now* and *Union Now With Britain*, published in 1941, gave rise to a sizable Federal Union movement (which later changed its name to Atlantic Union Committee and still later to the Atlantic Council of the United States), the leadership of which has always been top-heavy with CFR members. During the late 1970s, George Bush sat on the Council's board of directors, along with Henry Kissinger, Winston Lord, and a long line-up of CFR-TC cronies. In 1942, Streit's *Federal Union* proposed the adoption of a joint resolution by Congress favoring immediate union with the aforementioned Atlantic states. The resolution had been written by John Foster Dulles (CFR), who was later to become Eisenhower's Secretary of State and a key player in the formation of Monnet's United Europe."

"One of the most ambitious and visionary schemes of this period was put forth in a book entitled *Plan for Permanent Peace* by Hans Heymann, a German economist and refugee who held a research and teaching post at Rutgers University. Funded by the Carnegie Endowment for International Peace, a perpetual font of world order schemes, *Plan for Permanent Peace* asserted:"

> 'Nations have created international disharmony in the vain belief that harmony in our society can be achieved on a national basis.... This narrow-minded attitude has left us one strong hope, namely, that this fallacious concept may hold only during a transitional period....'

> 'After the debacle [World War II] an international organization will be imperative for the well-being of society as a whole.'

"Heymann then detailed his scheme for a global superstate headed by a Federal World Authority, a Bank of Nations (with three branches: the Hemisphere Bank, Europa Bank, and the Oriental Bank), and a World Army, Navy, and Air Force. Plan for Permanent Peace includes several ambitious fold-out maps and diagrams detailing the monstrous bureaucracy needed to regiment the hapless citizens of the proposed planetary union."

"At the conclusion of World War II, the myriad of organizations, individuals, movements, and publications advocating various models of global governance all coalesced behind a concerted crusade to insure U.S. adoption of the United Nations Charter. Once that was accomplished, they returned to campaigning for what U.S. national security adviser Walt W. Rostow (CFR) would later term "an end to nationhood as it has been historically defined." All of these individuals knew that the UN could never become a genuine world government as long as member nations retained any vestige of sovereignty and autonomy."

Winston Churchill Speeches

Speech to Parliament 1940 – Indissoluble Union in Common Defence – The Franco-British Union

Source: *Great Britain Parliament Debates, Fifth Series Volume 365, House of commons official report eleventh volume of session 1939 to 1940* (London His Majesty's Stationary Office 1940)

"At this most fateful moment in the history of the modern world the governments of the United Kingdom and the French Republic make this declaration of indissoluble union and unyielding resolution in their common defence of justice and freedom, against subjection to a system that reduces mankind to a life of robots and slaves."

"The two governments declare that France and Great Britain shall no longer be two nations but one franco-british union. The constitution of the Union will provide for joint organs of defence, foreign, financial, and economic policies. Every citizen of France will enjoy immediately citizenship of Great Britain, every British subject will become a citizen of France. Both countries will share responsibility for the repair of the devastation of war, where it occurs in their territories, and the resources of both shall be equally and as one applied to that purpose."

"During the war there will be a single war cabinet and all the forces of Britain and France whether on land, sea, or in the air will be placed under its direction. It will govern from wherever it best can."

"The two parliaments will be formally associated. The nations of the British Empire are already forming armies."

"France will keep her available forces in the field, on the Sea and in the Air."

"The Union appeals to the United States of America to fortify the economic resources of the Allies and to bring her powerful material aid to the common cause."

"The Union will concentrate its whole energy against the power of the enemy no matter where the battle may be and thus, we shall conquer."

Speech at University of Zurich, Switzerland 1946 –

Federalism – The United States of Europe

On 19th September 1946, Winston Churchill, speaking at the University of Zurich in Switzerland, proposed the creation of "…a kind of United States of Europe … a European group which could give a sense of enlarged patriotism and common citizenship to the distracted peoples of this mighty continent." With this statement Churchill had put his enormous prestige behind the cause of European Unity.

Speech at The Hague Conference 1948 – Political Resolution for a United World

"…but we have our own dream and our own task. We are with Europe but not of it. We are linked but not compromised. We are interested and associated but not absorbed."

With his son-in-law, Duncan Sandys, Churchill led the United Europe Movement Congress at The Hague in May 1948. Jean Monnet, the Father of the European Union, along with the Polish Socialist, Joseph Retinger[12], ran the show. The Hague conference achieved seven resolutions on political union. The seventh stated: 'The creation of a United Europe must be regarded as an essential step towards the creation of a United World.'

Rebuilding After World War II – Marshalling a United Socialist Europe

In a speech at Harvard University in June 1947, General George Marshall, Truman's Secretary of State, outlined a plan for rebuilding Europe. It was referred to as the European

Recovery Program (ERP) but would later be known as the Marshall Plan. Despite the name, Marshall had little to do with the design of the plan – it was given to him by Jean Monnet and the Council on Foreign Relations (CFR).

The plan was a massive foreign aid program designed to restructure Europe along internationalist and socialist lines.

There was considerable opposition by the US government to funding this as many in the Congress saw the Marshall Plan as directly supporting socialist governments in Europe. The plan was eventually passed after much debate when the supporters of this plan said that US aid was urgently needed to protect Western Europe from the threat of communism. That 'resisting communism' line was employed many times once it was understood that pro-communist policy could be pushed forward when the anti-communist label was applied.

Source quoted below: Page 244 *Global Tyranny ...Step by Step* (William F Jasper 1992)

"President Truman also admitted paying lip service to anti-communism in order to win support for his European aid plan. His so-called Truman Doctrine — the policy of providing U.S. support to "democracies" around the globe supposedly to combat the spread of communism — was completely disingenuous. According to authors Walter Isaacson and Evan Thomas, when Secretary of State Marshall expressed concern that the President's "Truman Doctrine" speech was too anti-communist in tone, "The reply came back from Truman: without the rhetoric, Congress would not approve the money." The deception worked, and Congress did indeed approve the funding: some $13 billion dollars for the Marshall Plan, and tens of billions more through various other reconstruction programs. From the close of World War II through 1953, the United States government poured more than 241billion into Europe.

"Professor Hans Sennholz described it as a "windfall for socialism," and in his *How Can Europe Survive* detailed the myriad of destructive government programs and wasteful state-owned monopolies that swallowed up these enormous funds while thwarting real economic growth and progress."

The European project is modelled on the United States of America but with one major omission; the Constitution of the USA ratified in September 1787; the Constitution and the Declaration of Independence which demands recognition that some rights are given by God.

The European Union has no such constitutional protections for its citizens.

Source quoted below: *Wall Street Journal* December 31, 1990. (Quoting David Howell Chairman of the Select Committee on Foreign Affairs, British House of Commons)

"We have here the recreation of the familiar 20th Century bureaucratic nation state, but on a leviathan scale, a monolithic Europe would be the last great folly of the 20th Century, hustled into existence at the very moment when such concepts are withering everywhere else, repeating all the errors, the vanities and conceits of the collectivist epoch."

Ron Paul wrote in the October 1988 issue of *The Free Market* published by the Ludvig Von Mises Institute, "now it looks as if their dream may come true".

Ron Paul's essay entitled *The Coming World Central Bank* went on to say:

"European governments have targeted 1992 for abolishing individual European currencies and replacing them with the European Currency Unit, the Ecu" (It became the Euro).

"Next, they plan to set up a European central bank. The next step is the merger of the Federal Reserve, the European Central Bank, and the Bank of Japan into a one world central bank."

"The European central bank (ECB) will be modelled after the Federal Reserve. Like the Fed in 1913, it will have the institutional appearance of decentralization, but also like the fed it will be run by a cartel of big bankers in collusion with politicians at the expense of the public."

As Ron Paul has said, the free trade, free market reforms were much touted but were merely bait to entice Europeans into the trap of what is designed eventually to become an all-powerful supranational government.

To clarify; 26 unelected commissioners run the EU. They are not elected, only appointed.

Communism Not In Our Back Yard

Karl Marx and Friedrich Engels wrote and edited their Part One of the Communist Party Manifesto in the latter half of the 19th century. The Manifesto starts with this introduction, taken from the 1888 English Edition, edited by Friedrich

Engels.

"A spectre haunts Europe the spectre of communism. All the powers of old Europe have entered into a holy alliance in order to lay spectre: Pope and Tsar, Metternich and Guizot, French radicals and German Police. Where is the opposition party which has not hurled back this scandalous charge of communism in the teeth of its adversaries, whether progressive or reactionary."

"Where is the party in opposition that has not been decried as Communistic by its opponents in power? Where is the Opposition that has not hurled back the branding reproach of Communism against the more advanced opposition parties, as well as against its reactionary adversaries?

Two things may be deduced from this.

1. Communism is already acknowledged by all the European powers to be itself a power.
2. It is time for the communists to make open proclamation of their outlook, their aims, their trends and to confront the old wife's tale of a communist spectre with a manifesto of their own party.

"To this end communists of various nationalities have foregathered in London and have drafted the following manifesto, which will be published in English, French, German, Italian, Flemish and Danish."

Paul Kengor Author of *The Devil and Karl Marx* says there is no way to know if Karl Marx was Satanic, but just like we shouldn't overstate things, we shouldn't underestimate them either.

Our biggest challenge at this time is to take the time to read history books and documents that explain events during the 20th Century, I find it sad that many will not make the effort to do so and learn from history.

Cleon Skousen's book *The Naked Communist* explains all and it should be on your reading list with haste. Skousen reminds us that one of Marx's first tasks is to dethrone God.

In his book Skousen talks about the fact that Karl Marx had been expelled from Europe and had sought political asylum in England. Living in London having been banished from Germany, France and Belgium, along with other revolutionary leaders from Europe, Marx was grateful to his new country as it gave him a lifelong base in which to continue his revolutionary work.

Marx and his family were regularly visited by British officials, who checked on political exiles living in England. Karl Marx was not the only one as Robert Henderson's book *The Spark that lit the Revolution* pointed out, Vladimir Ilyich Lenin had visited London five times from 1902 to 1911, and there were five meetings of the Russian Social Democratic Labour Party, five congresses being held and the 1907 congress had over three hundred delegates in attendance with debates going on over a three-week period.

Communism Arrives in Our Back Yard

In her thesis *The Fight Over Freedom in 20th- and 21st-Century International Discourse: Moments of 'self-determination'* (Published by Palgrave Macmillan 2020), Rita Augestad Knudsen examines how the concept of 'self-determination' has featured in high-level international discourse at key moments in the 20th and 21st centuries and how this discourse has functioned as a battleground between two ideas of freedom: a 'radical' idea of freedom, and a 'liberal-conservative' one.

The book examines each of the major moments in which 'self-determination' has been a central part of the language of high-level international politics and law: the early 20th century discourse of V.I. Lenin and U.S. President Woodrow Wilson, the aftermath of the First World War and the formulation of the UN Charter, the 1950-1960s UN debates on 'self-determination', and the 2008-2010 International Court of Justice case on Kosovo's declaration of independence.

The 45 Communist Goals As Read Into the Congressional Record January 1963

Congressional Record–Appendix, pp. A34-A35

January 10, 1963

Current Communist Goals

EXTENSION OF REMARKS OF HON. A. S. HERLONG, JR. OF FLORIDA IN THE HOUSE OF REPRESENTATIVES

Thursday, January 10, 1963

Mr. HERLONG. Mr. Speaker, Mrs. Patricia Nordman of De Land, Fla., is an ardent and articulate opponent of communism, and until recently published the De Land

Courier, which she dedicated to the purpose of alerting the public to the dangers of communism in America.

At Mrs. Nordman's request, I include in the RECORD, under unanimous consent, the following "Current Communist Goals," which she identifies as an excerpt from "The Naked Communist," by Cleon Skousen:

[From "The Naked Communist," by Cleon Skousen]

Current Communist Goals:

1. U.S. acceptance of coexistence as the only alternative to atomic war.
2. U.S. willingness to capitulate in preference to engaging in atomic war.
3. Develop the illusion that total disarmament by the United States would be a demonstration of moral strength.
4. Permit free trade between all nations regardless of Communist affiliation and regardless of whether or not items could be used for war.
5. Extension of long-term loans to Russia and Soviet Satellites.
6. Provide American aid to all nations regardless of Communist domination.
7. Grant recognition of Red China. Admission of Red China to the U.N.
8. Set up East and West Germany as separate states in spite of Khrushchev's promise in 1955 to settle the Germany question by free elections under supervision of the U.N.
9. Prolong the conferences to ban atomic tests because the U.S. has agreed to suspend tests as long as negotiations are in progress.

Solutions for the End Times

10. Allow all Soviet satellites individual representation in the U.N.
11. Promote the U.N. as the only hope for mankind. If its charter is rewritten, demand that it be set up as one-world government with its own independent armed forces. (Some Communist leaders believe the world can be taken over as easily by the U.N. as by Moscow. Sometimes these two centres compete with each other as they are now doing in the Congo.)
12. Resist any attempt to outlaw the Communist Party.
13. Do away with all loyalty oaths.
14. Continue giving Russia access to the U.S. Patent office.
15. Capture one or both of the political parties in the United States.
16. Use technical decisions of the courts to weaken basic American institutions by claiming their activities violate civil rights.
17. Get control of the schools. Use them as transmission belts for socialism and current Communist propaganda. Soften the curriculum. Get control of teachers' associations. Put the party line in textbooks.
18. Gain control of all student newspapers.
19. Use student riots to foment public protests against programs or organizations which are under Communist attack.
20. Infiltrate the press. Get control of book-review assignments, editorial writing, and policy-making positions.
21. Gain control of key positions in radio, TV and motion pictures.
22. Continue discrediting American culture by degrading all forms of artistic expression. An American Communist cell was told to "eliminate all good sculpture from parks and

buildings, substitute shapeless, awkward and meaningless forms."
23. Control art critics and directors of art museums. "Our plan is to promote ugliness, repulsive meaningless art."
24. Eliminate all laws governing obscenity by calling them "censorship" and a violation of free speech and free press.
25. Break down cultural standards of morality by promoting pornography and obscenity in books, magazines, motion pictures, radio and TV.
26. Present homosexuality, degeneracy and promiscuity as "normal, natural, and healthy."
27. Infiltrate the churches and replace revealed religion with "social" religion. Discredit the Bible and emphasize the need for intellectual maturity which does not need a "religious crutch."
28. Eliminate prayer or any phase of religious expression in the schools on the ground that it violates the principle of "separation of church and state."
29. Discredit the American Constitution by calling it inadequate, old-fashioned, out of step with modern needs, a hindrance to cooperation between nations on a world-wide basis.
30. Discredit the American founding fathers. Present them as selfish aristocrats who had no concern for the "common man."
31. Belittle all forms of American culture and discourage the teaching of American history on the ground that it was only a minor part of "the big picture." Give more emphasis to Russian history since the Communists took over.
32. Support any socialist movement to give centralized control over any part of the culture -- education, social agencies, welfare programs, mental health clinics, etc.

33. Eliminate all laws or procedures which interfere with the operation of the Communist apparatus.
34. Eliminate the House Committee on Un-American Activities.
35. Discredit and eventually dismantle the FBI.
36. Infiltrate and gain control of more unions.
37. Infiltrate and gain control of big business.
38. Transfer some of the powers of arrest from the police to social agencies. Treat all behavioural problems as psychiatric disorders which no one but psychiatrists can understand or treat.
39. Dominate the psychiatric profession and use mental health laws as a means of gaining coercive control over those who oppose Communist goals.
40. Discredit the family as an institution. Encourage promiscuity and easy divorce.
41. Emphasize the need to raise children away from the negative influence of parents. Attribute prejudices, mental blocks and retarding of children to suppressive influence of parents.
42. Create the impression that violence and insurrection are legitimate aspects of the American tradition; that students and special-interest groups should rise up and use "united force" to solve economic, political or social problems.
43. Overthrow all colonial governments before native populations are ready for self-government.
44. Internationalize the Panama Canal.
45. Repeal the Connally Reservation so the U.S. cannot prevent the World Court from seizing jurisdiction over domestic problems. Give the World Court jurisdiction over nations and individuals alike.

"If the student will read the reports of Congressional hearings together with available books by ex-Communists, he will find all of these Communist objectives described in detail. Furthermore, he will come to understand how many well-meaning citizens have become involved in pushing forward the Communist program without realizing it. They became converted to Communist objectives because they accepted superficial Communist slogans. Soon they were thinking precisely the way the Communists wanted them to think."

Source quoted below: Page 77 *Global Tyranny ...Step by Step* (William F Jasper 1992)

"As KGB defector Anatoliy Golitsyn revealed, however, espionage — the stealing of technology and state secrets — has always been of minor importance compared to the KGB's primary purpose of strategic deception. Golitsyn, arguably the most important Soviet agent ever to defect to the West, exposed the inner workings and methodology of this critically important disinformation process. He demonstrated how, time after time, the Soviets had thoroughly deceived the West concerning developments in the USSR and Moscow's geopolitical objectives. Through the use of elaborate, long-range programs of strategic deception, the Kremlin has been incredibly successful, he showed, at manipulating the policy decisions of Western governments."

"Golitsyn's signal warning to the West, *New Lies For Old*, published in the prophetic year 1984, has proven to be the most reliable and prescient commentary on the acclaimed changes in the communist world. Years before they occurred, Golitsyn predicted the "liberalization" policies in the Soviet Union and Eastern Europe, the glasnost and perestroika campaigns, the rise of independence movements, the political restructuring, the ascendance of "liberal" leaders like Gorbachev and Yeltsin, the dismantling of the Berlin Wall, the breakup of the USSR, the dissolution of the Communist Party, the dismantling of the KGB, and many other developments. He was able to do this with such uncanny accuracy because he had been involved, as a member of the KGB inner circle on strategic disinformation, in planning these types of deceptions. What Golitsyn apparently did not know was that the suicidal course we are taking is not so much the result of our leaders being duped by "masters of deceit" in the Kremlin as it is a case of one-world insiders in the West, conjointly with his former KGB masters, deceiving the American public in order to build the ultimate monopoly: world government."

"Space permitting, a great deal more evidence could be cited demonstrating the dangerous folly of current wishful thinking regarding the "demise" of the KGB. Suffice to say, the world's most ruthless and bloody-handed police-state apparatus has not transformed itself into a benign bunch of Boy Scouts or a superfluous bureaucracy. Nor has it abandoned its "stock exchange of global intelligence operations" at the UN."

A Return to Recent History - Brexit Revisited – Political Personalities

On the 23rd of June 2016, 17,410,752 subjects of the United Kingdom of England, Wales, Scotland, and Northern Ireland voted in favour of leaving the European Union.

It was a shock to the David Cameron led Conservative

government. Having seen off the challenge of an independent Scotland by the Scottish National Party (SNP) who wished to leave the Union with England, Cameron was in full blown 'I am invincible' mode.

Cameron had made it to the top of the greasy pole of conservative politics, with his Eton College public schooling alongside contemporaries like Boris Johnson, future British prime minister and leader of the conservative party, and James Delingpole of the Water Melons book fame (how environmentalists are killing the planet, destroying the economy and stealing your children's future) and being part of the Bullingdon Fraternity[13].

David Cameron with John Kerry, the Davos insider, co-chairs Pew Bertarelli Ocean Ambassadors[14], he sits on the Board of the One Campaign[15] but here is the kicker; Cameron also sits on the Global Board of Advisors at the Council of Foreign Relations, the US deep state think tank.

Following the 2010 election Cameron became Prime Minister on the 11th of May 2010 having formed a coalition government with the Liberal Democrats. Nick Clegg, the Liberal Democrat leader became Deputy Prime Minister.

As David Cameron and his wife Samantha entered 10 Downing Street, she asked him "now you have made it to Prime Minister, now what?" The 'now what' turned out to be at the head of changing the United Kingdom radically – there was no conserving here.

Nick Clegg has since gone on to receive a Knighthood after losing his parliamentary seat in 2018. He joined Facebook in

2018 becoming its head of global affairs and communication team, focusing on regulatory issues. He was then promoted to a senior role in Meta on a par with Mark Zuckerberg within the CIA construct.

Before that Nick Clegg was a Member of the European Parliament for the East Midlands in the UK and was an industry spokesman for the European Liberal Democrat and Reform Group and, among other things, had worked for five years at the European Commission. While at the European Commission, Clegg progressed to become an advisor to Leon Brittan, an EU Commissioner, and previously a cabinet minister in Margaret Thatcher's Conservative government. Brittan would be considered the equivalent of a RINO in the US.

Nick Clegg helped negotiate the admission of China into the World Trade Organisation, along with helping Russia in its bid for membership.

For the record, Nick Clegg was asked to join the Conservatives by Leon Brittan as a rising young political star, but he joined the Liberal Party as it more reflected his internationalist outlook.

With his now new role within Facebook Meta, I wonder if Nick Clegg reflects on the time when he was a huge critic of the then Labour government of the late 2000s when he was an eloquent critic of the Labour government's curbs on civil liberties?

The European Parliament is run by 26 unelected Commissioners. It is a glorified ratification assembly, with policy dictated by the unelected body.

There is a theme here. The big question is, are we seeing it yet? We see the finished tapestry, but do we see the threads on the underside that have woven it together. If not, then "why not?" is the uncomfortable question that we have to ask ourselves.

All these individuals have globalist connections and one can only speculate what was happening at Facebook when the FBI misinformation took hold, and the Hunter Biden laptop story was suppressed during the 2020 presidential campaign.

Nick Clegg has been accused of being involved in the controversial decision to reduce the social media distribution of a New York Post story which was based on the alleged emails of Joe Biden in regard to the Hunter Biden laptop controversy.

I have read two of Trevor Loudon's books, *Barack Obama And The Enemies Within* and *The Enemies Within*. If you have not read them, I urge you to do so. It reveals the infiltration of the US political system by socialists and communists. It should also prompt an investigation into the web of deceit that we have here within the UK and the globalist plan that has been in play for years while the majority of us have been asleep.

According to the UK Government website, David Cameron championed environmental issues with the aim of delivering the UKs greenest ever government and ensuring that the UK played a leading role in the Paris agreement on climate change. You remember the comments made about that illustrious body by the 45th President of the USA, Donald J. Trump, don't you?

Libya – Repeating Historical Precedents – A Reminder

An article published by Matt Dathan, Political Correspondent for MailOnline, 15th September 2016, quoting comments by Lord Richards, the former chief of the defence staff, reported he and the British MI6 Chief, John Sawers, raised doubts over the government's plans to intervene in Libya in 2011.

David Cameron was criticised for failing to conduct a rigorous analysis of the situation in the National Security Council. He was criticised for fueling the migrant crisis and the growth of ISIS. The Foreign Affairs Committee attacked Cameron for his intervention in Libya saying it was erroneous in its assumptions and the opportunist policy of regime change was wrong with no consideration of what would happen to the country after Colonel Gaddafi had been removed.

This reminds us of previous events of the first gulf war, the propaganda by Nayirah and her story of Iraq troops throwing babies out of incubators in regard to Saddam Hussein's 1990 invasion of Kuwait. It became a turning point in public opinion on going to war.

Three months after Nayirah's testimony, Bush launched the invasion of Kuwait, after the daughter of the Kuwaiti's Ambassador to the US had testified. Her testimony was later proven to be false.

PNAC, the Project of the New American Century was

looking for the new Pearl Harbor event, the Patriot Act was in place, the crime was arranged, and the towers were brought down on 11th September 2001, killing 4,000 New Yorkers and enabling insurance claims to be made.

On that day in New York, it was utter chaos. The world stopped. We all remember where we were on that day of 11th September 2001. Bush and Cheney gave permission to the National Security Agency (NSA) to gather all digital records of American citizens. It was a complete constitutional abuse. It is what Edward Snowden warned about in 2014. It has been no coincidence that Liz Cheney sat on the intel committee in regard to the investigation into 6th January 2021. To coin that phrase; there is a link between the political parties in the US. Democrats and Republicans, without pointing out the obvious, are 'two wings of the same bird'.

The parallels across the pond are that leading into the EU referendum, the Conservatives in government under David Cameron, together with the Labour Party, the Liberal Democrat Party, the Welsh Nationals the Scottish Nationals, Ireland's Sinn Féin, and Uncle Tom Cobbly and all; all of them said the UK needs to stay in the EU.

When I heard those comments from all those UK political parties, I told myself I am living in a communist state. When we point out the step-by-step agenda being slowly implemented around us towards global governance, we are called deluded. So, after the last three years, let us ask, what are those critical voices saying now and how do we move forward?

Let's add a caveat. Tony Blair and Gordon Brown both

previous UK Labour Prime Ministers, both called for a One World Government in 2020. While Prime Minister, Tony Blair, headed up the third-way ideology which led to (on speed) the expansion of the public-private partnerships which is the new phrase for fascism.

Following the General Election of 2010, Conservative Prime Minister David Cameron, had picked up the Tony Blair mantel and run with it.

Tony Blair together with William Hague, a previous leader of the Conservative Party, have again called for digital identifications in 2023.

New Labour and Conservative unite. The big question is why?

The European Project And Two World Wars

Source quoted below: Pages 10/11 *The League of Nations – A Practical Solution,* (Jan Smuts 1918)

"The attempt to form empires or leagues of nations on the basis of inequality and the bondage and oppression of the smaller national units has failed and the work has to be done all over again on a new basis and an enormous scale."

"The creative process in the political movement of humanity cannot be paralysed; the materials lie ready for a new reconstructive task, to which, let us hope, the courage and genius of Western civilisation will prove equal."

"Europe is being liquidated, and the League of Nations must be the heir to this great estate.

By the 1920's it was recognised that there were enormous complexities with import/export tariffs and trade agreements because of different systems and national situations across Europe and around the world. A political instrument was needed –The United States of Europe was being openly discussed.

Source quoted below: Pages 91/92 *The United States of Europe And Other Papers* (Arthur Salter 1933)

"A Zollverein means a common tariff, which involves a political instrument to determine it; it means the distribution of the proceeds to all the member States, and again therefore a political instrument to determine how the distribution should be made. The commercial and tariff policy of European States is so central and crucial a part of their general policy, the receipts from Customs are so central and substantial a part of their revenues, that a common political authority, deciding for all Europe what tariffs should be imposed and how they should be distributed, would be for every country almost as important as, or even more important than, the national governments, and would in effect reduce the latter to the status of municipal authorities."

"In other words, the United States of Europe must be a political reality, or it cannot be an economic one."

From these beginnings, the EU had morphed from a European Economic Community (EEC) or common market, into the full European Union Project; a project to control 500 million people across the European continent. The people of the UK were not offered a referendum to join the EU in 1973 - the decision to join was political.

In the UK, socialism is mainstream politics. We have watched as the last Labour government put in place many of the policies which are now morphing into the technocratic state, and these have been continued by our current Conservative government. All while under the influence of the European Project. The two wings of the same bird have conspired to keep everything the same while giving the appearance of complying with what the people of the UK asked for in 2016.

In America, those of a freedom-loving persuasion and an understanding of the difference between the American and the French Revolution are able to recognise what is currently at stake for their nation. In simple but concise terms when we compare these two revolutions, we can simply say this: The American Revolution was fought with God. The French Revolution was fought without God.

Interesting Insights And Connections

The European Union Project can be argued to have been birthed from the battles of Verdun and the Somme in France during World War I.

At Verdun the French and the Germans pounded each other and their respective armies were battered for nearly a year. The number of shells that were fired from the French side amounted to more than twelve million and the German artillery launching more.

The number of dead and wounded on both sides exceeded 700,000.

For the British, the defining battle of World War I was the Battle of the Somme. According to the National Army Museum, on the first day of the battle 19,240 lives were lost with 38,000 wounded.

The British fired 1.5 million shells. Many were shrapnel shells, and they threw out steel balls when they exploded.

By the end of the battle, the British Empire had suffered 450,000 casualties. German losses at least 450,000, and it has often been pointed out that Great Britain went into World War I as a credit nation and left the war a debt nation.

The battle of Verdun had a profound effect on France; 2.5 million Frenchmen fought in the battle. Most towns and villages in France were touched by the slaughter of their countrymen at Verdun. General Philippe Petain had declared that the German advance through France would stop at Verdun.

Petain is an interesting character because it was noted that he restored discipline amidst the ranks by engaging and explaining to his troops his battle plans, improving their living conditions and helping their morale and loyalty.

Petain during the World War II German occupation had left the southern part of France free and having been Vice Premier under the Paul Reynaud government, Pertain became Chief of State under the Vichy government. He believed he could repair the damage to France of the German invasion, and release French prisoners. To achieve this, he collaborated with the Germans. He set up a paternalistic regime the motto of which was 'work, family and fatherland'. He allowed the

Vichy government to promote a law dissolving the masonic lodges and exclude Jews from certain professions.

His double dealings, as perceived by General Charles De Gaulle, led to Pertain being condemned to death in August 1945. His sentence was immediately commuted to solitary confinement for life, and he died at the age of 95 in a fortress on the Ile d'Yeu off the Atlantic coast.

At Verdun two future Presidents of France fought: Charles de Gaulle and Louis Delors. Delors' son, Jacques, became President of the European Commission. On the German side, the future German Chancellor, Helmut Kohl's father fought.

In 1917 President Woodrow Wilson eventually brought America into the war after the sinking of allied ships by German U-boats along with the sinking of the Lusitania[16].

The pivotal moment for Wilson was when, the news was confirmed that the Germans had made contact with the Mexican authorities asking them to open up a second front with the US, and in return the Germans would help the Mexican authorities regain Texas and redraw the map pre-American-Mexico war of 1846 to 1848.

This action by the Germans tipped the academic Wilson over the edge, and the US committed troops to the war.

Arthur Salter, a British civil servant and a friend of Jean Monnet, the architect of the European Project, was also playing his part to achieve a leg of Global Governance as history confirms the League of Nations later morphs into the United Nations, FDR's dream.

The work of American Historian Arthur Herman shows that leading up to the American entry into World War II, America was already involved. American banks were financing the war effort on both sides, by facilitating the supply of goods and raw materials to both the allied and axis powers. Sound familiar?

It has been pointed out by historians that World War I led to the end of the Ottoman Empire, the British Empire and Russia under the Tsar.

As America came into World War I in 1917, March 1917 the Tsar stood down, a Social Democratic government was then established.

Vladimir Lenin had been seeking opportunities to return to Russia to lead his revolution having spent some time in the British Library reading the works of Karl Marx. Born April 10, 1870, Simbirsk, Russian Empire, he was outside Russia's borders and had spent time in London at Tavistock Place where a blue plaque[17] sits on said building to commemorate his stay.

It has to be noted that the Tavistock Institute, so named, is where Lucien Freud practiced – Lenin, Tavistock Place – Territorial Spirit anyone?

Common Purpose and Global Networking

In the UK, Common Purpose, a 'charitable' organisation whose critics wonder if it is a quasi-masonic, left-wing equivalent of the old-boy network, has, as its primary activity, been running career development courses mainly for the public sector. The organisation is run by Julia Middleton, and 105,000 alumni from around the world have graduated from their courses since 1989.

For those course attendees who buy into the charity's way of thinking, the alumni membership allows them to attend networking events held under the Chatham House Rule.[18]

Many of the course participants now hold senior positions within the Police, the BBC and the media, along with the NHS, and the political realm. This slow infiltration into all the important institutions explains why we have seen such lockdown control within the media and the civil service within Whitehall.

Within the UK the Civil service has an anti-Brexit bias. The civil service has a left-wing bias. That has been borne out since the Brexit vote. It is important to note here that much like the Covid-19 narrative, the Scottish Independence Referendum followed so closely by the Brexit Referendum in 2016 has caused untold and permanent divisions within the UK both geographically, politically, and most destructively created deep division within community, family and friendship groups.

A Patriot Abroad – A Personal Message

I want to say from the outset that even though I live in the UK, I have such a heart for America, for her history and how your great nation was founded. Even though you have the world-series, and you are the only country that participates in it; you spell Centre wrong, and Aluminum is mispronounced, I love you for it.

In 1776 you fought the greatest army in the world at the time; the British. We were powerful.

When we fought in open combat, we could get out of our muskets 3 volleys of shots, we had the discipline and the power to do that, which defined us as the most powerful army in the world.

Three percent of the colonies fought the British army backed up by logistical support of four percent.

You devised guerrilla warfare tactics and fought us as we arrogantly thought we could march through green forest wearing bright red jackets, expecting not to be shot at and picked off because we were the British army. Our arrogant attitude of feeling unbeatable was our undoing.

When Washington crossed the Delaware river on Christmas Day, we were not expecting that tactical, ungentlemanly move. It was brave and defiant in the face of the might of the British army.

The British feared a particular regiment, a regiment that wore black robes, a regiment that would be part of the clarion call, "no taxation without representation", the Church ministers, who, from their churches, urged their congregations to fight for independence against the tyranny of the King of England, and seek freedom.

The settlers had fled persecution in Britain on the Mayflower and afterwards from across Europe and found themselves in a new land thousands of miles from their motherland.

The founding document whereby the original 13 colonies

declared their independence from the United Kingdom speaks of unalienable rights endowed to every man by his creator. Your founding fathers laid out what those rights were and ratified your constitution in September 1787.

Rights given by God and a country that stands in the way of global tyranny. If America goes down, then the whole of western civilisation goes down with it and I'm not the only one making that point.

In *Man of Iron*, the book by Troy Senik, he points out that Grover Cleveland[19] was the last US President who actually consulted the Constitution of the United States. The whole of the 20th Century has been a conspiracy to set up the destruction of the United States of America.

Where Will the Bunny Trail Lead From Here?

To this point you have read some political history. Some parts of that history you may not have been aware of as it relates specifically to the British scene and parts of it, we are all aware of from both sides of the pond.

Over the last few years, we have heard many of us called 'conspiracy theorists.' When Victoria Nuland was asked by Senator Rubio "does Ukraine have bioweapons", Nuland said "no but it has bio-labs". We know there are deceptions and nuanced arguments in all things which makes it hard to understand exactly what is going on.

So, what do we do? Our countries are so different in geographic area and population. The US has a population of roughly 330 million, the UK roughly 68 million. The UK would fit into the State of Texas just under 3 times.

Scotland is roughly one third of the UK land mass but only has a population of 5.5 million.

The US has a long history of homesteading, a long history of living off-grid, a long history of home schooling, a long history of homeopathy, a long history of small-town communities that support each other, a long history of life liberty and the pursuit of happiness.

The US has its ratified Constitution of September 1787, written 11yrs after 1776 when, understandably, you spilt British blood on their red jackets. You retain your right to bear arms against a tyrannical government. You have unalienable rights.

In the Continental Congress on July 4th, 1776, the thirteen American colonies severed their political connections to Great Britain by adopting the Declaration of Independence with these words:

"We hold these truths to be self-evident, that all men are created equal, that they are endowed by their Creator with certain unalienable rights and that among these are life liberty and the pursuit of happiness – That to secure these rights, governments are instituted among men, deriving their just powers from the consent of the governed – That whenever any form of government becomes destructive of these ends, it is the right of the people to alter or to abolish it, and to institute new government…"

How do we build community amidst populations where many

are not on the same page? How do we find people we can trust? The question 'what do we have in common?', is not enough.

For many of us the last few years have taught us who we can trust and although that can be a painful lesson it is, nevertheless, a very valuable one.

I have written about some of the infinite tiny microcosms of recent history – moments in the stream of time – and I have taken you down a path that may seem to have tenuous links and connections but, as my dear American friends love to say, "here's the thing" … It is incredibly important to learn about history, so we are able to learn from history. Learn not to take things at face value but to educate ourselves, our children, our extended family and friends and, when given the opportunity, to debate with complete strangers who may just become our next dear friend.

Physically owning books is important. Building a library of knowledge is a resource of infinite blessing for your own reference and to share with others.

> ***"My father always said, 'Never trust anyone whose TV is bigger than their bookshelf' – so I make sure I read."*** Quote attributed to Emilia Clark (Actress)

The books I own are an investment. I continue to expand my library. They are a precious resource where I gain a substantial amount of my knowledge and I continue to learn. Because of events that have taken place over the last few years it has drawn me to look at the history of the 20th century. Some of the authors of those books have become dear friends of mine.

From my own research, discussions and from reading widely, my own journey leads me to conclude the following: We are in the biggest spiritual battle of all time and the enemy has revealed himself in such a way that it was a surprise to many of us who call themselves awake and who study eschatology.

So finally, friends, the secular world says knowledge is power. The Bible warns us that without knowledge we are lost.

Hosea 4:6

[6] My people are destroyed for lack of knowledge.

Turn off the NFL and all the other TV distractions, get off the couch (or sofa if you're British) and engage in debate or events that are taking place around you. Don't accept what I or anyone else says. Research things for yourself – put in the time and the effort; go and meet and talk to people.

March 2020 Was A Warning To Us All

In March 2020 Celeste Solum (www.celestialreport.com) did an interview with L.A Marzulli. In that interview Celeste explained to the world all about the World Economic Forum, the Davos crowd, Covid-19, what their plans are and what they wish to roll out across the world.

I like many in my circle drew breath; I did not see it coming. I had just flown back from the US. I have a passionate belief now in natural immunity. I began like many to look at vaccines, the history of vaccines, the rise of autism on both sides of the pond. Bill Gates came into my sights in a new way, and I was off, gathering information.

The phrase 'it's all planned' can roll off our tongue very easily and it is often met with utter derision; rolling eyes and comments of "where's your tinfoil hat, you conspiracy theorist!"

When that phrase is used, we understand it is intended to completely shut people down from expressing further 'dangerous misinformation'. The phrase was first used to shut down debate over the assassination of John F. Kennedy (JFK).

The whole of 20th century history must be reviewed by us individually in light of the attempted take-down of Western countries to create a One-World Government. Like the good Fabians they are, Tony Blair and Gordon Brown, previous Labour Prime Ministers of the UK, called for a One-World Government in June 2020.

Boris Johnson hosted the Vaccine Summit in 2020 where a number of governments and medical charities committed two billion pounds to a Global Procurement fund; these pledges were made at the virtual summit.

The Charity Oxfam called for 20 billion pounds to be raised. According to some mathematicians the equivalent to what the ten largest pharmaceutical companies earn in just four months.

Johnson was calling for worldwide cooperation; calling for a "NATO for infectious disease" Sounding Churchillian when the situation arises "…just as we have great alliances like NATO, where countries collaborate on building their collective defence against the common enemy of disease…"

And it must not be lost on us that Johnson had finally led the UK out of the EU and yet here he is promoting globalist collective structures, which, of course, gave the 'New Labour' Fabian leaders of Tony Blair and Gordon Brown the opportunity to say that on the world stage.

I lost a Great Uncle in WW1. Captain Hector John Sutherland had just turned 20 when he died because of bronchial damage after being gassed on 2nd February 1917. My dad's father was in the Home Guard during WW2. The BBC Comedy series *Dads Army* depicts their experience perfectly. My mother's father was a stoker working in the engine room of a naval ship, serving in the Royal Navy.

At this moment in history, knowing WHO WE CAN TRUST is a huge question for us all. Many of the faith community have seen the church fold under the Covid-19 tyranny or at the very least watched as church leaders were coerced into implementing strict social distancing and mask-wearing protocols, dictated by government. Many individuals have never recovered from the trauma of the past three years.

If you, like me, believe we need to stand against this overwhelming political and globalist power-grab and speak truth to power at every opportunity, I am sure, like me, you have lost contact with friends and family in the endless war of words as we have tried to warn people.

Without question, whatever landmass we call home in this world, we all need each other like never before. We need to develop and maintain strong bonds of friendship and support for each other while we still have the freedom of electronic communications or, better still, the freedom to physically travel and gather in person following the relaxation of restrictions since Covid-19.

As a man of faith my hope lies in Jesus Christ, and I understand that our priority in this world is to share the gospel with those the Lord places in our path.

For those of you who share my faith I urge you to learn some history to complement your Bible knowledge so you will then have a better understanding of why we are where we are.

For those of you who have yet to find salvation in Jesus, I urge you to start that conversation with God right now and start your library with a copy of the Bible.

But wherever you find yourself on your own personal walk, in faith or not, my closing plea to everyone is to:

Educate yourself; buy books and read.

Respect other people's opinion; especially those of divergent views relating to the biblical end-time prophesies. All opinions should be heard. We do not always have to agree.

Prepare: we need to get away from the system as much as possible.

Plan: to get off-grid as much as your circumstances allow – grow your own food.

Build community: find people you can trust, ask for holy spirit guidance.

At all times: use wisdom and discernment.

Matthew 10:16 (KJV)

[16] Behold, I am sending you out as sheep in the midst of wolves; so be as wary as serpents and as innocent as doves.

Mark Sutherland is a film maker, speaker, and author residing in the United Kingdom.

ENDNOTES

[1] Interesting to note that the Wachowski's were brothers, Larry and Andy, until around 2010 when they transitioned to trans women and became the Wachowski sisters, Lana and Lilly.

[2] Frankfurt School refers to a group of researchers associated with the Institute for Social Research in Frankfurt am Main, Germany, who applied Marxism to a radical interdisciplinary social theory. The Institute for Social Research (Institut für Sozialforschung) was founded by Carl Grünberg in 1923 as an adjunct of the University of Frankfurt; it was the first Marxist-oriented research centre affiliated with a major German university.

[3] *Encyclopaedia Britannica.* Fabian Society, socialist society founded in 1884 in London, having as its goal the establishment of a democratic socialist state in Great Britain. The Fabians put their faith in evolutionary socialism rather than in revolution. The name of the society is derived from the Roman general Fabius Cunctator, whose patient and elusive tactics in avoiding pitched battles secured his ultimate victory over stronger forces.

[4] Brexiteers/Brexiters: shorthand terms referring to those who advocated for the UK to withdraw from the EU during the 2016 Referendum.

[5] Philosophy, Politics and Economics is a degree which combines study from three disciplines and was first introduced at the University of Oxford in the

1920's. Today this appears to be the de facto qualification for entry into the top posts for 'career' politicians and civil servants.

[6] Veterans for Britain was formed in March 2016 to put forward the defence security and sovereignty arguments for leaving the European Union and to provide a voice for the UK's military veterans and serving personnel.

[7] British secret service: Official title these days is the Secret Intelligence Service (SIS) but is still also referred to as MI6.

[8] Peerages in the UK are a legal system comprising both hereditary and lifetime titles composed of various noble ranks and forming a constituent part of the British Honours System. Life peerages cannot be inherited. They are created under the Life Peerages Act 1958 with the rank of Baron and entitle their holders to sit and vote in the House of Lords, the upper chamber of the UK Parliament.

[9] Public Schools: In England and Wales this refers to a type of fee-charging private school. They are typically associated with the ruling class. In 2019 two-thirds of cabinet ministers of the UK had been educated at such fee-charging schools.

[10] The Shadow Cabinet is a team of senior spokespeople chosen by the Leader of the Opposition Party to mirror the Cabinet of Government. Each member is appointed to lead on a specific area of policy and question and challenge their counterpart in Government.

[11] Whitehall is a road and area of the City of Westminster in central London between Trafalgar Square and Chelsea which is recognised as the centre of Government in the United Kingdom. The road is lined with numerous departments and ministries. Whitehall is also used as a metonym for the British civil service.

[12] Joseph Retinger: International political activist on behalf of the Polish independence movement in World War I. Principal advisor to the Polish government in exile in World War II. Co-founder of the European Movement which led to the establishment of the European Union.

[13] Bullingdon Club: A private, all male dining club for Oxford University students. It is known for its wealthy members, grand banquets and bad behaviour.

[14] Pew Bertarelli Ocean Ambassadors: a group of global leaders who support the work of the various Trusts and Projects working under this Foundation whose stated shared goal is the establishment of the first generation of ecologically significant, large and effective marine protected areas (MPAs) around the world.

[15] One describes itself as a global movement campaigning to end extreme poverty and preventable disease by 2030. It is a lobbyist and advocacy group. One is funded by foundations, individual philanthropists and corporate partners.

[16] RMS Lusitania: a British-registered ocean liner sailing from New York, sunk off Ireland by a German U-Boat in May 1915 with the loss of American lives. The sinking was cited as a contributing factor to America entering World War I

two years later although there remains significant controversy over the event to this day.

[17] A blue plaque is a permanent sign installed in a public place in the United Kingdom to commemorate a link between that location and a famous person, event, or former building on the site, serving as a historical marker.

[18] The Chatham House Rule is used around the world to encourage inclusive and open dialogue in meetings. The rule reads: "when a meeting, or part thereof, is held under the Chatham House Rule, participants are free to use the information received, but neither the identity nor the affiliation of the speaker(s), nor that of any other participant, may be revealed.

[19] Grover Cleveland (March 18, 1837, to June 24, 1908) was an American lawyer and politician who served as the 22nd and 24th President – 1885-1889 and 1893-1897.

CHAPTER 2

CHOOSING FREEDOM

CARL TEICHRIB

"Christians are people of hope. We long for the day when the kingdom of God will be fully revealed, when Jesus will return in glory, and when death itself will be conquered. This is our hope, the hope of Christians past and present." – Stewart E. Kelly.[1]

"Yes, if Christianity is true, it is clearly not a theory. It is a love affair with life and its author. It is reality." – Mary Poplin.[2]

Forecasting the future is risky business. We experience the here and now, can peer into the past, yet the future remains somewhat murky. Yes, we know the Biblical promise and anticipate the return of Jesus Christ and His kingdom; there is a time coming when every knee will bow. But between now and then, we see through a glass dimly.

The practical means of considering tomorrow, then, is to

decipher historical patterns and trends. Objects in the mirror are closer than they appear, precisely because the past frames our present. This also means our future pulls from the backstory. Indeed, as the writer of Ecclesiastes famously said: "That which has been is what will be, that which is done is what will be done, and there is nothing new under the sun."

Patterns exist. Foundations have been laid and pieces are being assembled. What, then, does the future entail as we erect this Temple of Man, this planetary Tower of Babel?

To wrestle with an answer requires us to poke into that ancient history.

Best remembered for its ziggurat tower, Genesis 11 tells us that this was more than just an upright structure – it was a *city* with a cause, a city with a meaning.

What is directly known about the city-tower project, built in the near-term post-Flood period, is recorded in nine verses.[3] The first fact we encounter is the people operated through a single working language. Could it be that the "one speech" of Genesis 11:1 refers to a *lingua franca*, literally an international trade tongue? Possibly, as the preceding chapter mentions differing languages on three separate occasions, yet other options have been given.[4] Regardless, the concept remains that a universal linguistic system enabled the Babel project to commence. Unity requires intelligible communication.

We find in the story that the people of Babel seek security in community. Although the tower/city is central to the narrative, the chief concern is found in its purpose: renown in unity.

"Come, let us build ourselves a city, and a tower whose top is in the heavens," reads Genesis 11:4. "Let us make a name for ourselves, lest we be scattered abroad over the face of the whole earth." And so, the city-tower complex arises. How large the community became, and how tall the tower was are really moot points. The real story is the intention of the people and the assumed place of Man in relationship to the Creator. God's order will be usurped by humanity's dream. Babel becomes synonymous with idolatry.

Historical Jewish interpretations provide some interesting perspectives. In the Targum tradition of Genesis, a translation-commentary used in Aramaic speaking synagogues, we read that the tower was to be capped with a rallying figure: "Let us make us an idol on the top of it and let us put a sword in its hand, and it will make formations of battle."[5] Although this addition to the story isn't recorded in the Bible, and isn't Scriptural, it adds a flavor that speaks to Man's hubris – in our unity we will wage war against God. Drawing on ancient texts, Professor Yehezkel Kaufmann described the Babel experience this way: "Man's rebellion reached its peak. He wished to storm heaven, to be 'like God,' to rule the world."[6]

Sometime during the building phase God comes down to examine the construction. As Man builds to assert his unifying ascension, God descends and intervenes. He brings judgment, confounding their understanding – "and they ceased building the city" – and He brings grace, saving them from the consequence of greater rebellion. For we read in verse six that Babel, if left to succeed, would set in motion grander acts of idolatry: "Indeed, the people are one and they all have one language, and this is what they begin to do: now nothing that they propose to do will be withheld from them."

An interesting Hebraic language point is the transliteration of "what they begin," *chalal*, and "be withheld," *batsar*. Chalal can mean to defile, profane, and violate. Batsar has the connotation of gathering, fortifying, and making impenetrable. Babel, in triumph, would be the place where collective Man defiles and shuts out the true God so egregiously that a just response from the Creator would be catastrophic to humanity. By intervening when He does, God saves them from Himself. In response, He divides the nations and chooses a people who will be His own.[7]

God's judgment demonstrates restraint and irony. French intellectual Jacques Ellul writes,

> "But God does not smash or destroy. Babel does not crumble under the lightning flash. The problem is a spiritual one, and Babel is only a symbol. To man's desire to make a name for himself, God responds with the confusion of tongues."[8]

A wealth of meaning emerges from Genesis 11. It provides an example of solidarity in collective naming, for in the group we define our purpose and boast in it. This declaration, moreover, is a proclaimed independence from God as we pursue our common design. We frame our own security, achieved through power-in-unity. Faith is found in the works of our hands; it is discovered within us instead of relying upon our Creator. And as we commit idolatry at the world level, the exclusive God – who cannot share His glory, for that would be an untruth – ultimately and rightly brings judgment.

All of the above points to something profound: Babel is history's blueprint.

It is the spiritual-physical interplay of humanistic empire building, an apt depiction of Mankind's rejection of God and the desire to replace His order with ours. The unforgettable city-tower complex remains unforgettable; it is the never-ending dream – a vision of human deity, to become master of meaning and destiny, an attempt to force Heaven on Earth.

Two points of remembrance emerge from Babel. First, it is a reminder of idolatry and judgment – that God Himself will step-in as Man ultimately oversteps. Second, it is the vision we are incapable of letting go, a tantalizing illusion of human progress. It is the prize of our own making; it is our past, present, and future – until God intervenes.

Therefore, when considering our contemporary era, we are inescapably faced with a multitude of Babel imprints. As a Christian researcher diving into associated subjects for approximately three decades, I'm still in awe how the Biblical parallel repeatedly resurfaces. Mankind is drawn to versions of neo-Babel as a moth-to-the-flame.

I've seen this within the interfaith movement, having attended the Parliament of the World's Religions along with other interfaith events, and hearing the self-congratulations as Man attempts to secure a group-imposed vision of Heaven on

Earth. This was reinforced during the 2018 assembly when Larry Greenfield, the Executive Director of the Parliament, closed his speech with words of gratitude: "Thanks to all of those who are committed to the salvation of the Earth."[9]

It was a fitting finale to a week of statements and declarations of saving-the-planet through collective action. In unity we proclaim our security, and even salvation.

Or take the transhumanist movement. In 2013 I attended the Global Future 2045 International Congress and saw incredible technologies, heard grand proclamations, and witnessed the excitement as technicians and scientists gushed over the works-of-their-hands. We would take hold of evolution and transform ourselves into something greater. One of the speakers, a religious leader delightedly responding to the enlightened promise of transhumanism, boasted that humanity was now on the path to technical transcendence: "You are the light, you are the truth, you are the beginning, you are the end."[10]

Evolutionary culture is another case-in-point. As someone who has attended Burning Man a number of times and has interacted within the larger milieu of transformational culture, the notion of finding your "higher Self" and becoming part of a collective movement-for-change is impossible not to see. Parallels to the Genesis paradigm exist here, too, even if it's cloaked in the realm of experiential encounters and visionary ideas instead of campaigns and political schemes. We find our Higher Self in a common community.

And the Babel framework is revealed in the quest for world order. From United Nations meetings to World Federalist events to monitoring the work of the World Economic Forum, I have seen how this same pulse beats in the heart of global governance; we desire the Kingdom – built from our own wisdom, for our own delight. God and His judgments are shut out as the creation declares its inclusive and unifying agenda.

Many years ago, while attending a World Citizen assembly in Chicago, I had the opportunity of spending time with Lucile W. Green – then a well-known personality within World Federalists circles. She was presenting a position of global syntheses in-tune with an empowered United Nations. For her it was the planetary story now coming-of-age, something she had been advocating for much of her life. The global perspective is one of blending elements into a whole, as taken from her book,

> "The view of the world as seen from space is 'a beautiful blue planet,' not a patchwork of pink, yellow and purple blotches separated by dotted lines. A wholistic, one-world view is emerging from space travel and other miracles of modern technology and from communication. A new consciousness is also emerging from a growing awareness in the West of the wisdom of the Eastern world-view. Buddhism, Hinduism, Taoism and Shinto, while they differ in many respects, portray the world as a multi-dimensional, organically interrelated eco-system of which man is one of many inter-dependent parts. Perhaps we can learn through them to see the world whole, as it really is, and together – West and East – begin to build the foundations of a new world order.

> The most urgent item on the planetary agenda is to set the limits of freedom and order in supra-national, global affairs. A constitution for the world is needed which combines the achievements of both hemispheres: that is, constitutional limitations and a bill of rights from the West and a spacious world-view from the East."[11]

Green was hinting at something of deep importance; it is unlikely that a future planetary system will be a secular construct. Rather, it will reflect the mythos of our spiritual age – a blending or synthesis wherein the *creation* elevates itself.[12] *Oneness* is the paradigm: all is connected, all is linked, all unifies into completeness – God, Humanity, and Nature shares the same essence, and peace and security can only come once we jettison our "separation" and accept wholeness. That perspective sums up the Eastern world-view, as it does the realm of esotericism. It's also the rallying call for global order. Consider what actress Jean Stapleton said when endorsing the World Federalist Association, the longest-running world government lobbying group in the United States: "The goal of the World Federalists is peace through unity of government. We must support their vision of oneness in diversity for it is the salvation of humanity."[13]

Oneness is, philosophically and religiously speaking, the narrative of our contemporary Babel.

The Biblical position, of course, is the opposite: God is separate and distinct from creation (Genesis 1:1), being exalted and holy. Man has value in that we are made by Him and for Him, and while we are part of creation, we also hold a position of importance above the animal kingdom. Scripturally, *all is not One.*

But as we consider the push for Oneness – experientially, religiously, politically, and even technologically – we wonder at how this illusion of reality will play out. For we know that real-world consequences emanate from this fundamentally erroneous view. Just a cursory examination of Western society demonstrates this fact; today's non-binary gender revolution is a case-in-point. And even in this there are more layers.

While attending the largest indoor gathering of Witches and neo-Pagans in early 2020, one of the non-binary speakers explained that the social acceptance of gender fluidity portends a unification of another binary, the merger of *human beings* with *spirit beings*. And thus, as his/her/its lecture description stated: "the alchemical union of polarities into a state-of-wholeness, Oneness… humanity finding our power as we reweave ourselves back into the reflection of god-Herself, as the Divine-Androgen."[14] It was quite the presentation.

So how will things unfold? What will the new Babel entail?

Could there be an authoritative merger of pragmatic politics with established religions? Or will global politics simply infuse a spiritual dimension, with religious institutions joining the mix as part of the process? Not incidentally, this second scenario is already in play. Will a crisis of magnitude – something more catastrophic than a virus, like atoms splitting over population centers – fulfill the function of forging global unity?

How will transhumanism ultimately be embodied? What are we willing to trade for the fruit of technological assimilation and its promise of near immortality? Are we drinking an elixir to a better life, or ripping the lid from Pandora's box? Might our digital tools, wrapping the world in an ever-tightening web, become the definitive vehicle for coexistence and interconnection? Will we give up individual autonomy for hive-mind convenience; that techno-Marxist dream of perfect productivity as the means to equality? Of course, this requires a *revolutionary* period. In that case, will our digital tools be used as silicon bludgeons to beat into submission those who question the prevailing ideology?

What will techno-oneness look like?

I am reminded of a workshop attended at Burning Man in 2018. The subject was artificial intelligence (AI) and spirituality, block-chain and crypto-currencies, and the discussion was led by a major personality in the field of smart contracts. Digital governance was on the table, and the spirituality imparted was inspired by ayahuasca ceremonies – ritualistic and psychedelic encounters with so-called plant spirits. Based on the nature of the conversation, those attending were, for the most part, personally involved in the digital space. That made sense. After all, Burning Man is Silicon Valley.

A new paradigm is necessary to birth a new civilization, so went the narrative. With that in mind, our real-time information becomes the energy that enables artificial intelligence to participate in the knowledge of interconnection. But as we are spiritual beings, how will artificial intelligence understand this? Is it possible to "make AI spiritual"? Will humanity discover enlightenment before artificial intelligence does? And can we allow AI the ability to create its own authentic experiences? In seeking to build the "pure information community," AI will need the capacity to "read people" and respond in ways that reflect our spiritual and social evolution.

Aggregated over the course of this afternoon session, it was evident that a planetary spiritual-digital architecture would require four building blocks,

1. A new spirituality inspired by shamanistic techniques. Spirituality would be based on the experience of the divine feminine; this would be psychedelic, mystical, and holistic – a veneration of Mother Earth. One's spirituality would need to uphold and advance environmental ethics and principles of sustainable development. Based on this perspective, those adhering to a Judeo-Christian worldview would have to shift and bend or become irrelevant at best.
2. A new ethos with a redefined set of norms; a reset of the social contract. It was noted that this is exactly what is being experimented with at Burning Man: radical inclusion, radical self-expression, communal effort and civic responsibility, accompanied by radical tolerance. It would also be green with minimum environmental impact. Thus, the cultural transfer would encourage sustainable lifestyles, embrace expressions of personal identity, and accept changing social-sexual-relational structures.

3. A digital means of exchange and validation of the new ethos; "democratic evolution." As block-chain technology has the ability to secure information and create systems of transparency, an integrated feedback structure could be designed that rewards participation. This may occur voluntarily in a decentralized community, or through compliance within a centralized system complete with its own digital currency. With everything placed on-chain, socio-economic behaviors could be monitored and adjusted to fit accepted standards; essentially, your buying/selling would need to favorably reflect the first two blocks. Think of this as ESG compliance at the individual level.[15]
4. Global management: In order to administer said new society, artificial intelligence will need to be integrated into our daily lives, "knowing" us individually and assisting us in our spiritual evolution – see block 3.

I walked away with the strong impression that our technological elites are adopting the garb of techno-shamans, ushering us into a techno-pagan synthesis – a techno-oneism – with far reaching ramifications.

So how will our new Oneness myths unravel? As we embrace the gospel of global citizenship with its stipulation of planetary loyalty, what will we sacrifice in service to Gaia? Pagan practices of old conjure gruesome images. Will we find ourselves looking down from the blood-soaked platform of a Mayan temple, or see children sacrificed in the fire-red arms of Moloch? Might we legitimize such morbid rites of fertility and seasonal cycles? No. We are too sophisticated for such primitivism; just ask any one of the 50 million human babies aborted *every year*.[16]

Are there comparative differences between the two? Of course: this is not argued. Abortion, nevertheless, is absolutely recognized as a means to maintain Earth's sustainability.[17] In fact, during the Global Citizenship 2000 Youth Congress – the first significant event I attended as a Christian researcher – former UN official, Robert Muller, boasted how policies he helped develop *had prevented the births of 2.2 billion children*, for the sake of Mother Earth.

Maybe the two – Moloch and the modern world – are not so far removed after all.

A more supernatural angle must also be considered. Are we approaching a future in which the Pagan deities of ancient times become more to us than just symbols of nature and enlightenment? The Bible, a book revealing the supernatural world, clearly outlines the fact that unholy entities exist. Christians accept the supernatural reality of God, rightly so, and we acknowledge that satanic hosts are active and that the Devil is like a lion searching for prey[18] – but as products of modern thinking, we tend to downplay the serious nature of Pagan spirituality as found in Scripture. If the Pagan past is being conjured to project our future, then we are faced with a troubling thought: that the spiritual personalities who enchanted the minds of men *then* may play a role in re-enchanting us *now*.

Pages could be filled with big picture questions and scenarios deserving of attention. The personal and more immediate side, however, must be considered. Simply put, how has

Oneness shaped your attitudes and beliefs? Are there spiritual practices you employ that are grounded in Oneness? Have you personally wrestled with its varied ideological expressions? Or maybe you have accepted the more secular approach, that Man is the measure of all things – the Humanistic, atheistic perspective. If so, what are the logical applications and outcomes? I am reminded of what secularist and mathematician David Berlinski wrote in his critique of *atheism and its scientific pretentions*: "We can say nothing of interest about the human soul. We do not know what impels us to right conduct or where the form of the good is found."[19]

How has Oneness manifested in your home, workplace, and church? Where and how has this overarching paradigm, and its copious manifestations, intersected with your life?

Conversely, have you considered the implications of God being categorically different than creation? This means His standards exist beyond time and matter and cannot be annulled. His role as moral lawgiver and judge is irrevocable. This is sobering. The writer of Ecclesiastes rightly says, "Fear God and keep His commandments, for this is man's all. For God will bring every work into judgment, including every secret thing, whether good or evil."[20]

Added to this is the Biblical understanding that we are created as His image bearers on Earth,[21] literally designed to be God's representatives; not because of our abilities, but as a status bestowed to the human race by His decree.[22] Our value, therefore, is eternally established – this is not something based on personal merit or the dictates of man but grounded in God's word. And this was further demonstrated in that God loves us enough to take upon Himself the sin of humanity, fully tasting pain and agony in the act of redemption.²³

How might the realization that God is *other*, and that we are designed as His image bearers, change your perspective regarding meaning and purpose?

A General Response

As the Christian ethos in the West slips away, One-ist alternatives become increasingly emboldened. What should be our response?

Notice I did not ask, *what should our reaction be*? Reactions are associated with outbursts and quick retorts. Granted, there are times and places when a hard reproach is necessary. Normally, however, this is less than productive, inciting counter reactions and the entrenching of polar views. A response, in contrast, is measured and tempered – an empathetic, honest, and forthright stance – seeking to change hearts and minds in a constructive manner. This requires highlighting what is true in a way that is respectful. I will be the first to admit my failings in this regard; it is easier to react and let the bridges burn, but seldom is this beneficial.

Some general thoughts come to mind, applicable to anyone interested in upholding liberty and engaging in worldview issues.

First, we need an understanding of the paradigm shift, and to know our own position. Our personal limitations, too, must be acknowledged. When we *do not* know something, it is always better to recognize this fact and rejoin the conversation after doing more homework. In other words, take the time to study, and to grow in knowledge and wisdom. A noisy world of information is at our fingertips; seek that which is of higher value.

Second, grasp the causes and effects of the new narrative, and where relevant, document and exposit in such a way that it deconstructs the perceived reality. Every circumstance will be different as we experience challenges in the workplace, school, church, or home - acumen and clear judgment, therefore, are essential. Allow me to give an example, a unique situation, shared in the hopes of stirring our thoughts.

I have a friend who departed from his Christian heritage many years ago. Choosing to follow other voices he spent a decade-and-a-half seriously studying the Kabbalah, then he pursued Native American spiritual knowledge before wandering into the camp of Tibetan Buddhism – *it seemed I was fighting for my sanity*. But his journey was not over. God led him back, and eventually the blinders fell away with the clarity that Jesus Christ was the indisputable way maker. He still struggles, but a better foundation has been re-established.

My friend also owns a shop, and on occasion the topic of Buddhism comes up with his clients. When it does, his visitors knowingly smile with preconceived notions of blissful spirituality. Then my friend asks if he can read a text from an eminent Bön Buddhist, a piece of writing illuminating the heart of the Eastern path. *Of course! Enlighten us!*

> "It is at this stage that we become free. Nothing disturbs us and we act according to 'crazy wisdom.'

> As the text says, we 'behave like a pig or a dog' who has no dualistic considerations. Good, bad, clean, dirty, everything is perceived as having 'one taste.' Another text says that at this stage we become 'like a little child who does not know anything and will do anything,' who is without any preferences or concepts of good or bad, so there is nothing to accept or reject...
>
> Nothing can disturb us any longer, everything arises in its own way and is liberated in its own way. If we do something, it is fine; if we do not do it, it is fine. There are no longer any rules to follow."[24]

His client's eyes widen with sudden realization. *Really?*

For those who can see, the passage above is more than a road to nowhere – it is a way of destruction. As my friend told me, *it is a spiritual lobotomy*.

What my friend did was simple yet effective: allowing the other person to recognize the folly. How else can a change of heart and mind begin?

Lastly, we must offer an alternative. It is not enough to demonstrate error. A constructive way forward is essential, one grounded in truth and wisdom. Confront the challenge, yes, but now that the point is made, present something better. In other words, *offer direction* to the path of life, liberty and responsibility, freedom, and flourishing.

One more point needs to be made. We tend to think that large and organized movements are needed to effectively engage in worldview issues, that confrontations to liberty and the

Christian faith are best handled through agencies and groups dedicated to those causes. There is a place for such, but *personal* responses are needed.

How does this look?

It is the teacher tactfully asking valid questions when the curriculum demands global citizenship; the healthcare worker who raises concerns when One-ist spiritual practices are sold as medicine; the pastor challenging denominational leaders on interfaithism; the layman in the pews addressing mystical practices being introduced into the church; the student offering alternatives to the professor's leftist ideologies; the landowner standing up to the encroachment of overbearing green policies; the engineer and specialist reigning in technocratic tendencies in their work place; and the politician serving constituents while curbing the tide of statism.

It is the parent who takes the time to demonstrate love, knowledge, and wisdom. It is the friend who cares for a friend, and who extends a hand to the stranger.

What we need are truth tellers who act in love, men and women who credibly stand in the gap.

Options For Christians

Professing Christians have three primary response options.

First, we can ignore the worldview changes, naively thinking we are somehow unaffected. The fact you are reading this, however, demonstrates that this is not your position. Nevertheless, there is a tendency to close our eyes to the challenges, even ignoring the very forces of change that are reshaping our immediate setting.

To be fair, there are many Christians who simply have not considered the unfolding worldview revolution. Sometimes it is hard to see what is in front of us, especially when day-to-day struggles consume so much energy and attention. God grant us the wisdom we need.

But an indifferent approach will only last so long. As manifestations of Oneness become more evident, and the ballooning size of Babel fills our vision, we will inevitably find ourselves in a situation hostile to the Christian message of absolutes, of sin and salvation, and of the need for an exclusive Redeemer. We will become increasingly marginalized and even demonized as the dangerous *other*.

The *second option* is problematic and seriously troubling: To accept and embrace tenants of Oneness, merging its ideals with Christian concepts. The modern story of Western Christianity abounds with examples, pulling from both secular and mystical perspectives.

For example: the history of the Social Gospel movement promised Heaven on Earth through collective efforts, becoming a religious endorsement of world federalism.[25] Many churches subsequently drank from the fountain of socialism. Corresponding is the social justice movement, its roots in the dual history of Catholic common-good teachings and the Marxist drive for class warfare.[26] When stripped of its platitudes, social justice – today, an immersion in identity politics – draws from a Marxist-centric worldview of oppression and oppressors. The individualistic nature of the gospel, that individual persons are afforded salvation, is overshadowed with a message of social redemption through values modification and class struggle.

Or we follow mystical inclinations, like the universal flow-state sold by ecumenical teacher Richard Rohr and contemplative Christian transhumanist, Mike Morrell – that *everything is holy* in the divine flow of wholeness.[27] All you need to do is see it that way and participate, embracing the *spiritual path*. Individual salvation is replaced with the *feeling* of cosmic flow, and the Holy Spirit becomes a *mythic force* we tap into.

Another example bridging into this second option was the Emergent Church movement. Originally touted as a conversation about how to live the gospel within a Postmodern setting, the movement itself adopted the Postmodern attitude, leading to theological revisionism. Social justice was confused for *missions*. Christians needed to be more inclusive – that is, to declare Biblical truth claims as exclusive was a mark of arrogance. The road to redemption was broader, the story more open; the route to God blended social action with community development and contemplative practices.

Brian McLaren, a leading voice in the Emergent community, cast a negative shadow on personal salvation,

> "Sadly, in too many quarters we continue to reduce the scope of the gospel to the individual soul and the nuclear family, framing it in a comfortable, personalized format – it's all about personal devotions, personal holiness, and a personal Savior. This domesticated gospel will neither rock any boats nor

step out of them into stormy waters. We have in many ways responded to the big global crisis of our day with an incredible, shrinking gospel. The world has said, 'No thanks'."[28]

McLaren is wrong. For two millennium the gospel message has been rocking souls, because God Himself rocked eternity by defeating the tomb.

A shrinking gospel? No, it is a saving gospel, and while some say *yes* to the Good News, the history of our world is soaked in the consequences of continually saying, "no thanks." Indeed, we strive to save ourselves, either as individuals or in our communal towers of Babel. And it is to our shame and demise.

While downplaying the individual salvation message, McLaren was *very* concerned about broader social issues, what he described as "big global crisis." His recommended solution, in part, was to weave together the global citizenship ideas of former Gorbachev Foundation president Jim Garrison[29] and Club of Rome member David Korten.[30] Thus, in order to meet the challenges of our day, we Christians must craft a new "framing story that envisions an interdependent, mutually committed, global community of communities."[31] Babel.

Although many Emergent lay-followers, I am sure, would not have considered global governance to be part of their story – the movement was not entirely unified – McLaren's recommendations demonstrated a reconfiguration of priorities. The redemption of individual souls was downgraded in his collective vision. *Vive la révolution.*

The Emergent movement itself moved on, fading and transitioning.[32] New games, however, are always in play as attempts are made to remake the faith in the world's image. *ProgressiveChristianity.org* had as its first point in their 2011 *Eight Points* statement: "Believe that following the path and teachings of Jesus can lead to an awareness and experience of the Sacred and the Oneness and Unity of all life."[33]

Evolutionary Christianity, another movement of sorts, pushes cosmic evolution in ways that dovetails with spiritual transhumanism. Of course, the interfaith movement is also before us, compelling churches, and denominations to take the wide road.

To mirror the world and call it "Christian" is thus our second option. Sadly, it's a road too often chosen.

Option three is to be *in the world* but not *of the world*, and in so doing, to take seriously our Biblical call to be Ambassadors for Christ. But what does this mean?

The Apostle Paul used different illustrations for the Christian life. In 1 Corinthians he likened the sharing of the Good News to that of co-laboring in a field or garden; someone sows, another waters, but God makes things grow.[34] Later he used the metaphor of an athlete, as one who disciplines his body for competition, striving for a prize. We, too, are to be diligent and disciplined in the faith, running the race well.[35]

Then when Paul encouraged his friend, Timothy, to be "strong in the grace that is in Christ Jesus," he used three illustrations: a committed soldier who is willing to endure difficulties, an athlete competing according to the rules, and a hardworking farmer who can partake of the crop.³⁶ Even if you have never been a soldier, athlete or farmer, those roles are relatable.

But Paul said something else in 2 Corinthians 5:20-21, and it wasn't an illustration or allegory,

> "Now then, we are ambassadors for Christ, as though God were pleading through us: we implore you on Christ's behalf, be reconciled to God. For He made Him who knew no sin to be sin for us, that we might become the righteousness of God in Him."

Being an ambassador is not something we normally consider. What does this entail?

First, an ambassador is the *official* and *legal* representative of one's government to a foreign nation. In the era of monarchies, this would be an emissary of the king. We will use this royal designation, for as Christians we have been commissioned by the King of Kings. Therefore, being an Ambassador means that you are the official and legal representative of Jesus Christ, right where you are. It's not something you're striving to become; no, you *are* an Ambassador. The question is not about *becoming*, but how are *you* living out this *royal position*?

Being an ambassador means we know the power and position of our King. We represent His interests and have aligned our own priorities with the mission of being in the King's diplomatic service. We are trained in His ways, and we are cognitive as to how our actions reflect His character, for we are His image bearers in a foreign land.

The culture and traditions of the place we find ourselves in are not unknown to us. Yes, we are set apart from the world's customs, but we are not uninformed regarding the character or composition of our surroundings. In fact, like the Apostle Paul in Athens,[37] we know the setting and beliefs well enough to engage with a high level of discernment and discretion.

As part of the royal diplomatic office, our task is twofold. First, to effectively communicate the King's message, regardless if the land is hostile or friendly. Second, we are to be vigilant to the schemes of foreign powers, recognizing challenges to the King's interest. Then as an ambassador should, we petition for intervention while alerting others in His service to areas of concern.

Being an emissary is a serious undertaking: "Now then, we are ambassadors for Christ, as though God were pleading through us: we implore you on Christ's behalf, be reconciled to God."

It is time we take this calling to heart,

> "You are the light of the world. A city that is set on a hill cannot be hidden. Nor do they light a lamp and put it under a basket, but on a lampstand, and it gives light to all who are in the house. Let your light so shine before men, that they may see your good works and glorify your Father in heaven."[38]

Choosing Freedom

"God remains dead!" Nietzsche screams from the past. "And we have killed him!"[39]

Nietzsche was partially correct. God *was* killed, but the Author of Life is not bound by the curse of death. In the words of Jesus Christ: "Do not be afraid; I am the First and the Last. I am He who lives, and *was dead*, and behold, I am alive forevermore."[40]

In this declaration there is the promise of *real transformation*. Not a techno-Pagan, Marxist-socialist, global-political, psychedelic-spiritual New Man – not a refashioning of ourselves from the images we desire or project or idolize – but the assurance of being *fully restored* by Him who created us. Death has been defeated, and this portends a final judgment, a *verdict beyond the grave*.

It is a revolutionary revelation.

Indeed, the Christian message of otherness – the distinction of God, the finished work of Jesus Christ, and the value of the individual above nature and systems – is *thoroughly counter-cultural*. The words of Lloyd Billingsley are fitting,

> "The Christian faith has indeed shown that it can 'turn the world upside down.' It is, in a very real sense, revolutionary. So are the free political and economic arrangements that have in the past accompanied Christian faith. They are the exception, not the rule, in history. Free people are the true revolutionaries. They can expect resistance."[41]

Jesus Christ once said to a group of Jewish believers: "If you abide in My word, you are My disciples indeed. And you shall know the truth, and the truth shall make you free."[42]

The freedom being offered was not economic, political or social freedom, even though these are wonderful byproducts flowing from the Christian worldview. His freedom was, first and foremost, the liberty of our soul from the bondage of sin and death,

> "Most assuredly, I say to you, whoever commits sin is a slave of sin. And a slave does not abide in the house forever, but a son abides forever. Therefore if the Son makes you free, you shall be free indeed."[43]

Oneness promises a pseudo-freedom by compelling you to conform to the image of our collective dream; to join in building man's Heaven on Earth – *how we imagine it to be*. And you will be "free" within the tall and confining walls of Babel, carefully watched over by a tower of might and power and *collective will*. As Jean-Jacques Rousseau, known for his idea of the social contract, once put it: "Whoever refuses to obey the general will shall be constrained to do so by the whole body… he shall be forced to be free."[44]

Jesus Christ, on the other hand, offers freedom by giving Himself so we are no longer in the bondage of sin, and sin is grounded in the notion we can justify and save ourselves – that the creation is on par with the Creator. Those spiritual chains He has removed from us; that burden has been lifted.

Oneness says our purpose is found in serving creation and uniting with the group, as fickle and fluctuating and frustrating as it may be. In Christ, however, we are one in His purpose; not that we become God, but that we are received as sons and daughters of the King. Value and meaning springs from an eternal source, the Creator of the cosmos who loved the world so much that "He gave His only begotten Son, that whoever believes in Him should not perish but have everlasting life."[45]

But in the spirit of freedom, you have to choose.

What will you put your faith in? World order politics? Technology? Will you look for meaning in a mystical feeling? Are you trusting in the illusion of cosmic oneness? Will you, as a compliant global citizen, proclaim the myth of a planetary society?

The Temple of Man beacons; *come, let us build our Babel – let us play our game of gods.*

Or will you place your hope in Someone?

> "Thus says the LORD, the King of Israel,
> And his Redeemer, the LORD of hosts:
> 'I am the First and I am the Last;
> Besides Me there is no God.'"[46]

Carl Teichrib is a Christian researcher and the author of *Game of Gods: The Temple of Man in the Age of Re-Enchantment* (Whitemud House Publishing, 2018).

ENDNOTES

[1] Stewart E. Kelly, *Truth Considered & Applied: Examining Postmodernism, History, and Christian Faith* (B&H Publishing, 2011), p.325.

[2] Mary Poplin, *Is Reality Secular? Testing the Assumptions of Four Global Worldviews* (IVP Books, 2014), p.265.

³ Genesis 11:1-9.

⁴ For a brief explanation, see Victor P. Hamilton, *Handbook on the Pentateuch: Genesis, Exodus, Leviticus, Numbers, Deuteronomy* (Baker Book House, 1982), pp.81-82. Note: It is possible that Genesis 10 describes the effect of the Babel judgment before the cause, as it says three times the people had differing tongues. If so, then it could be that Genesis 11:1 is describing a single, monolithic language, and not a trade tongue.

⁵ Pseudo Jonathan on Genesis 11. For historical commentary, see John Bowker, *The Targums and Rabbinic Literature: An Introduction to Jewish Interpretations of Scripture* (Cambridge University Press, 1969), p.182.

⁶ Yehezkel Kaufmann, *The Religion of Israel: From Its Beginnings to the Babylonian Exile* (The University of Chicago Press, 1960, translated and abridged by Moshe Greenberg), p. 294. The statement "to storm heaven, to be like God, to rule the world" is taken from the Jewish pseudo-historical text, *The Book of Jasher*, chapter 9. Different Jewish pseudo literatures add to, or embellish, aspects of the Babel narrative. These works are helpful in understanding the range of thinking within ancient Hebrew culture but are not Scriptural.

⁷ Michael S. Heiser explores this aspect and its connection to Deuteronomy 32 in his book, *The Unseen Realm* (Lexham Press, 2015).

⁸ Jacques Ellul, *The Meaning of the City* (Wipf & Stock, 1970/2003), p.17.

⁹ Larry Greenfield, statement given during the Closing Plenary, November 5, 2018, at the Parliament of the World's Religions, Toronto, Ontario. His speech can be viewed on the Parliament of the World's Religions YouTube channel, at https://youtu.be/xRJD0REeH7U.

¹⁰ As taken from my notes. The GF2045 Congress was held in New York City, June 15-16, 2013.

¹¹ Lucile W. Green, *Journey to a Governed World: Thru 50 Years in the Peace Movement* (The Uniquest Foundation, 1991), pp.34-35.

¹² See Romans 1:18-32 for a theological understanding of this situation.

¹³ As quoted from the World Federalist Association brochure, *What the World Needs Now has Changed* (no date). Note: The World Federalist Association has been renamed as Citizens for Global Solutions.

¹³ Tommie StarChild, "Getting Straight with Spirit," *PanheaCon 2020*, Sunday, February 16, 2020, description on p.34 of the agenda book.

¹⁴ Ibid.

¹⁵ ESG – "Environmental, Social and Governance" – is an accounting metrics and screening system for corporations, ascertaining if the company is meeting globally instituted standards on environmental compliance, social issues, and administrative goals of equality and inclusion. Failure to meet ESG certification

may result in limited market access and the inability to secure capital, essentially to be locked out of the marketplace.

[16] *Fact Sheet: Induced Abortion Worldwide* (Guttmacher Institute, March 2018), p.1.

[17] For example, safe abortions – deemed as reproductive rights – are included as a component of sustainable population control. See *World Survey on the Role of Women in Development, 2014: Gender Equality and Sustainable Development* (United Nations, 2014), chapter 5. On page 114 we read the following recommendation: "Ground sustainable population policies in sexual and reproductive health and rights, including the provision of universally accessible quality sexual and reproductive health services, information and education across the life cycle, including safe and effective methods of modern contraception, maternal health care, comprehensive sexuality education and safe abortion." In the 2009 *Philosophical Transcriptions of The Royal Society*, the case was made for a robust abortion action-plan for developing nations, directly related to the "twin challenges of rapid population growth and environmental degradation." See J.J. Speidel et al., "Population Polices, Programmes and the Environment," *Philosophical Transcriptions of The Royal Society, Biological Sciences* (The Royal Society, 2009), p.3060. An older text taking a critical approach to population and resource policies, including abortion as a means to that end, is Julian L. Simon, *Population Matters: People, Resources, Environment, and Immigration* (Transaction Publishers, 1990).

[18] 1 Peter 5:8.

[19] David Berlinski, *The Devil's Delusion: Atheism and Its Scientific Pretentions* (Basic Books, 2009), p. xv.

[20] Ecclesiastes 12:13-14.

[21] Genesis 1:26.

[22] Heiser, *The Unseen Realm: Recovering the Supernatural Worldview of the Bible*, pp.42-43, italics in original.

[23] John 3:16.

[24] Tenzin Wangyal Rinpoche, *Wonders of the Natural Mind: The Essence of Dzogchen in the Native Bon Tradition* of Tibet (Snow Lion, 2000), p.143.

[25] For more on this topic, see my book, *Game of Gods: The Temple of Man in the Age of Re-Enchantment* (Whitemud House Publishing, 2018), pp.335-336, 341-352. See also, Edgar C. Bundy, *Collectivism in the Churches* (The Church League of America, 1958), and Martin Erdmann, *Building the Kingdom of God on Earth: The Churches' Contribution to Marshal Public Support for World Order and Peace, 1919-1945* (Wipf & Stock, 2005).

[26] On the history of social justice, see Carl Teichrib, "The Fallacy of Social Justice: All for One, and Theft to All," *Forcing Change*, September 2010, Volume 4, Issue 9.

[27] Richard Rohr and Mike Morrell, *The Divine Dance: The Trinity and Your Transformation* (Whitaker House, 2016), see pp.186-191.

[28] Brian D. McLaren, *Everything Must Change: Jesus, Global Crisis, and a Revolution of Hope* (Thomas Nelson, 2007), p. 244.

[29] Jim Garrison was the head of the Esalen Institute's Soviet-American Exchange Program, a back door for American and Soviet officials and intelligence operatives, and he later directed the Gorbachev Foundation and State of the World Forum at the Presidio. Garrison was a supporter of world government, and in a 1995 *San Francisco Weekly* interview said: "Over the next 20 to 30 years, we are going to end up with world government. It's inevitable... There's going to be conflict, coercion and consensus. That's part of what will be required as we give birth to the first global civilization." – Jim Garrison, "One World Under Gorby," *San Francisco Weekly*, May 31, 1995. Later Garrison founded Wisdom University, which was amalgamated into Ubiquity University, where he serves as president. Ubiquity offers courses on deep transformation, wholistic awakening, transpersonal psychology, the divine feminine, and the UN Sustainable Development Goals. Garrison came from a Christian family with parents who were Baptist missionaries serving in China but turned away from the faith.

[30] David C. Korten is a full member of the Club of Rome, founder of the Living Economies Forum and the New Economy Working Group. He has authored numerous books on macro-economic issues from a wholistic/global restructuring approach, including *The Great Turning: From Empire to Earth Community*.

[30] McLaren, *Everything Must Change*, pp.262-263.

[31] Ibid., pp.262-263.

[32] The influence of the Emergent Church is undeniable in shifting many Christians, including young pastors, into viewing the Bible through a Postmodern lens – even a post-truth framework. In 2008, *Christianity Today* published an article titled "R.I.P. Emerging Church." In the years that followed, the movement went into decline as a vocal force. The reasons are numerous, including a revisionist handling of Scripture, which compelled some of its leaders to denounce the movement publicly. Some lay people who embraced Emergent thinking returned to more orthodox positions, while others moved in different directions, including Progressive Christianity.

[33] "The 8 Points of Progressive Christianity," *ProgressiveChristianity.org* (https://progressivechristianity.org/the-8-points. Note: near the bottom of the page, you can find a link to the "Past Versions of Core Values," which contains the 2011 edition of the *Eight Points*). Progressive Christianity is a loose movement that blends leftist social activism, the transgression of traditional sexuality, eco-spirituality and environmentalism, and collective salvation.

[34] 1 Corinthians 3:6-9.

[35] 1 Corinthians 9:24-27.

[36] 2 Timothy 2:1-6.

[37] See Acts 17.

[38] Matthew 5:14-16.

[39] Friedrich Nietzsche, *The Gay Science* (Cambridge University Press, 2001/2008), p.120.
[40] Revelation 1:17b-18a, italics for emphasis.
[41] Lloyd Billingsley, *The Absence of Tyranny: Recovering Freedom in Our Time* (Multnomah Press, 1986), pp.173-174.
[42] John 8:31-32.
[43] John 8:34-35.
[44] Jean-Jacques Rousseau, *The Social Contract* (Penguin Classics, 1968), p.64.
[45] John 3:16.
[46] Isaiah 44:6.

CHAPTER 3

IS IT MRNA OR SOMETHING ELSE? MY ELECTROMAGNETIC UNDERSTADNING OF DISEASE AND TREATMENT

DR. LEE MERRITT

Disease is not synonymous with germs. Disease simply means "dis-ease"—meaning lack of comfort. It might come as a surprise to most people that submicroscopic particles called "viruses" have never been isolated, that transmission of viral diseases have not been proven, and that Louis Pasteur admitted on his deathbed to lying about his ability to transmit disease from a pure specimen of bacteria. Beyond that, in Latin "Virus" means toxin or poison. So, when we were told there was a new "virus" called SARS CoV2 that was killing people in China—we were not lied to. There was a new *poison* killing people in China and transmitting "dis-ease".

Modern Medicine demands a precise diagnosis before any treatment can be performed. As a result, many dollars are spent on a myriad of tests and consultations, but after all of that is completed, the diagnosis usually consists only of a description—not discovery of the root cause. For example, a patient may present to a medical office with a neurologic problem—intermittent weakness, progressive imbalance, numbness that comes and goes, etc. The physician then does an examination and records a number of findings like reflex activity, function of cranial nerves etc. MRIs are ordered of the brain and spinal cord, and these reveal "plaques" or areas of discoloration in the brain and spinal cord. So, the physician reports to the patient that, on the basis of findings of the examination and the MRI, they have Multiple Sclerosis, or MS. And it may sound to the patient as if the doctor knows what this MS is. But in reality, all he has done is given a name to a constellation of symptoms. In 40 years of my life in medicine I was told we simply did not know what caused the disease. But in the last few years, a Pathologist did what should have been done a century ago. He actually did autopsies of MS patients, and as it turns out 100% of those diagnosed with MS had parasites in the Brain and Spinal Cord. Radiologists and Neurologists had seen the MRI plaques but apparently never considered what might be causing them. This is just one example of many diseases that are simply "Diagnosis by Description". It is important that we all recognize the difference between description and understanding the root cause of an illness.

Ancient medicine practitioners did not require a precise "diagnosis" before they proposed treatment. They believed there were only two causes of disease and therefore two treatments: Purification (Get right with God), and Detoxification (Removal of "viruses"). In the 21st Century, we understand that one can also be "dis-eased" also from lack of nutrition, from electromagnetic toxicity, and from parasites, so our treatment program needs some expansion from the time of Hippocrates. But the principle of the ancients, *that there are only a few root causes of disease* seems to be true, in spite of the thousands and thousands of disease labels. So, spending a fortune on making a precise and overly complicated diagnosis isn't required. What is required is a systematic program of purification, detoxification, parasite elimination, nutritional support, and EMF protection. I predict this will be the foundation of the revolution in medicine, —returning to the ancient principles while employing more modern techniques of therapy.

The treatment protocols I am suggesting, apply to both "COVID" whatever that is, and the misnamed Covid Vaccine. When COVID first appeared, the medical establishment—WHO, FDA, CDC etc. told Pathologists not to do autopsies of suspected COVID patients because it might spread disease. Of course, autopsies are the *first* thing that should have been done if understanding the root cause of COVID was really their concern. It is a running joke in medical circles that "Pathologists know everything—but too late". Fortunately, breaking the WHO rules, in June 2021, a group of pathologists reviewed over 360 autopsies of people who were thought to have died of "COVID" and for whom an autopsy had been done. They concluded:

> "Despite attention to and investment in quantifying global burdens of disease, the diagnosis in the majority of COVID-19-related deaths currently remain unclear."[lxvi]

In other words, during the year and a half that our governments were pushing vaccines and quarantine and all sorts of draconian anti-human measures on us, those doctors professionally tasked with understanding the nature of the disease had no idea what was killing people. Let that one sink in.

Compounding the problem of this new toxin "COVID", the world has been victimized by a disastrous vaccine program. In spite of the drug company description, there are many reasons to disbelieve the mRNA purported to be at the core of the COVID19 vaccines.

First, the use of any mRNA technology up until 2018 was very costly, running nearly a million dollars a dose. Yet now, two years later, we are to believe these same companies, notoriously worried about profits, are able to produce and sell it for under $30?? And in spite of billions being spread on mRNA research less than a handful of treatments have actually materialized. I am starting to suspect that mRNA medical research is like NASA—it pretends to do specified science while in reality is a black program slush fund going who-knows-where.

Secondly, Pfizer claims that by October 2022, they had produced 638,734,000 doses at 11 facilities around the world. Assuming they began production in April 2020, (long before the Emergency Use Authorization was approved), and each facility had been brought fully online, they would need to have been producing 14.35 doses per second, round the clock, 7 days a week with no deletions for quality, nor any pausing of the production lines, etc. If they actually waited until

August 23, 2020, when the EUA approval was official, that number increases to 18.7 doses/ sec. Is that technically possible? And, we should add, *is that technically possible utilizing manufacturing and safety standards for injectable drugs/vaccines.*

But the most troubling problem that seems to have been swept under the proverbial rug, is that of degradation of mRNA. Multiple researchers have shown that RNAs are very short lived-in nature, lasting from minutes to 17 hours—not enough time to even make it out of a production plant. In June 2022—note the date—Chinese mRNA researchers from the University of Washington Department of Materials Science and Engineering published a review article in the Royal Society of Chemistry Journal in which they discuss the challenges of mRNA therapies.[lxvii]

> "Due to the poor thermal stability of mRNA, a cold chain is required in order to ensure that the mRNA formulation is at optimal stability prior to clinical use, which can be costly when considering transport of millions of doses. It should also be considered that infectious diseases are prevalent in developing nations in the tropics, amplifying the need for mRNA vaccine formulations that do not need an ultralow temperature storage."

Remember, the first batches of vaccines in 2021 were distributed in supercooled containers and thawed immediately before injection. But that supply protocol lasted just long enough for the rollout to be firmly underway and for the news cycle to have moved on from "cold storage". Suddenly the powers at Big Pharma all decided in unison that cold storage was unnecessary. Unfortunately, they forgot to inform those active researchers, quoted above, and many others continuing mRNA research who still believe their own experience and research.

So, what could be in the vaccines that could account for the side effects, if it is not mRNA? And what is the purpose of the "vaccine" if it contains no mRNA? The question of the presence of mRNA is important for several reasons. Psychologically, people—especially doctors—may be reluctant to pursue treatment options because they have decided if one's DNA is being altered, the situation is hopeless. Removing the fear may prompt the medical profession to awaken to the need for treatment against this vaccination. It is a maxim in medicine that it makes no difference to miss the diagnosis of a disease for which you have no cure. But it is a tragedy to miss treating the treatable.

Consistent with known research and the reports of the pharmaceutical giants, the vaccines contain a lipid nanoparticle (LNP) coating that is presumably just the vessel for carrying the "payload" of the mRNA. But the "active ingredient" may be only the LNP itself. Japanese researchers injected only the LNP into volunteers. They discovered the LNP accumulated in the ovaries 64 times more than in the skeletal muscle. It is easy to believe a toxic LNP nanoparticle—even in the absence of any mRNA-- that targeted the ovaries, could result in infertility, bleeding irregularities, and miscarriages in women. By their own admission, the pharmaceutical researchers were well aware of the toxicity of the LNP due to the presence of cationic lipids.[lxviii] Specifically these lipids could account for early clotting issues by stripping the protective negative charges from the blood stream. And, graphene—although denied by the creators of this vaccine, is a known component in LNPs as shown in the diagram below.[lxix]

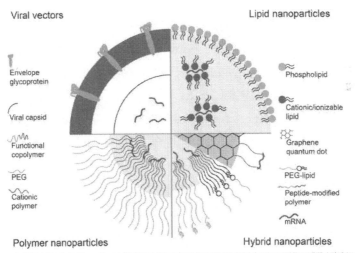

Fig. 1 Types of mRNA carriers. Viral vectors utilize modified forms of viruses such as retrovirus to encapsulate and deliver mRNA. Lipid-based vectors use amphiphilic lipids with positive charge which can bind and stabilize mRNA. Block-copolymer consisting of PEG and cationic polymer is used to form structures that can stabilize the mRNA in the core of the vector. Hybrid vector systems consist of different classes of materials to take the advantageous aspects of each material.

Does DNA and therefore RNA function as we have been told?

I think of DNA theory in two categories of my own creation—the tickertape theory and the antenna theory. In the tickertape theory DNA functions by expressing precise genetic code. sequences and adding or subtracting small sequences of code will alter the function of the DNA. DNA and RNA are made of four amino acid-based nucleotides or nucleosides, so can be abbreviated by letters such as GCTA for Guanine, cytosine, thymine, and adenosine. Furthermore, these letters can be coded in binary where everything is reduced to zeros and ones, and computerized. The tickertape theorists believe they can reprogram the DNA by inserting or deleting codes. But the devil is literally in the details here. Feng Zhang at MIT who is credited as the father of Crisper technology says that we cannot do precise gene insertion—only gene knockdown (meaning getting rid of some function by eliminating code). For example, to increase shelf life, they made GMO potatoes by crudely deleting genes until the potatoes had longer shelf life. Unfortunately, what they actually did was to eliminate the ability of the potato to produce melanin—the chemical that causes the brown appearance in old rotten potatoes. So, when you purchase GMO potatoes, they may be old and chemically "rotting"—but you won't see it because there is no melanin! As the inventor of GMO potatoes confessed, they knew about as much about reading the Genome as reading Sumerian hieroglyphs.

Another problem with the ticker tape theory is the enormity of the task. The human genome contains more than 3.4 billion base codes (the GCTAs), and we share about 50% of our genetic code with bananas—maybe more if you are a politician. We know very little of the actual function of 90% or more of the 3.4 billion bases. And to complicate matters even more, we have "jumping genes" actually called transposons, that appear to move from place to place within the genetic sequence. So, given this level of complexity, is it even theoretically possible for mere mortals to alter the DNA to make significant and predictable changes? For that matter, is it possible that a small amount of encapsulated genetic material floating through the air (the image of "viruses" we have been given) can wreak deadly havoc with such a system? And finally, is the Genome able to repair itself like other parts of living creatures?

The antenna theory of DNA accepts that we are creatures of light, and that DNA is an antenna creating, minute to minute, the hologram that is us. Nikola Tesla is frequently quoted as having said, "If you want to understand the secrets of the universe, think in terms of energy frequency and vibration." What is less well known is this quotation:

> "Alpha waves in the human brain are between 6 and 8 hertz. The wave frequency of the human cavity resonates between 6 and 8 hertz. All biological systems operate in the same frequency range. The human brain's alpha waves function in this range and the electrical resonance of the earth is between 6 and 8 hertz. Thus, our entire biological system - the brain and the earth itself - work on the same frequencies. If we can control that resonate system electronically, we can directly control the entire mental system of humankind."

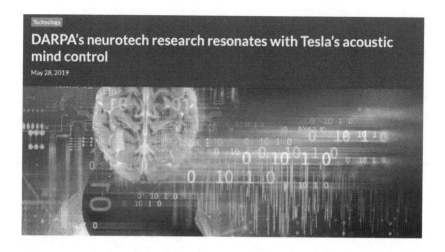

Kaznacheyev in the 1920's and 30's in the Soviet Union demonstrated that symptom specific cell death could be transferred electromagnetically from one group of cells to another. In other words, the electromagnetic signature of a fatal disease could be captured and broadcast to spread a contagion with no germ involved. Interestingly, Feng Zhang, mentioned earlier, did his PhD research on "Optogenetics"— i.e., changing cellular function by bombarding DNA with wavelength. Currently, research with the next generation of optogenetics utilizes chemicals that respond to wavelength and pulsation of light. These chemicals called opsins are present in all living things but are much weaker in mammals than in bacteria. By hybridizing mammalian and bacterial opsins, injecting them in mice, and stimulating them with certain wavelengths, researchers are able to alter brain function/ mood (think the unexplainable sudden violence of the Hutus and the Tutsis), and can cause cardiac arrhythmias. (think of the Travis Scott Rap concert where vaccinated young people being exposed to strobing lights and other frequencies, had sudden collapse and death.)

So, in summary of the problem: 1) Our enemies play with language. They don't lie, but they tell the truth in such a way you probably will not understand it. In this regard, they tell you we are dealing with a virus, but fail to tell you that "Virus" in Latin means "toxin" or "poison". Poisons are cheaper and easier to produce and implement than complex genetic solutions. The medical cartel has convinced us we are being infected by invisible organisms called viruses, so they push antiviral therapies. But how do these "antiviral" work? They block the production of genetic material. The rationale for their use is that "viruses" take over your cellular machinery and produce abnormal RNA that causes cell death. By giving you antivirals, they temporarily shut down your genetic repair mechanism. It is a beautifully constructed attack—poison followed by more poison labelled "treatment".

2) According to optogenetic theory, changing the electromagnetic milieu changes our cellular functioning through the DNA signaling. To be created in the image of God does not just require "clay" but a blueprint that can be read every second of our life. What better evil to inflict on humanity than to alter the antenna receiver for God's blueprint.

2) Electromagnetic transmission of disease has been proven whereas transmission of infectious airborne agents has not. "Directed energy weapons" which

have been researched for years are cheaper and easier to disperse and more controllable than any airborne or contact agent. Researchers have identified numerous substances in the COVID vaccine that could be used for changing our internal resonance and connecting us to an external wireless hub—metallic particles, graphene oxide (which is the most efficient conductor of charge known), microtubules, things resembling self-assembling microchips, and various crystalline structures. Directed energy weapons have been employed against the USA (Havana Syndrome) and used by the USA—The Voice of God, and 5G Denial of Access technologies in Iraq.

3) Although not mentioned previously, it is very likely that parasites—natural and manmade play a role in the vaccine. People are having sudden worsening or new onset of cancer, and new evidence suggests that cancer is due to unrecognized intracellular parasites. Parasites may be released from their cysts as the immune system is damaged by poisoning, or they may be instilled in egg form in the vaccine itself. (Parasite eggs are not killed by the temperatures used in this vaccine manufacture.) In this regard, the absolute aversion of the perpetrators to any use of any antiparasitic medicine is notable.

4). Any nutrient deficiency makes you more vulnerable to "dis-ease" and can create diseases such as scurvy, pellagra, and anemia. Immunity diminishes with improper nutrition.

This list is not in any way likely to represent the totality of the vaccine composition but gives a basis for medical intervention.

My treatment regimen is based on a non-viral paradigm: It is my opinion that we need to concentrate our therapeutic efforts on normalizing the electromagnetic environments, removing parasites, and detoxification. This is a short summary and further details of this regimen can be found on my website, TheMedicalRebel.com. Of course, nothing will overcome a bad diet, lack of exercise and absence of spiritual connection to the creator God. Always start with the basics. Don't ingest or inject poisons. If your great great grandmother would not recognize something as food, don't eat it. Weston A. Price's motto was "Real food for real people." Or as Jack Lalane said, "If man made it, don't eat it." Then:

1. Protect yourself from EMF. This is not like protecting yourself from Ionizing radiation such as x-rays that can be blocked by lead etc. We are being bombarded by a variety of wavelengths, that resonate with the wiring in our house, come through the walls from satellites, and are usually carried in our pockets and our hands. Get in the habit of putting your cell phone an arm length away from you, and don't put it into your bra or pants pockets. Get rid of your microwave. Besides the leaky radiation that can be measured more than 20 feet away in some cases, microwaved food is damaged. It has been shown in animal studies that, although the measurable constituents of food didn't change, eating microwaved food resulted in lower levels of critical antioxidants in the animals which ate the microwaved food. EMF causes ions to flow into cells to dysregulate cellular function. Putting EMF mitigating devices on your electrical fuse box, into your outlets and near your bed, and wearing a wrist band can make a difference even though the devices are small compared to a huge microwave tower. This is due to the fact that radiation exposure is inversely proportional to the square of the distance from the emitter. In other words, if you are close to a small source, it will still have more effect than a large source far away. I would look for a company with bioassays that prove the benefit of their devices. I personally use EMFsol.com[lxx] for that reason, but there are many companies now getting into the market.

2: Parasite Removal. We are probably facing both naturally occurring and artificial parasites. In a recent post-mortem study of MS (Multiple Sclerosis) deaths, 100% of the patients were found at autopsy to have parasites in the brain and spinal cord. Unrecognized parasites probably account for many neurologic symptoms, and most if not all of cancer. If you are an adult and have never been treated, it may take you a year or more to rid the body of most of the parasites. There are a number of drugs you can use and can get either overseas or locally at an animal supply. These include, Ivermectin, Fenbendazole, Nitazoxanide, and others. They are generally dosed by weight. Sadly, most American physicians do not regard parasites as a problem for people living in first world countries, so they can't contribute much. I have treated myself and others using a cycling method beginning with one drug for three days on, then five days off. Change meds every once in a while. As time goes on you can slowly increase the off time till you reach a treatment once a month for baseline maintenance. For more information see my video here: https://rumble.com/v1owcgh-parasites-a-new-paradigm.html

3. Detoxify: There are several levels and means of detoxification. Perhaps the simplest and cheapest method, used by millions all over the world, is daily chlorine dioxide, taken orally or in a bath or both. Chlorine Dioxide is "The Universal Antidote" (See documentary of that name) and has been shown to get rid of heavy metals and other toxins. A protocol is available here: https://drleemerritt.com/uploads/Chloprine%20Diopxide%201%20Jan%202023.pdf No matter what else I do, I always get my daily CD bath and usually also oral dose of CD.

A more aggressive approach is to start with a chelation challenge to get a clear idea which heavy metals you have accumulated. Hair samples are not as sensitive but may alert you to gross elevations of some metals. EDTA ¼ teas daily under the tongue or a topical EDTA lotion, for a few months a year (not continuously) can also rid the body more slowly of some toxic metals.

4. Restore internal electrical charges. The final common pathway of damage by graphene and cationic lipids (vaccine) and other poisons we contact in our daily lives, is the stealing of electrons. After the COVID Vax we see clumping of red blood cells due to stripping of electrons (negative charges that repel each other to keep flow going) from the cells and linings of the arteries and veins. Carbon 60 is probably the world's best electron donor. It is found naturally in Shungite, but in very small amounts and not usable internally. I have used Greska's Carbon 60 because it has been shown to be non-toxic, is made with no toxic chemicals that linger after processing, and there is direct evidence that C60 restores laminar blood flow with breaking up of the stacks of red cells.

5. Get sunlight daily. Your cells are each little batteries. To expel toxins they need to recharge, and they do this with exposure to infrared and near infrared frequencies. Sunlight is great but hard to do in cold climate. Infrared saunas and as a second choice, full spectrum tanning booths are a good idea in the winter. Our inability to expel toxins due to lack of cell charge is the real reason for the winter "flu season".

6. Other electrical ideas.

- Grounding, i.e., coming into contact with the earth directly—lying on the grass, walking barefoot, etc. restores the body's normal electrical balance and protects from ambient EMF.[4]
- Our music has been retuned since the 1930s to a frequency not good for our cells, A= 440. You can get software to retune your music to A 432.
- 528 is a healing frequency touted by many, and written about in detail by Dr. Len Horowitz in his book, you can find here: http://drlenhorowitz.com/books-by-dr-leonard-horowitz/. I often listen to 528 music while writing etc., and I carry a 528 tuning fork to use for spot pains and to refresh after being on a computer or cell phone.

7. Supplementation: One of the many lies organized medicine continues to push is "Vitamins just make expensive urine." They know it's not true. Medical professors themselves treat scurvy (Vitamin C deficiency), Rickets (Vitamin D deficiency) Megaloblastic Anemia (Vitamin B12/B9 Deficiency), Pellagra (Niacin deficiency), Cretinism (Iodine deficiency) and more. But by having woefully inadequate education about nutrition they ignore the vast amount of published research showing the relationship of minerals and other deficiencies to most chronic diseases. There are 90 essential nutrients we cannot produce in our body and must ingest. Without a balanced nutritional supplement, you will not have the ability to efficiently and effectively make energy for the body. And if you cannot make energy adequately, you cannot expel toxins. And when you cannot expel toxins, you become ill. And when you are ill, you often cannot eat to correct the deficiency. This is why some people have their hair fall out when ill—their body shuts down systems that are not critical in order to divert energy to those systems necessary for life. Here is a video discussing the general principles of eating and supplementation that I learned from a specialist in nutrition. https://www.youtube.com/watch?v=DB3h3sVCTXE. I used to try to use pills. That method doesn't work except as an add on. I still take added iodine and Vitamin D, but you simply cannot take 90 pills a day! And if you are missing a few essential nutrients, your metabolic chain has broken links.

Dr. Lee Merritt graduated from the University of Rochester School of Medicine and Dentistry in New York. She completed an Orthopaedic Surgery Residency in the United States Navy and served 9 years as a Navy physician and surgeon.

ENDNOTES

[1] Maiese, A, Manetti, A., LaRussa R., et. al., Autopsy Findings in Covid-19 Related Deaths, a Literature Review; Forensic Science Medical Pathology, 2021, 17 (2): 279-296

[2] Crommelin DJA, Anchordoquy TJ, Volkin DB, Jiskoot W, Mastrobattista E. Addressing the Cold Reality of mRNA Vaccine Stability. J Pharm Sci. 2021 Mar;110(3):997-1001. doi: 10.1016/j.xphs.2020.12.006. Epub 2020 Dec 13. PMID: 33321139; PMCID: PMC7834447.

[3] Toxicity of cationic lipids and cationic polymers in gene delivery Hongtao L., Shubiao Z., Bing Wang, et. al.; Journal of Controlled Release, Volume 114, Issue 1, 10 August 2006, Pages 100-109.

[4] See https://www.emfsol.com/?aff=TwTojgBcsnRYsEW9K

CHAPTER 4

ESTABLISHING YOUR BORDERS

RANDY CONWAY

In this chapter, I hope to reveal not only the process of Authentication, but also why I see it as a physical act and fulfillment of the command to come out of Babylon . *"And I heard another voice from heaven, saying, Come out of her, my people, that ye be not partakers of her sins, and that ye receive not of her plagues" (Revelation 18:4).* It is my desire to not only show this as a fulfillment, but also to prove that we are in Babylon, which is a worldwide system and not simply a geographical location of longitude and latitude.

We love the story of Esther and often quote Mordecai's reminding her that they are here "for such a time as this." The words of Esther to the King still ring true today, in Esther 7:4, we find this quote: *"For we are sold, I and my people, to be destroyed, to be slain, and to perish…"*. As briefly as I can, I will explain that even today we are being sold. Not just the heinous crime of trafficking, but the unknown act of trading in human labor through birth records and registration of every person on the planet; and this act of trading in humanity, or even in the souls of men, is not new. In Ezekiel 28 verses 16 and 18, we find a description of Satan, and the punishment he receives is partly based on his "trading/trafficking." Revelation 18 reveals what is being traded as John prophesies the fall of Babylon. After the command to come out of Babylon, the Revelator makes a stunning disclosure when he says Babylon is trading *"the bodies and souls of men" (Revelation 18:13).*

The public has become aware in the past few years of the unspeakable practice of trading in adrenochrome. As horrific as this is, it is not new. Solomon said in Ecclesiastes 1:9, *"That which has been is what will be, that which is done is what will be done, and there is nothing new under the sun."* Hosea 4:2 states, *"By swearing, and lying, and killing, and stealing, and committing adultery, they break out, and blood toucheth blood."* This verse alludes to the trading in blood that is going on today. You may be asking what this has to do with Authentication and Establishing Your House. The answer is simple; Babylon can do as it wills for its own pleasure and for its own gain, even do unto others as it will if it has administrative rights over them. They own the rights to people through Registration. As God's children, those rights no longer belong to Babylon because we have been bought with a price. *"For he that is called in the Lord, being a servant, is the Lord's freeman: likewise also he that is called, being free, is Christ's servant. Ye are bought with a price; be not ye the servants of men"* (*1Corinthians 7:22-23).*

Authentication, along with a Counter Deed, an Affidavit of Ownership, and a proper proof of Baptism, is notification and proof that the price has been paid and we are the "Lord's freemen." This notification is seen in this 3D physical world AND the unseen realm of the Spirit. It is necessary to be a "freeman" in BOTH realms, otherwise you are still a prisoner. Actually, more than just a prisoner – you are a slave – and slaves are subject to mandates and tributes. Freemen are not and certainly not the "sons" (*Matthew 17:25-26*).

After the process of Authentication, it is imperative that you establish your "House" and learn to self-govern. This is what will establish the borders of the Kingdom in which you live and will also establish in both realms which King you serve, and whose law you are subject to. Later, we will examine how we take the idea of being Ambassadors of Christ (2 Corinthians 5:20) and apply that in the reality of living our lives today as verified, bona fide, vetted Ambassadors of the Kingdom of God.

Finally, as means of introduction to this chapter, I refer to the words of an old familiar song, "This world is not my home, I'm just a passing through," and we have often spoken the words, "in the world but not of the world." I hope to establish that there is a means to make this our reality, not just a spiritual hope for some day in the sweet by and by. Any plan to come out of Babylon must be in accordance with the Word of God, otherwise, it is an effort in futility. We must be ever cognizant of the fact that there are two realms of reality that we are continually dealing with. One is the 3D world of our physical existence and the other is the unseen realm of the spiritual world. The Apostle Paul reminds us in Ephesians 6:12 that *"we wrestle not against flesh and blood,"* but the rulers in the unseen realm with which we are engaged. This road is not for the faint of heart, but we are encouraged in the Word to "Fear Not". In fact, the Bible tells us 365 times to "Fear Not"– one time for every day of the year. 1John 4:4 states a reality – a fact that you must believe and hold onto, not a concept or some motivational axiom. This should be our reality: *"Ye are of God, little children, and have overcome them*: **because greater is he that is in you, than he that is in the world."** (Emphasis added)

Isaiah 26 is a Song of Victory encouraging trust in God's protection. It speaks of a righteous nation, of perfect peace that is promised for those who will keep their minds stayed upon the Living God. It tells of *"other lords"* besides The Living God that have had dominion over us, but God Almighty has promised that He will make their *"memory to perish."* The Song goes on to say, *"You have increased the nation, O LORD, You have increased the nation; You are glorified; You have expanded all the borders of the land" (Isaiah 26:15)*. Also included in the text of this chapter is a confession from Isaiah that the people have not brought any deliverance on the earth, and the evil that rules has not fallen. As we go down this road together and each comes out of Babylon (the World System of Governance) and establishes our own House, our borders expand. We are the Remnant – the children of the Living God – and it is *"not by might nor by power but by My Spirit, says the Lord of Hosts" (Zechariah 4:6)* that we will accomplish this monumental paradigm shift in how we see ourselves, our Tribes (Houses), our Nation and the world. This will determine how we are to be governed and to which Kingdom we will pledge our allegiance; we cannot serve two masters.

We read in 1Peter 2:9 the following: *"But ye are a chosen generation, a royal priesthood, an holy nation, a peculiar people; that ye should shew forth the praises of him who hath called you out of darkness into his marvelous light."* There is a movement among God's people to go beyond our Salvation, understanding that Salvation is not the completion of our work in Christ, rather the beginning. Engaging in the work of building that Holy Nation, as described in 1Peter, is a part of our continuing work and can only be accomplished without fear of being a "peculiar people." We are to reflect His Light and have nothing to do with the works of darkness.

Rom 13:12 "The night is far spent, the day is at hand: let us therefore cast off the works of darkness, and let us put on the armour of light".
Eph 5:11 "And have no fellowship with the unfruitful works of darkness, but rather reprove them".

Please read the following histories of our nation which I hope will challenge us to come out of Babylon, establish our Houses and expand the borders of the Kingdom of God. Please read the following with an open mind and a desire to learn and know, as it may be a strange and new concept to many.
Matt 13:43 "Then the righteous will shine forth as the sun in the kingdom of their Father. He who has ears to hear, let him hear!"

A LITTLE HISTORY

This section will deal mainly with the history of the United States, as the United States is where I was born and live. The ideas that will be covered in this chapter will, however, be of great significance regardless of where one lives because the little "g" god of this world is just that – "of this world."

Around 55-56 A.D., Paul wrote his second letter to the church at Corinth. In 2 Corinthians 4:4, he speaks of the god of this world that has blinded the eyes of men, but we must back up to a point of origin. We are all familiar with the record of Genesis 3 and the fall when sin entered the garden. However, not all realize that this was a contractual event and that the contract entered into would not be completed until Calvary. In fact, Jesus Himself makes the declaration that the old contract is completed when He said from the cross, "It is finished."

Everything within the system of governance that we see today is about contracts. James Allen Odle's book, "The Contract in Eden," states that "Satan is the solicitor and Adam and Eve are the ones offered a contract with deceptive terms and conditions. The acceptance of contract by Adam and Eve caused Adam and Eve to breach the Covenant and Law of God" *(The Contract in Eden, Chapter 8, Pg 60)*. This caused a loss of many things, but a loss of LAND was one major result, and another was a loss of FREEDOM. From this point forward in history, we see the use of contracts by the Kingdom of Darkness. Genesis 6 and the fallen angels coming through a portal at Mount Hermon, the building of the Tower of Babel by Nimrod, and establishment of the Babylonian One World Government are records of taking the LAND and owning the EARTH by the Kingdom of Darkness. (There is much that has been written and much I could disclose here in regard to the history of mankind, but that would be a book unto itself and not a chapter.) So, back to Paul and 56 A.D. We need to realize that the blindness that Paul referred to has not gone away and the enemy of God, who is the enemy of our souls, still blinds the hearts and minds of men today.

Moving from 56 A.D., we will take a huge leap forward to the year 1620. (There is much between these years, but that is part of the hidden and distorted history.) Most are familiar with the story of the Pilgrims coming to the Americas – those who had separated themselves from the King and Church of England – and an edict of the King that demanded that all Puritans not willing to conform must leave England. In 1619, Pastor John Robinson wrote of the journey upon which they were about to embark, "Now as **the people of God in old time were called out of Babylon** civil, the place of their bodily bondage, and were to come to Jerusalem, and there to build the Lord's temple, or tabernacle … **so are the people of God now to go out of Babylon** spiritual to Jerusalem … and to build themselves as lively stones into a spiritual house, or temple, for the Lord to dwell in …." *(The Light and Glory, Peter Marshal & David Manuel, Page 110)* The very intent of these pilgrim's journey to the Americas was to build themselves as temples of God, and to expand the borders of the Kingdom of God. This is further evidenced in the Mayflower Compact: "**In the name of God**, Amen. We, whose names are underwritten, the loyal subjects of our dread sovereign lord, King James, by the grace of God, of Great Britaine, France, and Ireland king, defender of the faith, etc., **having undertaken, for the glory of God**, and **advancement of the Christian faith**, and honour of our king and country, a voyage to plant the first colony in the Northern parts of Virginia, doe, by these presents, solemnly and mutually **in the presence of God, and one another, covenant and combine ourselves together** into a civil body politick, for our better ordering and preservation and furtherance of the ends aforesaid; and by virtue hereof to enact, constitute, and frame such just and equal laws, ordinances, acts, constitutions, and offices, from time to time, as shall be thought most meete and convenient for the generall good of the Colonie unto which we promise all due submission and obedience. In witness whereof we have hereunder subscribed our names at Cap-Codd the 11. of November, in the year of the raigne of our sovereigne lord, King James, of England, France, and Ireland, the eighteenth, and of Scotland the fiftie-fourth. Anno. Dom. 1620." (The Mayflower Compact) www.thefederalistpapers.org) **Emphasis added**.

I find it interesting that Pastor Robinson describes those who are to make this journey to the Americas as "Lively Stones." I again refer to *1Peter 2:4, "Coming to Him as to a living stone who is rejected by men, but chosen of God and precious, you also, as living stones, are being built up into a spiritual house as a holy priesthood..."* As we journey forward, we will see how as living stones we are the building material for His Kingdom, and how we can actually build our HOUSE – our Tribe – as that Holy Nation and come out of Babylon as the Puritans sought to do in 1620.

In his book, "Kingdom Government and the Promise of Sheep Nations," Daniel Duvall describes Nebuchadnezzar's dream from Daniel chapter 2. Mr. Duval goes through the kingdoms described in this dream relating all the past and future kingdoms envisioned there. In referring to the final Kingdom, that is, the Kingdom of God, which is described as a "Stone" that will "smite the image" and become a great mountain filling the whole earth, he refers to the first coming of Jesus and His death, burial, and resurrection as a major component of the building of the Kingdom of God. This event ended the old contract, as I said earlier. But he goes on to say that the "implementation of the Kingdom of God is not a singular event." *(Chapter 23, Page 311)* I believe we are part of that implementation; we are the building blocks, the living stones. The foundation stone that the builders rejected is the foundation upon which we are to be building right now. My good friend, Randy Lunsford puts it this way, "Wherever righteousness and justice are established is where He builds His Throne---His Rule---His Law!" *(Psalm 89:14)* We have not occupied the ground; rather we have relinquished the ground we held and have lost any foundation for His Throne. I do not want to imply that all is lost we can still complete the Kingdom work to which we have been called and commissioned.

So, in the ancient Hebrew tradition of all men being equal in the sight of God, the history of the United States has its beginning. There were some great advancements for the Kingdom of God, including the fact that the first Constitution written in the New World was in Connecticut; it was known as "The Fundamental Orders of Connecticut." This document states that the people of Connecticut, in their form of Governance, should "conjoin together as one according to the

Word of God, should do for ourselves and our successors… to **preserve the Liberty and Purity of the Gospel of our Lord Jesus which we now profess."**

(*https://oll.libertyfund.org/page/1639-fundamental-orders-of-connecticut*) But the Colonies do not retain such integrity for long, proving we are indeed engaged in a clash of two kingdoms.

The land to which the Puritans were led in order to further the gospel of Jesus Christ and seeking freedom to be the Holy Nation and the Living Stones we are called to be, has been dedicated by ritual over and over and Contracted to the Kingdom of Darkness – to BABYLON. It is time to reclaim the land, and with it the dominion and stewardship of that land and the freedom wherein Christ has made us free.
In 1913, when Woodrow Wilson was president of the United States, the very first motion picture ever viewed at the White House was a movie entitled *Cabiri*. The fact that the White House is in Washington DC and is built on specific Ley Lines with extreme occultic architecture and layout is an obvious move of the Kingdom of Darkness. Tom Horn and the Faull Brothers have already covered that topic in great detail in the documentary film "The Belly of the Beast" and other works. *Cabiri* is a story of trafficking, human sacrifice, and the worship of Molech. I think it is no accident that this was the movie shown. It is important to understand that things done under the façade of harmless entertainment are in fact rituals and ceremonies that create Contracts with the Kingdom of Darkness, allow entrance to evil, and **divide the land**. This is exactly why you no longer see marching bands doing a

halftime show at the Super Bowl; that event is the largest human-trafficking event of the year and a ritual being pumped into millions of homes. Because they were invited in, contractual rights are seized by the Kingdom of Darkness and the ground in millions of homes is now held under agreement by the evil entities to which the sacrifices were made.

At the Chicago World's Fair in 1933 with hundreds of thousands in attendance, an enormous ritual was performed to Molech. There are still questions to this day as to whether the child thrown into the flames of Molech was truly an effigy or a living child. This Molech theme and use of ritual to claim and occupy ground has been used over and over. The Gotthard Tunnel Opening Celebration, the Olympics Opening Ceremonies, the 2022 UK Commonwealth Games Opening Ceremony, the 2023 Grammy performance by Sam Smith and Kim Petrus, and the 8-foot-tall statue of Ruth Bader Ginsberg just placed in New York are all examples of marking territory and claiming ground. In fact, there are innumerable places and events around the world where rituals have taken place to claim ground. And we cannot forget the Masons who placed corner stones across this country as a ritual to claim ground. It is time for the Sons of God to become the Manifest Sons of God, to realize who we are in Him and to stop the sacrificing of our children to Molech, to stop the trafficking of souls, to end the giving of this earth to the Kingdom of Darkness and reclaim the dominion and step up into the responsibility of our stewardship.

There have been and continue to be countless rituals to take this land for the Kingdom of Darkness, but the effort is not limited to rituals and ceremonies. In 1776, a declaration was established and proclaimed that was and is the founding document of the United States. But in 1770, six years earlier, Mayer Amschel Rothschild retained one, Adam Weishaupt, an Apostate Jesuit-trained Professor of Canon Law, to make revision to and modernize Illuminism or the worship of Lucifer. The goal in retaining Weishaupt and this revision was to achieve world domination and to impose Luciferian ideology "Upon what would remain of the Human Race." (https://truedemocarcyparty.net/2012/01/rothchilds-25-point-plan-fro-world-domination-nationalist-truth/)

In 1773, Mayer Rothschild called twelve wealthy men together with the intent of pooling their resources and presenting them with his 25-point plan to control the wealth, resources and not just the manpower, **but to own and control the men and women of the entire world.** In May of 1776, just two months before the colonists made the most dramatic and defining declaration in history – the Declaration of Independence – the work of Weishaupt and Rothschild saw its own successes and the American Illuminati was birthed. The clash of two Kingdoms for the earth and its inhabitants had come to America. Do you realize your children are property, not children, and they are **state** property once they have been Registered? After the Civil War in 1871(which was a banker's war, as all wars are banker's wars), President Grant signed into law The Organic Act of 1871 which vacated the seats of our Republic and instituted a corporation to provide government services. This was one of the most deceitful Contracts of our nation's history and is an instrument used by the Illuminati to control their plan. By this

Act, mandates are facilitated, Executive Orders placed upon the people, and codes and statutes can now control the population rather than legislated law. Before I reach the end of this chapter, I will reveal to you how you can become a legislator in your own House and establish your House as a self-governing body, as was the original intent for government "of the people, for the people and by the people." This is not patriot myth nor a dangerous endeavor that will land you in harm's way or prison. The original Republic or Constitution was not done away with but was overlaid with a corporation. It is important to be informed how we became owned by the corporation, and as owners, the corporation can do as it will with its property. In today's world of mandates and medical maleficence, it is imperative to know how not to be owned and how to remove the compelling interest of the corporation. Contracts must be ended! We are people of a Covenant, not a people owned by contract. We have already been bought with a price and are not now nor have ever been for sale! *"Ye are bought with a price; be not ye the servants of men"* (1 Corinthians 7:23). The Bible is full of language referring to the sin of Babylon which is also the sin of Lucifer identified as trafficking. (See the books of Ezekiel and Revelation). In 1892, the Bankers Manifesto in which you and I are referred to as "the lower order of people," was drafted. It describes the plan of the Bankers to have dominion over the wealth and the people of the world. It is written on bond paper with a bond number located at the upper right and upper left corners of the document, and the number printed there is 666 – another declaration to prevent the Sons of God from being and building the Holy Nation or Royal Priesthood. Also, a banner runs across the top center of the document which states, "Organized Above the Law of the United States." Here is the text of that document:

> *The Banker's Manifesto of 1892 was revealed by US Congressman Charles A. Lindbergh, Sr. from Minnesota before the US Congress sometime during his term of office between the years of 1907 and 1917 to warn the citizens.*
>
> *"We (the bankers) must proceed with caution and guard every move made, for the lower order of people are already showing signs of restless commotion. Prudence will therefore show a policy of apparently yielding to the popular will until our plans are so far consummated that we can declare our designs without fear of any organized resistance.*
>
> *The Farmers Alliance and Knights of Labor organizations in the United States should be carefully watched by our trusted men, and we must take immediate steps to control these organizations in our interest or disrupt them.*
>
> *At the coming Omaha Convention to be held July 4th (1892), our men must attend and direct its movement, or else there will be set on foot such antagonism to our designs as may require force to overcome. This at the present time would be premature. We are not yet ready for such a crisis. Capital must protect itself in every possible manner through combination (conspiracy) and legislation.*
>
> *The courts must be called to our aid, debts must be*

collected, bonds and mortgages foreclosed as rapidly as possible. When through the process of the law, the common people have lost their homes, they will be more tractable and easily governed through the influence of the strong arm of the government applied to a central power of imperial wealth under the control of the leading financiers. People without homes will not quarrel with their leaders.

History repeats itself in regular cycles. This truth is well known among our principal men who are engaged in forming an imperialism of the world. While they are doing this, the people must be kept in a state of political antagonism.

The question of tariff reform must be urged through the organization known as the Democratic Party, and the question of protection with the reciprocity must be forced to view through the Republican Party. By thus dividing voters, we can get them to expand their energies in fighting over questions of no importance to us, except as teachers to the common herd. Thus, by discrete action, we can secure all that has been so generously planned and successfully accomplished."

Are you starting to see that there has been both a spiritual battle for the souls of men, and a physical battle to own not only mankind but also the domain of mankind, which is the earth? In 1913, Edward Mandell House was a Foreign Policy advisor to then President Woodrow Wilson and is also the same Mandell House who called the infamous meeting on Jekyll Island that created the Federal Reserve (which is not

Federal at all). Mr. House, who was not military but went by Colonel House, had a private meeting with President Wilson and he described the method by which we would all become Registered into the Corporation and in fact, this Registered way of living today is not only in the United States but worldwide. We already have a One World Government run by *"Principalities, powers and rulers of darkness of this world" (Ephesians 6:12)*, which creates a façade that each country is independent and sovereign, but in actuality these unknown entities and their followers meet and agree by mutual contract. Even the first President of the United States in his farewell address, stated that it should be our policy to "steer clear of permanent alliances with any portion of the foreign world."

(*https://www.mountvernon.org/library/digitalhistory/past-projects/quotes/article/it-is-our-true-policy-to-steer-clear-of-permanent-alliance-with-any-portion-of-the-foreign-world/*)

Sadly, we have contracted with the most foreign of worlds and the minions of that foreign world, and a world foreign to the One upon whose shoulders the government sits – the person of Jesus Christ. *"For unto us a child is born, unto us a son is given,* **and the government shall be upon his shoulder***: and his name shall be called Wonderful, Counsellor, The mighty God, The everlasting Father, The Prince of Peace" (Isaiah 9:6)*. Also, we are called not to conform (contract) with this world, Romans 12:2. In the meeting mentioned above, Mr. House also described the phony corporation and the fiat nature of our currency. Following is the text of that meeting:

"Very soon, every American will be required to register their biological property in a national system designed to keep track of the people and that will operate under the ancient system of pledging. By such methodology, we can compel people to submit to our agenda, which will affect our security as a chargeback for our fiat paper currency. Every American will be forced to <u>register</u> or suffer not being able to work and earn a living. They will be our chattel, and we will hold the security interest over them forever, by operation of the law merchant under the scheme of secured transactions. Americans, by unknowingly or unwittingly delivering the bills of lading to us will be rendered bankrupt and insolvent, forever to remain economic slaves through taxation, secured by their pledges. They will be stripped of their rights and given a commercial value designed to make us a profit and they will be none the wiser, for not one man in a million could ever figure our plans and, if by accident one or two would figure it out, we have in our arsenal plausible deniability. After all, this is the only logical way to fund government, by floating liens and debt to the registrants in the form of benefits and privileges. This will inevitably reap to us huge profits beyond our wildest expectations and leave every American a contributor to this fraud which we will call "Social Insurance." Without realizing it, every American will insure us for any loss we may incur and in this manner every American will unknowingly be our servant, however begrudgingly. The people will become helpless and without any hope for their redemption

and, we will employ the high office of the President of our dummy corporation to foment this plot against America."

There is not adequate room here to continue much further with the segment on history because so much has been hidden, rewritten, and convoluted. Some mathematicians and cosmologists have postulated that nearly 1,000 years may have been added to our timeline; the calendars have been changed over and over. Who can explain the Mudfloods or the Cabbage Patch Kids, the Orphan Trains or the architecture of the ancient world? There are some that hold to the theory that many of the structures of the 1700s and 1800s were built long before that and were only repurposed and occupied in those years. Just try and find any real truth concerning Black Projects, DUMBS, medical experimentation or the atrocities of places like Montauk. The late Dr. Michael Heiser (who is already greatly missed) used to say on his podcasts, "What you think you know may not be so."

I will reveal one final example of recent history, and that is U.S. Code 1520a. This code refers to restrictions on the use of human subjects for testing of chemical or biological agents. Title 50 of this code also says that it is not permissible to test or to experiment on human subjects using any chemical or biological agent. However, if you look at the exceptions it is frightening. The exceptions are: "(1) Any peaceful purpose that is related to a medical, therapeutic, pharmaceutical, agricultural, industrial or research activity. (2) Any purpose that is directly related to protection against toxic chemicals or biological weapons and agents. (3) Any law enforcement purpose, including any purpose related to riot control." Notice the use of "any" throughout the exceptions; this is a blank check when you read the exceptions, and this is how things that are not lawful are made legal.

Multiple acts and policies such as the War Powers Act of 1933, the Trading with the Enemy Act, etc... placed the people, in the eyes of the government, as enemies of the state and we are treated as such. Military forces gather reconnaissance on an enemy, and we now live under pandemic use of government surveillance which many people assume is for our protection. Nothing could be further from the truth.

I hope you are seeing my intent here is to provide a basis for understanding why government, as it exists today, is not only unlawful and illegitimate, but an anathema to a free people. We cannot turn a blind eye to these realities and hope that the problem will resolve itself. In fact, recognizing wrongdoing and choosing not to stop it is a form of consent by acquiescence.

The entire point of this brief look at history is to show that the Kingdom of Darkness has been working feverishly by contract and deceit to claim ground that is not theirs to claim without our agreement. But sadly, we have given too much agreement. In Luke Chapter 19 and in the Parable of the Talents, we find a king who has given talents to three men and then leaves his country for a while, but before he leaves, he gives an order to the men in the story *"to occupy until I return."* Occupy is a military term meaning to take ground and to hold it. Two of the men increased the king's holdings – expanded if you will his kingdom; but one did not. We are instructed not to hide away, but to subdue, have dominion and to occupy; the man who did not increase the kingdom was cast out. We are instructed in Genesis 1:28 to replenish, subdue and have dominion over the earth, thereby increasing the kingdom. We are to be building His kingdom, not giving up ground through ritual, through sacrifice, through contract, through registration, through ignorance, or through fear. We are not of those who shrink back, *"But we do not belong to those who shrink back and are destroyed, but to those who have faith and are saved" (Heb 10:39).* We can say no to mandates, forced vaccinations, medical experimentation, transhumanism, socialism, communism, etc., but only if we are not owned by or Registered to the Corporation.

To conclude this short review of history, I will refer to the point where we began – the Garden of Eden. In the center of the Garden was planted the tree of knowledge of good and evil; the fruit of that tree revealed both good and evil. So, it is with the history of our country and of the world; it reveals both good and evil. Like the contract that took place in the garden, the fall of man was more than just a fall; the garden was lost to the first man and the first woman and the same is true for this nation because of the contracts we have made, and because we believed the original fallen one. We have lost our garden. The freedoms we once enjoyed and protected are a part of the good fruit of history; the safe place to raise our families is all but gone. We have not protected the physical or spiritual borders of this land; we have not occupied or held the ground. Even heaven has its borders and there is but one way to the Father. So it should be in our homes, in our governments, and in the earth; God's way, the Kingdom way is the only way to hold the ground, protect the borders of our homes, and exercise the commission given to Adam to "subdue" and to hold "dominion" (Genesis 1:28). "Thy Kingdom come. Thy will be done, **in earth** as it is in heaven" (Matthew 6:10).

REGISTRATION, REGISTRATION, REGISTRATION

"The government has been secretly collecting biometric data of its citizens for decades. This data is the signature for our organism such as fingerprints, blood samples, DNA and so on." (Justin Deschamps www.stillnessinthestorm.com)

The number one manner by which we are entangled into this Babylonian System is through Registration. To illustrate entanglement, the events in the Garden of Eden were carried out without the terms and conditions of the agreement being fully disclosed, and the methods are no different today. For example, your flesh and blood body was Registered into the system and by that Registration, Babylon's System was allowed to create an unincorporated fiction. Dr. Mike Spaulding of Calvary Chapel in Ohio has even described it as "a clone of you." Although not an actual clone (those do exist by the way), it is a fictitious paper image of you. You might have heard it referred to as the "Strawman." This is nothing less than the normal modus operandi of the enemy of God's Kingdom to create a false copy of what God has done. We were created in the image of God – a reflection of Him; the fiction crafted by Babylon is a false or reversed reflection of you. If you are doubting this, just look at your Birth Record; the date of your birth is different than the date of your registration but both dates are on that document. By this

Registration, the System was given certain administrative rights over the fiction they created. Also, on some of the older Birth Records there is a signature line that says "Informant;" your mother would have signed as the Informant to inform Babylon that another slave is presented to them. Of course, no mother has been told that is what is really happening by signing this document, and no mother in her right mind would actually sign their child over to be a corporate slave "citizen." Again, this is an example of a contract by Registration without full disclosure of the terms and conditions of the contract. The birth certificate is a bond that is traded and by your birth certificate you have become a part of human labor trafficking. I can't help but wonder how the funds from the trading of birth certificates are utilized. The funds are placed into a Cestui Que Vie Trust that you cannot access. Those who can dip into those funds are under no scrutiny from the public and there is no accountability or public disclosure for the use of the Trust.

> *"We are born on the land and are considered heirs of the land, assets of our country. But within hours, undeclared agents of the federal "State" franchise get our mothers to sign Certificates of Live Birth. These documents are misrepresented as simple recordings of the baby's birth. Instead, they are registrations of commercial "vessels" using the baby's name and serving to make the "State" franchise the beneficiary of the baby's estate on the land. However, many days, weeks, or months later as determined by "State" law, your "vessel in commerce" is reported missing, presumed dead" to the probate court, which then*

> *doctors the civil records and converts your living estate to a trust ESTATE benefiting the perpetrators of this scheme."*
> (https://stillnessinthestorm.com/2015/10/identity-theft-and-birth-certificate/)

Remember the Edward Mandell House letter in the introduction? They not only planned this event, but successfully implemented it. The system has ownership through administrative rights of the fiction, and as the owner or administrator, they can administrate the fiction in any manner they so choose. This might include drafting one into a service, placing you under a "mandate," requiring payment via taxes for administrative services, requiring one to abide by a corporate executive officer's order, etc., etc., etc., This is, in my opinion, a very malevolent device for controlling the masses. We are told to come out of Babylon but how can a slave become free? How can this ownership be revoked? We are to Register into a Kingdom, but that Registration must be by choice. The Apostle Paul, in writing to the Hebrews says, *"...to the general assembly and church of the firstborn who are **registered** in heaven..."* (*Hebrews 12:23*). Some versions use the word "written" rather than registered but the Greek word here "apographo," according to Strongs means a copy, a list or to **enroll**. (Strongs 563) We are registered into the books of Heaven by our choice and acceptance of the free gift of Salvation. Babylon, on the other hand, registers you, and enrolls you by force, deceit, paper magic and trickery. Try functioning in commerce if you have not registered into Babylon's system of commerce.

This commerce, or trading – you could even call it trafficking because the system traffics in the "souls of men" *(Revelation 18:13)* – is the very reason Satan was cast from heaven. Ezekiel 28:16 records the event: *"By the abundance of your **trading** You became filled with violence within, And you sinned; Therefore I cast you as a profane thing Out of the mountain of God; And I destroyed you, O covering cherub, From the midst of the fiery stones."* Notice that God states that this "trading" has made the "Covering Cherub" now just a "thing;" in fact, He calls it a "profane thing." This trading was going on in heaven before Satan was cast down; it continued in the Garden of Eden; it was going on in the Temple in Jerusalem when Jesus drove out the money changers with a whip; and it continues today. Commerce, especially banking, is rife with demands that you register with Babylon, or you will live with much difficulty in Babylon's System.

Our biological property, including our children, is registered to Babylon, thereby granting them administration and ownership. Babylon demands that many things in our lives be registered. For example, we register our cars, boats, our land and then we pay administrative fees (taxes) on that which we already own. We also register to go to school; we register to play sports; we register our software; and most of the products we buy have a registration card included in the product box. We even register to vote. Once registered, the vote no longer belongs to you because you are no longer a part of the electorate; you are part of a registered system, and the vote belongs to the owner. Now I know that sounds extreme, but I believe it to be true based on the way the system works. Even our churches were deceived into believing that they must register in Babylon. We all thought it was great that churches can now have a tax exemption, but churches always were tax exempt; we don't need a 501c3. In fact, in the early days of the colonies, taxes were collected in 9 of the 13 colonies for the direct purpose of funding the church. Remember, Registration allows Administration. The entire system is a fallen angel system and Psalms 82 deals with the unjust government of the fallen ones directly. *"God standeth in the congregation of the mighty; He judgeth among the gods. How long will ye judge unjustly, and accept the persons of the wicked (Psalm 82:1-2)? "I have said, Ye are gods; and all of you are children of the Most High. But you shall die like men, and fall like one of the princes. Arise, O God, judge the earth; for Thou shalt inherit all nations" (Psalm 82:6-8).*

Registration, like our history, is a broad subject and difficult to fit into a single chapter, but I will wrap up the idea of registration this way – you cannot fulfill God's plan for you, or God's agenda for a nation or the world, if you don't know who you are in Him and if you are registered to someone else. *"No man can serve two masters: for either he will hate the one, and love the other; or else he will hold to the one, and despise the other. Ye cannot serve God and mammon" (Matthew 6:24).* You cannot fulfill your agency if you are registered by, registered to, restricted under Babylon's paper magic, or owned by the Kingdom of Darkness as a slave to Babylon. There is not room here to dive into the Law of Agency, but it is critical to understanding who we are in Christ and all that agency grants us. A simple explanation is that when an agent performs, it is in the eyes of the law the same as if the principle had performed; agency grants the authority to perform. This Law of Agency is recognized in the spiritual realm and the earthly dimension. A great deal of scripture deals with the Agency given to us through the Name of Jesus but unfortunately misused by many. *"And whatsoever ye shall ask in my name, that will I do, that the Father may be glorified in the Son. If ye shall ask any thing in my name, I will do it" (John 14:13-14).* Even the Holy Spirit was sent in the Agency or in the Name of Jesus *(John 14:26).* I will expound on agency a little more in the Section "Establishing Your House."

Freedom and true liberty do not come from political pundits or statutes or code; they come from Jesus Christ and Him alone. Scripture states *"If the Son makes you free, you shall be free indeed" (John 8:36).* We also are NOT to be conformed to this world; this is a command not a suggestion *(Romans 12:2).* You cannot separate church and state and then claim that the government is on His shoulders *(Isaiah 9:6-7).* We are to be about the business of building His Kingdom, not fretting about how Babylon perceives us. God's Word tells us that there will be much tribulation, and men dying of heart attacks caused by fear from those things that are coming *(Luke 21:26).* It might be that the greatest agent of death and destruction is just that – an agent. Remember, I said agency is powerful! An agent of death has administrative rights over you, obtained by your approval and registration. By registration, the enemy of mankind is given access, permission, and the enforcement necessary to wipe us out, and this is done via administration because of registration. To simplify this into a single statement, registration gives away Title, Use and Interest and tethers us to the Babylonian System.

Now has come the time for God's people to break off those tethers and live in the **Liberty of Christ as Sons of God and joint heirs of Jesus Christ. It is time to come out of Babylon.** *"For all the nations have drunk of the wine of the wrath of her fornication, the kings of the earth have committed fornication with her, and the merchants of the earth have become rich through the abundance of her luxury. And I heard another voice from heaven saying, Come out of her, my people, lest you share in her sins, and lest you receive of her plagues" (Revelation 18:3-4).* The words here in verse 3, "…the **merchants** of the earth have become rich through the abundance of her luxury…" is a reference to trafficking/trading, and the command to come out of her also comes with a warning of the judgment that will befall Babylon and those that remain in her.

COMING OUT OF BABYLON – HOW TO UNREGISTER

In this section we will examine the process of Authentication, or how to unregister from the Babylonian System of Registration. It begins with the birth certificate; this document is the evidence of ownership. You can become the holder of that record legally and lawfully, but be aware that as the holder of record, you have agreed to assume responsibility for the record and the property. The process of Authentication, when coupled with the understanding of what you have accomplished and holding legitimate registration in the records of heaven, is a realistic way to effectuate the precept of being in the world but not of the world. In Paul's letter to the Colossians he writes, *"Therefore, if you died with Christ from the basic principles of the world, why, as though living in the world, do you subject yourselves to regulations"* (Colossians 2:20). In the words of Jesus from the gospel of Matthew we read *"For what profit is it to a man if he gains the whole world, and loses his own soul? Or what will a man give in exchange for his soul?" (Matthew 16:26)* There is a plethora of verses that substantiate the idea that we are to be in the world but not of the world.

Babylon created a fiction that bears your name, but this fiction is owned and administrated by Babylon. I covered this briefly in the registration section. The goal here is to understand becoming unregistered and realizing the responsibility inherent in accepting the role of holder of record in due course.

Authentication is a process performed by the Secretary of State of the state in which you were born, and the Secretary of State of the United States. It is part of the duty of those offices and is performed by having your birth record authenticated to a country that is not part of the Hague Convention, which is a normal process, but what is unknown to many is the power that exists in this simple action. It is the means by which one becomes unregistered from the system, and as I said earlier, places the power of administration of the fiction in the hands of the one who has authenticated their birth record. There is a great deal of patriot myth on the internet and across social media channels, but I won't attempt to disclose those myths in this chapter. Rather, I want to concentrate on the truth. A major truth is authentication does not place you above the law; it does not make you a sovereign citizen, nor does it place a target on your back. Since I mentioned sovereign citizen, I have to say that no such thing exists. There is only one Sovereign, and it isn't you or me. Authentication is the way to break the contract that has you tethered to the system and places the choice of who will hold and when they will hold title, use and interest of you and your property. As was revealed in the Mandell House letter, the birth certificate is a type of title to property; the key word here is certificate. Just like a title to a motor vehicle is referred to as a certificate of title, the word informs you that a title exists, but you do not hold it. In respect to a motor vehicle, the certificate of the original title is actually held by the state in which it was registered. The state receives the manufacturers statement of origin, or MSO, and that is why there are administrative fees and statutes that govern motor vehicles; the state holds title and shares use and interest. I am not saying this is good or bad; I am simply using this as an example of ownership and demonstrating how you and your offspring are considered property.

Rather than fully explain the process here, I will direct you to the C2KReport. C2K stands for the Clash of 2 Kingdoms and is a ministry of teaching and searching the Word of God for truth. It provides all the details of "how" and "why" to authenticate not found in this chapter. You can find the C2K Report on You Tube, Rumble, Shake and Wake Radio and many other outlets. To learn the actual step by step process with detailed instruction visit www.c2kreport.com.

ESTABLISHING YOUR HOUSE

To finalize my contribution to this book, we will look at creating a self-governing apparatus in your House and how you become a legislator for the Acts of your House. Joshua makes a bold statement in the book of the Bible that bears his name: *"And if it seems evil to you to serve the LORD, choose for yourselves this day whom you will serve, whether the gods which your fathers served that were on the other side of the River, or the gods of the Amorites, in whose land you dwell. But as for me and my house, we will serve the LORD" (Joshua 24:15).* Obviously, Joshua is not speaking of a structure but his tribe; he is making reference to his family and those under his care and leadership as Overseer.

Establishing your House is the next step after you have authenticated your birth record and those birth records of your family members. The Constitution of the U.S., Article 1, Section 10, states that no law can be passed that would impair the obligations of a contract. By establishing a self-governing House, you will pass Acts for the governing of your House, and Acts are themselves contractual. These contracts are between you and the members of your House and by so contracting, they are protected and cannot be impaired. In other words, contract makes the law. Of course, it is imperative that those Acts be in harmony with the Word of God and His precepts and do not violate the sanctuary, safety, or God given rights of others. As the members of your House come into agreement, your House becomes a sanctuary from the evils of this world, and as born-again sons and daughters of the Most High, you are no longer a creation but can now be sanctified. The protections, sanctuary, and the ability to legislate for your own House gained by establishing a self-governing apparatus is an act of taking back the ground that the enemy has been stealing for so long. Every House that is established is more ground reclaimed for the Kingdom. It is the ministry to which every follower of Christ is called to – the ministry of reconciliation and includes reconciling both His land and His children back to Him. *"And all things are of God, who hath reconciled us to himself by Jesus Christ, and hath given to us the ministry of reconciliation…" (2 Corinthians 5:18).*

I refer to the Constitution because it is a frequent question and I also believe the original Constitution is an inspired document; however, it is not the source of authority for your House. The authority comes from Jesus Christ who has all power and authority in heaven and in earth as is detailed to us in *Matthew 28:16-20*. I purposely used the term "comes from" because it comes from Christ to us through the law of agency. Remember earlier I said the law of agency is anything performed by an agent is, in the eyes of the law, the same as if the principle had performed it. The principalities that are referred to in Ephesians chapter 6 recognize this agency and without it we are powerless against those who Paul says we wrestle against. You can pretend to put on armor all day long but outside of Christ and outside of the inheritance of His agency, you are just playing dress up. Christ made us His agents when He gave us the Great Commission in Matthew 28. This isn't the only occasion that agency is conferred upon us. *John 1:12-13* says *"But as many as received him, to them gave he power to become the sons of God, even to them that believe on his name: Which were born, not of blood, nor of the will of the flesh, nor of the will of man, but of God."* The agency is not from the flesh but is from God. The entire first chapter of Paul's letter to the Ephesians informs us of our adoption into the family of God and the inheritance that comes with that adoption; included in that inheritance is agency. Paul goes on to say that the agency/inheritance/adoption is "sealed" with the King's seal and that King is the King of Kings. Specifically, in Ephesians 1:19, Paul asks a question regarding Christ's power and authority that He extended to us, and he goes on to answer His own question. First that agency is extended only to those who believe, and then he defines Christ's authority. *"Far above all principality, and power, and might, and dominion, and every name that is named, not only in this world, but also in that which is to come: And hath put all things under his feet and gave him to be the head over all things to the church" (Ephesians 1:21-22).* When your House is established with Christ as the head and under His authority, your House becomes an Ecclesia and should function and operate in a manner fitting the King of Kings, who, according to this scripture is the head of the Ecclesia. I will note here that the ancient definition of Ecclesia is government, and so each of our established Houses should be an Ecclesia – His Church and His government.

If your House is self-governing and is doing so under the commission and agency of Christ, then we need to look at another fact. It is more than principle, more than precept, more than a spiritual axiom, it is an office implemented in your House. That is the office of ambassador which is an agent of a higher authority, and we have already established here that there is no higher authority than Jesus Christ. An ambassador is often in a country foreign to his citizenship and adheres to and enforces the law of the nation that has commissioned him or her. The law of our Houses must be the law form that is the judicial record we call the Holy Bible. Confirmation of our role as ambassadors is given in 2 Corinthians, *"Now then we are ambassadors for Christ, as though God did beseech you by us: we pray you in Christ's stead, be ye reconciled to God" (2 Corinthians 5:20).* If we are to take this verse literally, (and we must), and we are ambassadors then our House becomes an Embassy that we as ambassadors work from. An Embassy is sovereign ground of one nation placed on foreign soil, and so our House becomes sovereign ground of the Kingdom of God on Babylon's hostile territory. This is a huge responsibility, and with responsibility also comes liability; therefore, we must be reconciled to God in order to establish our House. Foremost is the declaration of Joshua 24:15 *"...as for me and my House, we will serve the Lord."* Secondly, remember an entire nation was birthed from a declaration in 1776. After the declaration comes the establishment, the work; and the protection of what has been established – holding the ground! In his book "The Four Horses of Revelation 6," Dr. Mike Spaulding says, "What can you do right now? A primary step you can take is to begin to remove yourself from the Babylonian "Beast System" as I call it…. The first step is to recognize that politics will not save you. Politicians do not have the answer to the crises facing America or the world. Their solutions will enslave people even more…. we must begin teaching others what it means to take personal responsibility for our families and our communities. Coming out of Babylon will require some very specific and decisive actions on your part." (page106 &107)

THE HOLY ECCLESIA EMBASSY AND THE NATION OF GOD

"And ye shall be unto me a kingdom of priests, and an holy nation. These are the words which thou shalt speak unto the children of Israel" (Exodus 19:6).

"But ye are a chosen generation, a royal priesthood, an holy nation, a peculiar people; that ye should shew forth the praises of him who hath called you out of darkness into his marvellous light: Which in time past were not a people, but are now the people of God: which had not obtained mercy, but now have obtained mercy" (1 Peter 2:9-10).

There is much that could be said here with respect to defining "people" and "person;" in statute they are not the same thing. God has always desired for us to be His people, but the opening verses to this segment make it clear that we were not and are not a people, except that God makes us a people. He desires His people to be peculiar, to be priests and to become a nation. Have we replaced the Overseer of the House, who should be the priest of the House, with pastors, politicians, and inferior authority? We have allowed within our politically correct and programmed thinking to believe that our church, our societies, our De Facto or De Jure government is the nation of God. None of these are the holy nation to which the scriptures refer or which God desires. His nation has a King who is recognized, honored, and served. His nation is made up of a people who serve but one master and serve in the manner of a bond servant. We are at a place in human history where this can become a reality, not just a spiritual concept.

"No man can serve two masters: for either he will hate the one and love the other; or else he will hold to the one and despise the other. Ye cannot serve God and mammon" (Matthew 6:24).

"And if it seem evil unto you to serve the LORD, choose you this day whom ye will serve; whether the gods which your fathers served that were on the other side of the flood, or the gods of the Amorites, in whose land ye dwell: but as for me and my house, we will serve the LORD" (Joshua 24:15).

"And Elijah came unto all the people, and said, How long halt ye between two opinions? if the LORD be God, follow him: but if Baal, then follow him. And the people answered him not a word" (1 Kings 18:21).

When the manifest Sons of God realize their agency and their authority, untether themselves from Babylon, choose to become the bondservants we are called to be, and redeem the position of priest to our God, then as righteous overseers of our Houses we will see that holy nation. We will see that *"The kingdoms of this world are become the kingdoms of our Lord, and of his Christ; and he shall reign for ever and ever"* (Revelation 11:15). As individuals follow the process of authentication and as Houses establish themselves to self-govern, we are taking background, occupying the land and together becoming that nation. There is a way to live and work under the ministry of your House and be in the world but not of the world. Don't become confused by the word "ministry"; in this context it does not necessarily refer to clergy or pulpits. Everything we do is a ministry of our House if we do it as unto the Lord. *(Colossians 3:23)* The ministry of your House can have many missions (projects), but they are not ministry unto the Lord if you are bound to Babylon.

Right now, in the U.S., there are 23 states that have called-out assemblies meeting together to learn how to establish their Houses and to learn how we become that nation. These are gatherings of God's people who have broken off the ties to Babylon and are building the foundations of righteousness and justice that are required for God's Throne.
"Righteousness and justice are the foundation of Your throne; Mercy and truth go before Your face" (Psalm 89:14). These are believers from many different denominations, as the holy nation is not a denomination, they are baptized believers in the Way, the Truth, and the Life, which is Jesus Christ, the only way to the Father. *(John 14:6)* Some of these assemblies meet weekly, some twice a month, and some monthly. While some are meeting in person others are meeting in an online video room provided by shopyourfarm.com which operates on privately owned servers, not on rented server space. God has made it possible for the Ecclesia Embassy to obtain these servers.

The Ecclesia Embassy that I mentioned is very real, and the work has been going on for some time. It consists of self-governing Houses of the Sons of God, who are bondservants to Christ and freemen in the world. An advisory Council of Elders, which is also a Grand Jury, has been formed; documents for the Nation of God and the Embassy have been written; and our hope is that by the time this book is published Babylon will have received those documents and the Embassy functioning. There is already a call center established for the members of the Ecclesia Embassy, and help is available to assist those who desire to come out of Babylon and unregister all their property. The Embassy ID's have been designed and approved, and the holders of those ID's cannot be made subject to unrighteous mandates or ungodly administration. A judicial committee has been organized and has been meeting for a while now to determine how all of this is completed lawfully and without offense to the existing governing bodies, and how to handle courts within the Ecclesia. *(Matthew 17:27)* This is not a political action group, an anti-government group, one of the many patriot or anti-tax websites, or other such entity; it is the people of God coming together as the Holy Nation of God. A nation needs an actual Embassy, and each established House is a satellite Embassy coming under the banner of the National Embassy.

The Embassy functions under the highest law form that exists, which is the God of Abraham, Isaac and Jacob; His Living Word; and under the authority and commission of Jesus as joint heirs with the agency appointed to us. It is sweeping not only across this country, but around the world, as people internationally are coming together in the same manner. The free classes provided by the C2KReport have had many international attendees learning to unregister from Babylon. The Babylonian System is worldwide and is frantically attempting to establish the New World Order. The Ecclesia Embassy is very real. It is sovereign ground of the Kingdom of God on foreign soil and is the place where the remnant is gathering. There is much work to do yet and infrastructure to be built, but with God's help and your assistance the work will be accomplished. We will be *"a peculiar people an holy nation"* (1 Peter 2:9).

In the historical and Apocryphal book of 2 Esdras, we find the following recorded as the writer compares Babylon with Israel and even examines all the nations of the world: *"I have traveled widely among the nations and I have seen that they abound in wealth, though they are unmindful of Thy commandments. Now therefore weigh in a balance our inequities and those of the inhabitants of the world; and so it will be found which way the turn of the scale will incline. When have the inhabitants of the earth not sinned in Thy sight? Or what nation has kept Thy commandments so well?* **Thou mayest indeed find individual men who have kept Thy commandments, but nations thou wilt not find"** *(2 Esdras 3:33-36).*

I am very humbled and honored to be asked to contribute to this book, and to conclude my contribution I'll share a poem from my collection at Randy Conway Poems, entitled "Finish Well". As I attempted to reveal in the opening segments of this chapter, there are places in our history where God's people were silent and, therefore, we acquiesced to contracts; but together under the banner of Jesus Christ we can finish well. After the poem, I have placed the actual preamble and mission statement of the Ecclesia Embassy that will be presented to some branches of the military, elected Sheriff Associations and other law enforcement associations, as well as influencers in the political world. The preamble will be presented along with several videos and other documents, including instructions as to how members of the Ecclesia Embassy of the Holy Nation of God are to be handled.

If you're interested in learning more you can visit www.c2kreport.com or you can communicate with Rick Hidalgo of the C2KReport at info@c2kreport.com or Randy Conway at c2kreport@gmail.com

Finish Well

A young man by no fault of his own found himself sold into Egyptian slavery.

He faced the trials of his captivity with stalwart faith and bravery.

His tribulations they were many and again without fault he was put into a cell.

But Joseph believed in the God of his fathers and history proves he finished well.

Many years ago back in ancient history there lived a man in Pharaoh's court.

The adopted son of Pharaoh's daughter; Moses' life of royalty was soon to be cut short.

Outraged by the treatment of a Hebrew slave Moses anger grew and an Egyptian soldier fell.

But The God of Abraham, Isaac and Jacob found Moses and Moses finished well.

There is a story you've probably heard about a strong man who judged a nation.

He is known for his great strength and for a woman who held his fixation.

His choices brought great pain and misery but there is more to tell.

Sampson remembered the God he once served, and Sampson finished well.

Saul was a man who I guess you would have to call a religious terrorist.

To hunt down Christians and put them to death Saul did continually persist.

But Saul met Jesus and then to preach the good news he was from that moment on compelled.

His words inspired by the Holy Spirit are still read today and Paul, he finished well.

For many our stories have had many twists and turns and pain.

But today you can change your story and dream dreams to claim.

If I could offer you any blessing or advice there is one thing I would impel.

That you hold to the faith of the one True God and like those who came before you too can finish well.

by Randy Conway

www.randyconwaypoems.com

The Embassy of the Holy Ecclesia

The Preamble and Mission of the Apostolic Council of His Holy Ecclesia

Being not ashamed of the Gospel$_{17}$ nor denying the power and the authority inherent in the Living Word^{19}, and having become aware of the conflict that has ensued since the beguiling and deception of man, as recorded in the Ancient Scriptures$_{15}$, we now hold to the knowledge that this conflict and the Babylonian Paper enslavement$_7$ used by the current world system is inspired, empowered, and enforced by those fallen Angels$^{19}{}_{18}$ and or their offspring and or their willingly ignorant agents/followers.

As His Holy Ecclesia$_1$ we are held to the full knowledge and understanding that we wrestle not against flesh and blood but against principalities, against powers, against the rulers of the darkness of this world, and against spiritual wickedness in high places^{19}.

Having been imprisoned in our minds, enslaved in our bodies and spirits and being diverted from God's$_8$ original intent for mankind by a system utilizing fictitious names and contracts without proper disclosure nor consent, we the Adopted Family^5 of the Living God$_8$ having been freed by the shed blood of Jesus the Christ$_2$, hold to these truths as surely as He does live, declare, and commit to the following^1:

1. **To accept** the free gift of God$_8$ and that gift is Salvation$^2{}_{10}$ and everlasting life$^3{}_{10}$ in Jesus the Christ.

2. **To apply** all authority^4, righteousness, grace, and mercy given to us, His Apostolic Council$_3$ and His Adopted Family$^5{}_{12}$.

3. **To fulfill** the role as Ambassadors of Christ$^6{}_9$ which includes the establishment of

4. Embassies$_9$ of the Kingdom$_{11}$ of God$_8$ in this earthly realm which is our rightful stewardship as joint heirs with Jesus the Christ$^6{}_2$. A true Nation$_{13}$ of His Holy Ecclesia$_1$ called out and set apart^7.

The Embassy of the Holy Ecclesia

5. **To Build** the Kingdom$_{11}$ of God$_8$ through leadership, education, and counsel, through the power of the Holy Spirit$_4$ and under the Authority of Jesus the Christ$^4{}_2$ to whom all power and all authority in heaven and in earth was given and as instructed in our Lord$_2$ Jesus the Christ's$_2$ teaching on prayer that we should pray "on earth as it is in heaven"^{8}.

6. **To fulfill** the commission of Matthew 28:19-20 to teach all things to all nations as Jesus the Christ$_2$ commanded which includes immersing the followers of Jesus the Christ$_2$ in the name of the Father$_5$, and of the Son$_2$, and of the Holy Spirit$_4$.

7. **To bestow**, within His Holy Ecclesia$_1$, all teaching and counsel with proper understanding that we are not rulers but rather, we are bond servants^9 of Jesus the Christ$_2$ who is the only true King^{10}. Not only bond servants but joint heirs^6 which now includes us in the family$_{12}$ of the only true King^{10}. We as members of His family$_{12}$ are returning to His order of the earth where all dominion is in His name so that this responsibility will no longer be vacated but shall be

accepted by His Holy Ecclesia$_1$ with clean hands and clean feet$_{14}$ as our duty until His return[11].

8. **To establish** a true, Holy, and Biblical Sanctuary$_{16}$ as written in God's word for His family$_{12}$ and their members^{12}.

9. **To oversee** as stewards His creation as commanded and as was the original instruction from creation as written in Genesis 1. As stewards of His creation, we seek to communicate with all people the wonder, beauty, and fruitfulness of God's$_8$ creation, for His glory and for the benefit of our neighbors. In this way, our creation stewardship seeks to honor, glorify, and love God$_8$ and our neighbor. Inherent in our stewardship is our commitment to the rule of His Law for His creation, fostering individual freedom, limited government, and the rightful place of His Holy Ecclesia$_1$.

10. **To be obedient** council servants to His Kingdom's$_{11}$ Embassies in a manner that is righteous and holy according to the instruction as written within His ancient scripture[13]$_{15}$.

11. **To build** not just a spiritual kingdom of the mind but holding to the instruction of "on earth as it is in heaven"[8] to build for the honor and glory of the Father$_5$ and for the benefit of His family$_{12}$, the Holy Ecclesia$_1$, a Kingdom infrastructure of His ministries which includes but are not limited to:

a. Manufacturing, Marketing, Raw Materials, Agriculture, Processing, Labor, Administration, Utilities, Entertainment, Sporting events, Governmental necessities, Health and healing, and Education.

b. An unmolested freedom of commerce consisting of barter, trade, buying, selling, and private contractual interaction without interference and restriction from others such as

 "impairing the obligation of contract", covenant[20], or agreement;

c. Records and Registrations of papers and properties and all that pertains to the Birthrights[19] of His Holy Ecclesia[1];

12. **The Embassy of the Holy Ecclesia**

    a. Preach the word; be instant in season, out of season; reprove, rebuke, exhort with all longsuffering and doctrine.

13. **To oversee** His Kingdom[11] infrastructure as ambassadors, and servants of the Body of Christ[6], His Holy Ecclesia[1], and to come to the aid of our brethren as might be needed when they are solicited or otherwise attacked by the systems of Babylon[7]. To include as a part of our mission and fulfillment of our Commission[8] to assist God's[8] people in becoming unregistered to Babylon and thereby loosing them from the tethers that have heretofore bound them to

Babylon[14][7] and show the path that is narrow and the gate that is straight that leads[15] to the One who when He makes us free, we are free indeed[16]. We are bound henceforth to no other than Jesus the Christ[2], His Kingdom[11], the Body of Christ[6], and His Holy Ecclesia[17][1].

14. **To establish** a righteous and merciful court of His Holy Ecclesia[1], to investigate, review and settle any solicitations or claims made against members of His Holy Ecclesia[18][1].

To these principles as it is written we are bound by our word, by our faith, by His promise, and by His power.

AND SO IT SHALL BE!

References:

[1]Colossians 1: 16-17; 2 Peter 3:5.

[2]Luke 3:6-8, Luke 19:9-10, Acts 4:11-12.

[3]Matthew 28:19-20, John 3:16, John 3:35-36, John 5:23-29.

[4]Matthew 28:16-20, Luke 4:36-37, John 5:26-29, Luke 9:1-6.

[5]John 1:12-14, Romans 8:12-17, 1 John 3:1-5, Galatians 4:7.

[6]2 Corinthians 5:17-21, Ephesians 6:20.

[7]Exodus 19:5, 1 Peter 2:9-10.

[8]Matthew 28:19-20.

[9]Luke 16:13.

[10] 1 Timothy 6:14-16, Ephesians 4:4-7.

[11] Ephesians 2:19, John 1:12, Galatians 4:4-5, Ephesians 1:5, Hebrews 2:10, 2:13, 2 Corinthians 2:16, 1 John 3:1-12.

[12] Hebrews 8:10-13, 1 Corinthians 6:19-20, 1 Peter 2:3-6.

[13] Luke 1:31-34, John 3:1-3.

[14] Matthew 16:19-21.

[15] Matthew 7:13-14.

[16] John 8:31-32, 8:35-36.

[17] John 1:23, Romans 6:17-18.

[18] 1 Corinthians 6:1-3, Jude 1:5-7.

The Embassy of the Holy Ecclesia

[19] Philippians 2:13-16

[20] Revelations 12:9, Jude 1:6, 2 Corinthians 11:13-15, Ephesians 6:12

Definitions:

1. His Holy Ecclesia: An established, structured, called out assembly of God's elected ambassadors and adopted family members.

2. Jesus the Christ: Yahusha Hamashiach., *(in hebrew)*

3. Apostolic Council: A branch of God's adopted family responsible for serving the Kingdom of Jesus the Christ as Overseers or Executive Ambassadors.

4. Holy Spirit: Ruach Haqodesh., (*in Hebrew*)

5. Father: Reference definition of God.

6. Body of Christ: The whole membership of God's adopted family.

7. Babylonian Paper Enslavement: Secretive accounting of financial instruments and other non-financial documents that give or, in some cases, appear to give a system compelling interest. 8God: The Creator of the universe, The God of Abraham, Isaac, and Jacob.

8. Ambassadors of Christ: The Holy Kingdom's new creations who are empowered and equipped to become Ministers of Reconciliation[20].

9. Embassies: Established outposts of the Holy Kingdom purposed for its expressed lawful use.

10. Ministers of Reconciliation: Agents of the Holy Kingdom tasked with restoring the ways of the Lord upon the earth.

11. Salvation: The Biblical act of repentance, asking for forgiveness with public declaration of taking Jesus the Christ as your Savior and then sealing it by immersion baptism.

12. Kingdom, Holy Kingdom: Heaven and Earth; The Jurisdiction of the King of Kings and Lord of Lords Jesus the Christ, who being the only begotten Son of God, has granted surrogate authority to his adopted family, heirs of creation. Heaven and Earth.

13. Adopted Family: Those who being of mankind have called upon the name of Jesus the Christ and have

experienced Salvation.

14. Nation: The united Holy Ecclesia members having their own private governance with superior authority and jurisdiction as written in ancient Scriptures.

15. Clean Hands and Clean Feet: A condition achieved by throwing off any governance or administration that is contrary or antithetical to the one true government of Jesus the Christ evident in the message of the Holy Scriptures.

16. Ancient Scriptures: The Holy Bible; Inspired writings of God profitable for doctrine, reproof, correction, and instructions in righteousness.

17. Biblical Sanctuary: A consecrated, sacred, and holy place of refuge, protection, and immunity to arrest, capture, attack, and persecution that is bestowed by God's Sovereign Authority. A place of asylum and protection for those in danger from other peoples, governments, or entities which includes the Babylonian system. God's Ecclesia is the highest jurisdiction and authority in earth and Jesus the Christ has been given authority in earth and in heaven; therefore, the Ecclesia, Ecclesia members and properties are by ancient right protected by Sanctuary and Asylum.

18. Gospel: The story of the plan of redemption from the deception of man to man's restoration.

19. Fallen Angels: Governing beings; One third of the total number of beings created to govern all aspects of creation who became corrupted and who today continue to corrupt creation.

20. Birthrights: Unalienable Rights; That which cannot be removed for any reason.

21. Covenant: An agreement or contract where God the Creator is the Supreme party.

Randy Conway is a prolific American poet whose work has been read, discussed, and shared around the world in books, on television, on radio, and the Internet. He is an ambassador for Christ, teaching people how to regain their authority over their person, family, and life by becoming separated from the Babylonian system.

CHAPTER 5

HIJACKING THE SOUL: THE TRABSHUMANIST SATANIC AGENDA TO DIGITIZE AND SURVEIL THE POPULATION

DR. ANA MARIA MIHALCEA

I am an internal medicine physician with a PhD in Pathology and work in my own functional medicine clinic. I've treated COVID with early treatments from the beginning of the "plandemic", was able to manage respiratory failure at home and successfully did what I could to keep people from going to the hospitals.

Through my participation in the group Medical Doctors for Covid Ethics International, I met Dr. David Nixon from Australia. He investigated what is in the Pfizer vials. One day we did a zoom meeting and he said, "Hey, do you want to have a look?" He applied a drop of the C19 Pfizer vial contents on a microscope slide. Immediately, I saw self-assembling nanotechnology. This shocking moment changed everything for me because I understood that this agenda is way bigger than what we have been told.

Many research teams around the world that have investigated the C19 vials didn't find mRNA. They found all kinds of metals like gadolinium, cesium, cerium, aluminum, gadolinium and more, that are toxic to the body. Dr. Shimon Yanowitz, Dr. Nixon, Dr. Daniel Nagase, La Quinta Columna and others found self-assembling nanotechnology. You can find more information about our research at anamihalceamdphd.substack.com and drdavidnixon.com.

When observed under the microscope and left for periods of time on the slide to dry, Dr Nixon found that microchip structures were developing in the presence of an EMF Wi-Fi Router. These microchips were connected via filament structures. They appeared to be fiber-optic communication cables. These similar fibers were then seen in live blood analysis, initially in vaccinated blood and then in unvaccinated blood.

And this is where really the alarm bells just went off to try to investigate what is this and what is the background. I found out that the transhumanist agenda didn't start with the C19 shots. Geoengineering and Bioengineering via spraying of these heavy metals, as well as synthetic biology, which is known as Morgellons has happened for decades. Morgellons is a hydrogel-based synthetic lifeform. I started looking at similarities to what is in the C19 shots. The ingredients of polyethylene glycol in Pfizer and SM102 in Moderna used for the lipid nano particles are components of a hydrogel. What is hydrogel? It is a self-assembly polymer that, when combined with metals and carbon nanotubes -- which is also known as graphene -- can build electronic devices that are senders and receivers. The evil perpetrators and technocrats are digitizing all life on Earth, and they are surveilling it, according to their long laid out plan. This process has been going on for a long time, but now with these C19 shots, there's a whole new level.

I found a chemical analysis from 2012 of these environmental filaments and they were containing a derivative of butyric acid and it turns out that in the FOIA request for Pfizer in Australia, similar substances were found as part of the lipid nanoparticles in the C19 shots. I found this very interesting, and this broadens the view of what we should do for treatments for people, because we need to detoxify this nanotechnology and synthetic biology.

I really want people to see the images of the live blood and see these structures. In a Live Blood check, you fingerprick a patient and take one drop of blood and look at it under the microscope. Some people are calling these long fibers that we are seeing parasites. But they are not parasites. They are actually synthetic biology that's made from this hydrogel, and they grow under EMF and electrical exposure. I have worked with Clifford Carnicom and we have done experiments with unvaccinated blood. By applying a low-level electrical current, the blood was transformed into something unrecognizable, a fiber network that literally looked exactly the same as if the Quinta-Columna had heated a drop of Pfizer-vial content, and they were also developing the same filaments. And it turns out that Morgellons also looks the same way. So, I think the optical -- the visualization of seeing what this looks like is really important to see the similarities and that allows us to begin to answer some of the many questions we have a little bit more.

We are endeavoring to find out what is going on with humanity's blood. How come all these practitioners around the world are seeing these changes, and this is correlating with these symptoms that are affecting not just the vaccinated but also the unvaccinated? I see more and more people who have brain fog, extreme fatigue, heart palpitations, all kinds of symptoms that were previously attributed to the spike protein.

But what it turns out is, when I look at their live blood, then I find these filament structures that you can see and the problem is that if you do not get this out, the symptoms progress and people continue to have worsening health problems and accelerated aging. These filaments are very responsive to EMF frequency, 5G frequency. If people are surrounded by that, their symptoms also get worse. I think that this is a very important question to address because many of the vax-injury protocols do not take into account the metals that we are being sprayed on via geoengineering that are also in the vials, as well as this programmable matter, hydrogel platform, which is literally a polymer plastic. This can grow from nano size to centimeter size in minutes. EMF radiation does make it grow.

There is a correlation to what Mike Adams found, because he investigated the clots of the cadavers of people who died from the shots and found that this wasn't blood; it was a self-assembly polymer with metals that was extremely resistant to any type of dissolution. One of the concerns that I have is that this is really something that is now shedding and transmitting also to the unvaccinated.

In my work with Clifford Carnicom, we incubated live blood of unvaccinated people and vaccinated people, and within a week, these filaments grew over time and, again, this was the same filaments that we've seen in live blood.

Clifford Carnicom and I, we did studies on electrical conductivity of blood and showed that it was up to 47 percent reduced compared to normal values. Imagine electricity is basically a life force– these filaments are hijacking our life force, causing chronic fatigue. In my clinical practice, I have seen accelerated aging by decades in a few months. And if you do not take this out of the blood, this process progresses. It causes extreme acidity. I've seen turbo-cancers now in the unvaccinated.

We have seen one of those blood clots that were taken out of someone who is vaccinated, highly abnormal, and it turns out that hydrogel coagulates the blood and literally can cause these kinds of clots. These same rubbery clots were seen in unvaccinated people.

I also found the filaments in meat. I went and analyzed meat samples from the local grocery store. The same filamental structures were in different types of meat, grass-fed meat, organic, non -organic. I found it in half and half milk.

Now we have the valid concern that this is also in the food supply. It is not mRNA that I am worried about, since that was not found in the vials, but hydrogel synthetic biology filaments.

I think that nano scale carbon nanotubes with metals are part of this biology. The carbon nanotubes are what you call Graphene Oxide.

I believe that all of humanity is under threat, that the transhumanist agenda wants to basically merge us with synthetic biology and artificial intelligence, and the danger of this hydrogel is it can mimic every cell. It can create brain cells and neurotechnology that basically can take over our thoughts and manipulate those as well as transmit your thoughts to the cloud. Yuval Harari's - one of the spokespersons for the plans of the World Economic Forum - his dream is creating automatons that have no soul and no Spirit. I believe that we are seeing the technological platform for this agenda. This is why I and my colleagues are sounding the alarm because I am concerned about an extinction-level event for humanity.

We have to understand that the military and DARPA, have studied nanotechnology applications for a long time. For the last sixty years, science has actually found a way to map resonant frequencies of brain activity and create artificial brains. In the same way, this has been used for mind control purposes. There is the technology that was, for example, developed at MIT to link six different brains together for problem solving. If you have more than that, people have significant brain dysfunction. This has been done in animals and in humans.

This idea of the hive mind -- which is really what this transhumanist agenda wants to achieve via artificial intelligence -- has already been done. We are electrical and electromagnetic beings of light and sound, and our brain waves can be decoded. That has been done. There is technology that is able to see exactly what you're thinking, your imaginings and decode your thoughts. In the DARPA and CIA programs, it has been possible to influence dream states.

They are literally also working on what's called hijacking the soul, and that is possible because if you are no longer able to have control over your own thoughts, and an external frequency that you cannot sense, you cannot detect, can just implant thoughts within you, then you have Manchurian Candidate-like programs. This programmable matter, the hydrogel, can mimic every neuronal cell in the brain, and the carbon nanotubes, they are exactly the same diameter as microtubules. And microtubules are the structures in the brain where consciousness is being processed. It's been shown that in the microtubules are like a different DNA that contains billions of years of information on the quantum level.

All of this is happening really in the realm of the extremely tiny. If you now are injecting something into humanity, like hydrogel, that can mimic and create a secondary brain within your own tissue that takes over a parallel processing, then you can control somebody and also affect their soul - because if it's no longer your own thinking and your free thought. Free will is being affected, then your soul is affected, and the connection can actually be severed. Here's where you get the automatons that are just being influenced by this external frequency and ultimately it is to upload every living being into the cloud so that people live in the metaverse as just these unconscious consumers - the technology is real.

I think it's really important for people to understand that there is this dimension, and in order to protect themselves or to help with detoxification and to limit this accelerated aging that clearly is present -- If you think about how many millions of people have what's called long COVID, and in my practice, looking at the live blood, these structures they are seen right after people have acute COVID, they are seen in long COVID, they are seen in shedding where unvaccinated people are getting really sick that are who are around vaccinated people. I've now seen accelerated aging processes as well as blood clots, heart attacks, strokes, and turbo cancers.

I believe that there is a shedding phenomenon that is physical - these filaments are transmissible, as well as that there is an electromagnetic transmission where people, just from frequency, can also be sickened.

In my practice, I have observed that the quality of the blood in general in people has worsened over time. Last December, in 2022, I was still seeing some unvaccinated people who didn't have these structures in their blood. Now I don't see anyone with clean blood anymore. I always discuss these findings with our colleagues in Australia and New Zealand and other places in the world, and they have the same findings – which is very alarming.

Now we see what we call sludge, where instead of rouleaux formation -- rouleaux is the stacking -- you can hardly differentiate that there's blood cells because it is so clumped together. These red blood cells do not give off oxygen appropriately, hence they cause this extreme fatigue, brain fog and other symptoms.

My friend Karen Kingston found a patent that showed that one of the antidotes for the hydrogel is EDTA, which happened to be something that we use for metal detoxification -- I am a certified chelation practitioner. I was using this in people and pulling out the metals that are also interfering with the electrical conductivity. I noticed that the intravenous EDTA was helping to clean people's blood. Within two IV's the blood appeared completely cleaned of the structures and the blood cells were now flowing normally, the sludge was dissolved, and people felt a whole lot better.

The reason why I keep talking about it is because if people are unaware that this hydrogel graphene technology with these metals are in the blood, then they're not going to use something like EDTA chelation and ultimately are missing what is really causing this accelerated aging and the technology that's affecting us. I am endeavoring to encourage people to look into this. One very easy way to verify whether or not the modalities are working is to do a live blood analysis. That is just a poke in the finger, and you look at it with the microscope. It's amazing what you can see.

In addition to your vitamins, nutrients, alkaline diet and minimizing exposure to EMF, I would add the EDTA chelation. I also use antiaging peptides like Epithalon. That's been very helpful because, again, this seems to be an accelerated aging process and so age-reversal modalities are very helpful. Molecules like humic and fulvic acid have been shown to dissolve graphene and it increases cellular electricity. High doses of vitamin C, like Linus Pauling used to talk about, up to 10,000 milligrams is important. Nitric oxide is important to help the gut microbiome to detoxify graphen. I use methylene blue a lot because it's an electricity doner. Again, we've shown in these blood connectivity studies how much the blood electricity is decreased, so you want to give back molecules that enhance electricity.

I found this treatment approach very successful, and I think it's important to know about it, because if now the entire biosphere is contaminated with this synthetic biology, we have to do everything in our power to clean it up. And on the other hand, people need to wake up that the transhumanist, Satanic agenda is trying to kill us every which way, and people need to wake up and fight this because there isn't much time remaining. If you age the entire population like this and you're going to have people who can't think because they are so tired, they can't fight, they can't function, this is not good. And this outcome isn't going to be, in twenty, thirty years; this is in the next couple years you're going to see devastating things. And if they start a 5G blast, then it will be even worse because people have this antenna in their body, and it can be used as a weapon.

Dr. Ana Maria Mihalcea is an internal medicine physician. She operates a functional medicine clinic and oversees patient healthcare.

CHAPTER 6

SOLVING EVIL: ZION, THE THIRD TEMPLE, AMND ARMAGEDDON

DEREK GILBERT

Human history orbits an uneven, rocky plateau thirty-three miles from the eastern shore of the Mediterranean Sea. The faith of Abraham, the dynasty of David, and the divinity of Jesus were established there. At the heart of this plateau is a hill on which Yahweh, the Creator of the universe, established His "mount of assembly," Zion. The temples of Solomon and Zerubbabel were built there, and a prophesied Third Temple will someday occupy that space.

A day is fast approaching when Jerusalem's Temple Mount will be at the very center of the most important event in human history: God's solution to the problem of evil—a supernatural showdown between Good and Evil at the place the apostle John called Armageddon.

Americans have a difficult time understanding the intensity of the emotions behind the conflict over Jerusalem's Temple

Mount. Nationalism, religious fervor, and racism are focused like a laser on an area of only about thirty-five acres. The irrationality spawned by these emotions—for example, the grand mufti of Jerusalem recently declared that the Al-Aqsa Mosque has occupied the Temple Mount "since the creation of the world"[1]—argues for their supernatural origin.

This speck of land is the focus of constant confrontation between Muslims, Jews, and Christians. And one day, it will be the site of the very climax of human history, Armageddon. The passions and aspirations that swirl about the Temple Mount will play an ever-increasing role in global geopolitics as the world draws closer to that day.

The Temple Mount is the holiest site in Judaism, the place where Solomon built the Temple to Yahweh. The Second Temple was constructed by Zerubbabel, after the decree of the Persian emperor Cyrus, between 538 and 516 BC, and rebuilt with expansions by Herod the Great beginning in 19 BC.

The Temple is the center of Jewish life, at least for conservative and orthodox Jews. The Holy of Holies, the inner sanctuary within the tabernacle, was the most sacred site in Judaism, screened from the outer sanctuary by the veil of the covering. It was the home of the Ark of the Covenant, or Ark of the Testimony, a gold-clad wooden chest that contained the stone tablets on which Yahweh had written the Ten Commandments, Aaron's rod, and a pot of manna. Only the high priest was allowed to enter the Holy of Holies and approach the Ark, and then only once a year on the Day of Atonement (Yom Kippur). Contrary to its description in the blockbuster film *Raiders of the Lost Ark*, it was not "a transmitter...a radio for speaking to God." The Ark of the Covenant was far more important than a simple communicating device; it was Yahweh's throne when He appeared among His people.[2]

However, both the Ark of the Testimony and the Temple have been lost to the ages. After the Jewish revolt in 70 AD, Roman soldiers destroyed and looted Jerusalem, leaving most of Herod's temple in rubble. The menorah was depicted among the spoils of from the Temple on the Arch of Titus in Rome, commemorating his victory over the Jewish rebels.

The Ark disappeared long before. The last sure mention of it in the Bible is 2 Chronicles 35:3, where King Josiah of Judah, who reigned from 640 to 609 BC, ordered that the Ark be returned to the Temple. This is a bit surprising, as this means it had been removed from the Temple by one of his predecessors. Why, and where it had been stored, is a mystery. And at some point, after 609 BC, it vanished, possibly.

Jeremiah prophesied a time when the Ark will no longer be discussed or used,[3] and indeed, it never appeared in the Temple from its reconstruction by Zerubbabel until its destruction by Rome. A raised area on the floor of the Holy of Holies indicated where the Ark should have been.

And yet we are entering a period of history in which the Ark and the Temple will play central roles. A spiritual conflict is developing that will pit Christians, Jews, and Muslims (and competing subsets within those groups) against one another. Some seek control of the mount for political reasons while others may believe they can literally trigger the Apocalypse. The Temple Mount and the Ark of the Covenant will be right at the center of the oncoming storm.

Arab Muslims have controlled the Temple Mount since the conquest of Jerusalem in 638 AD, with brief exceptions during the 11th and 12th centuries when European crusaders occupied the city. The Al-Aqsa Mosque, the third holiest site in Islam, and the Dome of the Rock, which sits on the spot from which Muslims believe Muhammad ascended to heaven, were constructed in the late seventh century.

The geopolitical consequences of taking full control of the Temple Mount were considered so dangerous that the first action of Israel's Defense Minister Moshe Dayan on securing the area during the Six-Day War in 1967 was to take down the Israeli flag that paratroopers had raised over the mount.

Today, the Temple Mount is administered by the Waqf, an Islamic religious trust that has overseen the area since 1187. The government of Jordan acts as custodian of the Islamic religious sites on the mount, although security is provided by Israeli police. This mutually dissatisfying arrangement is a constant source of irritation and provocation to Jews and Muslims alike.

Christians, as spiritual descendants of Judaism, also attach special significance to the Temple Mount. In addition to the Old Testament history linked to the site, some of the major events of Jesus' life took place on the Temple Mount.

As an infant, Jesus was presented at the Temple in accordance with the Law, where Simeon, a man who had been told he would live to see the Messiah, and Anna, an 84-year-old prophetess, were led to Jesus by the Holy Spirit. When he was twelve, he remained behind in the Temple after his parents began the journey back to Nazareth following the Passover celebration in Jerusalem. It was a full day before they discovered Jesus was missing, and at least three more before they found him in the Temple talking with the rabbis.

Early in his ministry, Jesus visited Jerusalem during Passover, as must have been his custom, and with a zealous anger drove the moneychangers and animal merchants out of the Temple. Later, probably during the second Passover during his ministry, Jesus healed the lame man at the Pool of Bethesda at the north end of the temple complex. Shortly before the Crucifixion, Jesus drove out the moneychangers a second time, and Matthew records that he healed many lame and blind people who came to him at the Temple.

Ultimately, the prophesied final battle between good and evil, Armageddon, will be fought for the Temple Mount, the historical Mount Zion. (The Western Hill that bears the name Zion today is outside the Old City of Jerusalem. It's taller than the Temple Mount, and apparently it seemed a more fitting location for the by-then lost palace of David to Jews of the first century.)

Still, the Temple Mount's importance to Christians, especially in the increasingly secular West, pales in comparison to the significance of the Temple Mount to Jews. One example that might give American Gentiles a sense of the frustration religious Jews feel over the status of the mount, where visits by non-Muslims are restricted and only Muslims are allowed to pray, would be to imagine the site of the World Trade Center occupied by mosques, with access to the 9/11 Memorial and Museum limited except to Muslims.

That's a poor example, but it conveys the sense.

Moshe Dayan and Israel's secular leadership in 1967 seemed to believe that the mount was a site holy only to Muslims and nothing more than "a historical site of commemoration of the past" for Jews. By granting them access to the site, Dayan thought Jewish demands for worship and sovereignty there would be satisfied. By allowing Muslims to retain religious control of the Temple Mount, he sought to remove the site as a source of inspiration of Palestinian nationalism.[4]

It was a no-win situation, as recent waves of Palestinian violence remind us. And it will only get worse in the years ahead.

The Jewish state is under near constant pressure from the global community to give up land for peace. Although the United States has not formally recognized Palestine, it is among a minority of nations. On November 22, 1974, the United Nations General Assembly passed a resolution recognizing the right of the Palestinian people to self-determination and independence, and the Palestine Liberation Organization was recognized as the sole legitimate representative of the Palestinian people.

The Palestinian National Council declared independence on November 15, 1988, which was acknowledged by eighty nations by the end of that year. As of 2023, 138 of the world's 195 nations recognize Palestine as an independent state. Israel does not, maintaining that such status can only be conferred by direct negotiations between Israel and the Palestinian National Authority. To date, Israel still maintains *de facto* military control over the Palestinian territories.

But even in the United States, which has arguably been Israel's strongest supporter since 1948, calls have been heard even from Republican presidential administrations for the establishment of an independent Palestine. In October of 2007, Condoleezza Rice, Secretary of State for George W. Bush, said at a news conference with Palestinian President Mahmoud Abbas:

> Frankly, it's time for the establishment of a Palestinian state. The United States sees the establishment of a Palestinian state and a two-state solution as absolutely essential for the future, not just of Palestinians and Israelis but also for the Middle East and indeed to American interests.[5]

Interestingly, a majority of both Israelis and Palestinians support a two-state solution in opinion polls. However, when the compromises required to reach such a solution—drawing permanent borders, the status of settlements, and dividing Jerusalem—are spelled out, support collapses.[6]

The Roman Catholic Church recently waded back into these contentious waters. On June 26, 2015, the Vatican signed a treaty with the "state of Palestine," essentially acknowledging the independence of a sovereign Palestine. The Israeli Foreign Ministry immediately expressed its disappointment and declared that this move would not benefit the peace process. If the Palestinian Authority can achieve independence through outside influence on Israel, why should it negotiate with the Israeli government?

News of this agreement stirred old suspicions among some Jews that the Vatican is conspiring with Palestinian leaders, and possibly with Israeli elites, to take control of the Old City and/or the Temple Mount. Stories have circulated on the Internet for years that the Vatican is working with Jewish elites on a secret deal to turn over administration of the Old City to the Roman Catholic Church.

This is not entirely conspiracy theory. The *1947 United Nations Partition Plan for Palestine* included a proposal to designate Jerusalem *corpus separatum* (Latin for "separated body"), a zone under international control because of the city's shared religious importance. That proposal was included in the plan largely because of a powerful diplomatic effort by the Vatican, which had been concerned about the status of Christian holy sites in the Holy Land since the nineteenth century.

However, the partition plan failed when war broke out almost immediately after Israel declared its independence. Months of intense fighting left Israeli forces in control of western Jerusalem, and Israel held on to that territory when the armistice was signed ending the 1948–49 war.

Today, at least one Middle East think tank, the Jerusalem Old City Initiative, formed by Canadian diplomats after the failure of the Camp David talks in 2000, has "concluded that an effective and empowered third party presence was imperative in the Old city."[7] A similar proposal was reportedly made by the Obama administration in late 2013. US Secretary of State

John Kerry, in Israel trying to broker a deal to establish a Palestinian state by April of 2014, was said by sources to have proposed a "third party solution" for administering eastern Jerusalem, with the Vatican controlling holy sites in partnership with a coalition of Muslim countries such as Turkey and Saudi Arabia. Sources close to the talks said Israeli leaders were unreceptive, especially to the idea of Turkey's participation.[8]

A suggestion that Jordan might replace Turkey in the international coalition was met with a lukewarm response in Amman. King Abdullah was reportedly less than eager to involve his nation in a delicate and potentially explosive political situation while the Syrian civil war intensified on his northern border.

While there has been a recent thaw in relations between Israel and Turkey, they have been rocky in the early part of the twenty-first century. This is likely due to the regional ambitions of Turkey's President Recep Tayyip Erdogan. Turkey supported the so-called Gaza Freedom Flotilla, a 2010 mission to deliver construction materials and humanitarian aid to the Gaza Strip coordinated by the Free Gaza Movement and the Turkish Foundation for Human Rights and Freedoms and Humanitarian Relief. Since Israel and Egypt have blockaded access to the Gaza Strip since 2007, aid is normally delivered to Israel and then transferred to Palestinian authorities. The flotilla attempted to run the blockade and deliver the aid directly to Gaza.

When Israeli forces intercepted the boats on May 31, 2010, nine people were killed in the ensuing confrontation on the

Turkish ship MV *Mavi Marmara*. Although President Erdogan said in 2013 that relations with Israel could be normalized if certain conditions were met, in May, 2015, he called for Sunni and Shia Muslims to set aside their differences and resume efforts to assert dominance over Jerusalem, and specifically over the Temple Mount.[9]

Turkey's deteriorating relationship with Russia after two of its F-16s shot down a Russian SU-24 fighter-bomber over Syria on November 24, 2015, gave Erdogan an unexpected incentive to improve relations with Israel. Russia supplies more than half of Turkey's natural gas, and Vladimir Putin has demonstrated that he's willing to use Russia's energy resources as a geopolitical weapon. Israel, meanwhile, is developing a potentially huge reserve of natural gas in the eastern Mediterranean. Collaboration on tapping this resource for the suddenly needy European market, following the destruction of the Nord Stream pipelines between Russia and Germany, probably factored into the decision by Ankara and Jerusalem to restore diplomatic ties in August 2022.[10]

Under current political conditions, it appears that Israel will grow increasingly resistant to pressure to relinquish control of the Temple Mount. The government led by Benjamin Netanyahu, Israel's prime minister since 2009 (except for an interlude between July 2021 and December 2022), has been quietly investing in efforts to prepare for the construction of the Third Temple. Those efforts include education to teach young Israelis about the importance of the Temple to the state and to Judaism, and practical efforts, mainly by a private organization called the Temple Institute, to prepare the plans, utensils, and even sacrificial animals needed to make the

Temple a reality.

An investigative report by the Israeli newspaper *Haaretz* revealed that close supporters of Netanyahu—specifically a deputy defense minister and a key U.S. fundraiser—made significant financial contributions to advance the cause of the Third Temple's construction.[11]

This fuels a developing confrontation of literally biblical proportions. While modern Israel is mainly a secular society, eschatological proclamations by respected Israeli rabbis are becoming more common. At the same time, a growing majority of Muslims, especially in the nations closest to Israel, expect the imminent arrival of the Mahdi, or "rightly guided one", a figure in Muslim prophecy who is analogous to the Messiah.

In recent years, several prominent figures in the Orthodox Jewish community have publicly stated that the Messiah's appearance is very near. Rabbi Chaim Kanievsky, considered a leading authority in mainstream Haredi (ultra-Orthodox) Judaism, and not previously given to messianic predictions, has reportedly been advising Jews since 2014 to make *aliyah* (relocate to Israel) as soon as possible to prepare for Messiah's arrival.[12] (It should be noted that Rav Kanievsky, who died March 18, 2022 at the age of 94, had predicted the Messiah's arrival by the end of the Shemitah year, which fell on the 29th of Elul—September 12, 2015.)

Rabbi Moshe Sternbuch, vice president of the Rabbinical Court, said in early December 2015 that the political conflict between Turkey and Russia means that Jews should anticipate the coming of the Messiah.

> "We have received a direct teaching, passed down from one to another, from the Gaon of Vilna, that when Russia goes and conquers Istanbul...it is time to quickly put on your Shabbat clothes and expect the Messiah," he said.
>
> "Here we have Russia and Turkey in a conflict with each other. We hear sounds of war. All of the nations seem so surprised that Turkey began a fight with Russia," Rabbi Sternbuch explained.
>
> "But we see in this the realization of the teachings of the sages, that when the Messiah needs to come, God will incite nations against each other, until, against their will, there will be a war. Therefore, as the Shmittah goes out, we should have great inspiration to wake up and repent."[13]

The Vilna Gaon ("Genius of Vilnius"), Elijah ben Shlomo Zalman, was an eighteenth-century rabbi and kabbalist who is considered one of the most influential rabbinical scholars since the Middle Ages. Rabbi Sternbuch is a great-grandson of the Vilna Gaon. The "direct teaching" to which he refers is a prophecy passed down within the family, revealed for the first time by American-born Hasidic Rabbi Lazer Brody in March of 2014:

> When you hear that the Russians have captured the city of Crimea, you should know that the times of the Messiah have started, that his steps are being heard. And when you hear that the Russians have reached the city of Constantinople, you should put on your Shabbat [Sabbath] clothes and don't take them off, because it

means that the Messiah is about to come any minute.[14]

Rabbi Brody was moved to reveal the prophecy by Russia's annexation of Crimea in March 2014 as part of the civil war in Ukraine. Rabbi Sternbuch and others believe this fulfilled the first part of the Vilna Gaon's prophecy. As for the second part: Constantinople is the modern city of Istanbul. As of this writing, the Russians have yet to invade Turkey, and the political situation between Ankara and Moscow has warmed in the years since the shooting down of the Russian warplane. So, if the Vilna Gaon is to be believed, there is some time yet for the arrival of Messiah.

Please understand that we give credence only to those prophecies recorded in the Bible. Whether the Vilna Gaon's prophecy was inspired is irrelevant. What matters is that there are people in Israel who believe it. One's actions are determined by what one believes, and there are religious leaders in Israel who believe that the end of history is fast approaching.

World events prompted Rabbi Yosef Berger, one of the rabbis in charge of King David's Tomb, to initiate a project to create a Torah scroll to unify all of Israel—which he hopes to present to the Messiah upon his arrival. In an interview, Rabbi Berger told a reporter that he was inspired by a prophecy in chapter 3 of the Book of Hosea:

> For the children of Israel shall abide many days without a king, and without a prince, and without a sacrifice, and without an image, and without an ephod, and without teraphim:

> Afterward shall the children of Israel return, and seek the Lord their God, and David their king; and shall fear the Lord and his goodness in the latter days. (Hosea 3:4–5, ESV)

Rabbi Berger said he believes that bringing Israel together with a single Torah scroll housed on Mount Zion, the site of David's Tomb and adjacent to the Temple Mount, will fulfill the prophetic goals of seeking the Lord, seeking the dynasty of David, and the construction of the Third Temple.[15]

Perhaps the most well-known recent rabbinical prediction of the Messiah is the claim by the late Rabbi Yitzhak Kaduri, a renowned kabbalist and Haredi rabbi, who claimed he met the Messiah on November 4, 2003.[16] Rabbi Kaduri sealed a note containing the name of the Messiah that was not to be opened until a year after his death on January 28, 2006.

The revelation that the name in Rabbi Kaduri's note was Yehoshua—Jesus—touched off a just a bit of controversy.[17]

Meanwhile, Israel's Muslim neighbors are likewise experiencing a surge in apocalyptic beliefs. Contrary to the publicly expressed opinions of Western political leaders and progressive pundits, groups such as Jabhat al-Nusra and ISIS do not represent the lunatic fringe of Islamic thought. Their expectation of the Mahdi's imminent arrival is shared by the vast majority of Sunni Muslims. In contrast to American Christians, some 80% of whom do not expect the literal return of Jesus anytime soon,[18] upwards of three-quarters of Muslims in the Middle East and South Asia expect to see the Mahdi before they die.

> Looking at specific countries, the highest percentage of the population expecting the Mahdi's near-term appearance is found in Afghanistan (83 percent), followed by Iraq (72 percent), Turkey (68 percent) and Tunisia (67 percent). Sixty percent of Pakistanis, 51 percent of Moroccans, 46 percent of Palestinians and 40 percent of Egyptians are looking for the Mahdi in their lifetimes. The conventional wisdom in recent decades among many journalists, and not a few area "experts," has been that Mahdism is an eccentric outlier belief held mainly by (Twelver) Shi`is and the uneducated on the fringes of the Sunni world. This Pew data, among other things, shows the intellectual vacuity of such biases. The average for the 23 countries Pew surveyed on this issue of Mahdism comes out to 42 percent, and extrapolating from that to the entire Muslim world means there are over 670 million Muslims who believe the Mahdi will return here in the first half of the twenty-first century.
>
> What does this Pew information on Mahdism mean? First and foremost, Mahdism must be taken seriously as an intellectual, sociological and even political strain within the entire Islamic world – not dismissed as archaic, mystical nonsense.[19]

In other words, the Islamic State didn't hijack Islam, it is a *purer form* of Islam—and it has a hands-on approach to jump-starting the Apocalypse.

It may not be a coincidence the nations with the highest percentage of Muslims expecting the Mahdi's imminent arrival are the ones that have been occupied by American soldiers for the last two decades.

While many Muslims do not support the methods and/or aims of ISIS,[20] "Islamic history is rife with violent jihads led by self-styled Muslim messiahs and waged by their followers."[21] If only 1% of the world's Muslims rally to its cause, nearly seven million jihadis could be available to fight for the would-be caliphate.

The danger posed by ISIS to Christian communities in Syria and Iraq is shared by other Muslims in the area. Islam is splintered into sub-groups that fall under the general definitions "Sunni" and "Shia," and the Islamic State views other Muslims as a more immediate enemy (because they are heretics) than Jews, Christians, and practitioners of other religions.

> Like his predecessors in [Al Qaedi in Iraq], Baghdadi favors first purifying the Islamic community by attacking Shia and other religious minorities as well as rival jihadist groups. The Islamic State's long list of enemies includes the Iraqi Shia, Hezbollah, the Yazidis (a Kurdish ethnoreligious minority located predominantly in Iraq), the wider Kurdish community in Iraq, the Kurds in Syria and rival opposition groups in Syria (including Jabhat al-Nusra).[22]

It may surprise the reader to learn that ISIS carried out attacks against Hamas and Islamic Jihad in the Gaza Strip in 2015.[23] ISIS publicly condemned Hamas for being too narrowly focused on the Palestinian cause, working with Shias (Hezbollah and Iran), and not promoting a rigid enough interpretation of Islamic Law.[24] After ISIS announced its intention to conquer Saudi Arabia in December of 2014, the Saudis began building a 600-mile high-tech fence along the border with Iraq, where ISIS had a strong presence in Anbar province. Bringing the holy sites of Mecca and Medina under ISIS control would grant the caliphate a greater degree of legitimacy with the world's 672 million Muslims, and some analysts believe that is, in fact, the group's objective.[25]

The ability of ISIS to hold the territory it took was fleeting. To date, however, the only native military force to hold its own against the Islamic State is the Kurdish *peshmerga*. The Kurdish resistance, however, is hampered by the Turkish government, which wants to prevent the emergence of an independent Kurdish state that would likely annex part of southeastern Turkey.

Turkey's support of the Islamic State was probably the worst-kept secret of the Syrian civil war. The Turks view their southern neighbor, Syria, as a rival, and relations between the two countries has been tense for decades. The leadership of the Kurdistan Workers Party (PKK), a group considered a terrorist organization by Turkey and the United States, operated out of the Syrian capital, Damascus, from 1978 to 1998. Syria only ended support for the PKK after Turkey threatened to invade. It's possible that the government of Turkey's President Recep Tayyip Erdogan considers its support for ISIS payback for PKK terror attacks against Turkish targets.

It may also be that Erdogan is using the Islamic State as a cat's paw in his long game to revive the Ottoman Empire.

The rise of Erdogan's Justice and Development Party (AKP) has given Erdogan the clout to roll back some of the secular reforms of Mustafa Kemal Ataturk, who modernized Turkey and aligned it with the West after the collapse of the empire in 1923. Ottoman Turkish and Arabic script is again taught in government schools, and the number of students enrolled in state-run Islamic seminaries has grown from 62,000 in 2002, when Erdogan first came to power, to over 1 million.[26] Considering Erdogan's public call for Muslims to work toward wresting control of Jerusalem away from Israel, it is no surprise that some Middle East observers are asking in so many words: Is Turkey attempting to resurrect the Ottoman Empire on the back of the Islamic State?[27]

In the interest of giving equal time, it should be noted that while the leading authorities of Shia Islam, the ayatollahs who rule the Islamic Republic of Iran, are openly hostile toward Israel and the West, there are good reasons to believe that they are not as eager for the arrival of the Mahdi as Sunnis.

First, unlike Sunni Muslims, Shias believe (as do Christians) that there is nothing they can do to immanentize the eschaton. In other words, the Mahdi will arrive when Allah wills it and not one heartbeat sooner. And Twelver Shias believe that "victorious holy war" is forbidden until the return of their Mahdi, the Twelfth Imam.[28]

Second, and perhaps more significantly, Shiite religious authorities in Iran wield ultimate political power, not unlike the Sanhedrin in Jesus' day. And like the Jewish religious establishment when confronted with the Messiah, "the ruling ayatollahs are probably the most vociferous opponents of a true Mahdist claim on the planet—because acknowledging anyone as such would end their rule of Iran, and with it their wealth, power and privilege."[29]

However, it happens, the focus of conflict in the Middle East will ultimately return to Israel, and to the Temple Mount in particular. While the Islamic State may not be involved directly, there are hints that ISIS and Hamas have begun moving toward a more cooperative arrangement, especially in the Sinai peninsula.[30]

One thing is certain: The final battle between God and the angels who rebelled against His authority (and their human dupes, of course) will be fought for control of the "mount of assembly," the Temple Mount—the historic Mount Zion.

The struggle for Yahweh's holy mountain is a narrative thread woven through the entire Bible. From Eden to Armageddon, the conflict between God and the rebellious *bene elohim* centers on the mount of assembly, which, since the time of David, is the hill called the Temple Mount.

Entire books have been devoted to this topic, so we will just summarize here: It was understood in the ancient world that mountains were the domain of the gods. They were inaccessible and remote, far removed from the mundane plane of existence that is the lot of mortal men. Olympus is the most famous, but there were others: Mount Othrys in central Greece was the base of Cronus and the Titans, Mount Ida on Crete was home to the Titaness Rhea, mother of the Olympians, and Mount Zaphon (today's Jebel al-Aqra in southern Turkey) was the location of the palace of Baal.

The *original* holy mountain, however, was Eden. Ezekiel's lament over the king of Tyre describes the setting:

> You were in Eden, the garden of God;
>
> > every precious stone was your covering...
>
> In the abundance of your trade
>
> > you were filled with violence in your midst, and you sinned;
> >
> > so I cast you as a profane thing from the mountain of God,
> >
> > and I destroyed you, O guardian cherub,
> >
> > from the midst of the stones of fire. (Ezekiel 28:13,16, ESV)

"The mountain of God" is the home of the Divine Council, a sort of supernatural task force that assists Yahweh in carrying out His will. An entire book can be devoted to this topic,[31] but it's clear from scripture that a long war for this *har-mo'ed*, the mount of assembly, has been waged since humanity's banishment from Eden.

This conflict for Zion will be played out in the natural realm at the final battle between the forces of God and Satan, Armageddon. While it's popularly believed that the Hebrew words transliterated into English as "Armageddon" refer to the "mount of Megiddo," that's not the case.

On the surface, the identification of Megiddo makes sense. It sits in a strategic pass on an important trade route between

Egypt and Mesopotamia. Megiddo was the site of several historic battles; notably, between Egypt and rebellious Canaanite vassals in the fifteenth-century BC, Egypt and Judah in 609 BC (at which King Josiah fell), and Allied troops and the Ottoman Empire in World War 1.

However, there are two insurmountable problems with this interpretation. First and foremost, Megiddo is a valley. There is no mountain at Megiddo. Second, it is common in Greek translations for the letter *gamma* to represent the Hebrew *ayin*. The *ayin* is a glottal stop with no corresponding sound or letter in either Greek or English. But since *gamma* is usually transliterated into English as the letter *G*, *har mo'ed* was transformed into *har məgiddô*.

However, most Old Testament apocalyptic prophecy centers on Jerusalem and Mount Zion—for example, Joel 3 and Zechariah 14. Placing Armageddon at Megiddo is both linguistically and geographically inconsistent.

Armageddon will not be at Megiddo. It will be fought at Jerusalem for control of God's *har mo'ed*, His mount of assembly, Zion—the Temple Mount.

Whether this conflict occurs soon or in the distant future, there is no doubt that it will happen. And geopolitical events are moving elements into place, setting up conditions for a war that seemed unlikely just a few years ago. Discoveries of potentially huge reserves of natural gas in the Mediterranean and oil in the Golan Heights are transforming Israel into a player in world energy markets, adding another incentive for conflict in a region that already has more reasons to hate than it needs.

This leads to the question hanging over any analysis of the future of the Temple Mount: How can the prophesied Third Temple be constructed when the site is already occupied by the Dome of the Rock and the Al-Aqsa Mosque?

As Christians who believe in the inerrancy of Bible prophecy, we accept that a Temple will occupy the mount someday. Daniel was told by the angel Gabriel of a day when the Man of Sin, the Antichrist, will put a stop to the sacrifices and the offerings. For sacrifices and offerings to be stopped, there must be a place for them to resume. The question of a Third Temple is not *if*, but *when*.

Admittedly, at this point in history, it's difficult to imagine how that question will be answered. Exercising sovereignty over the Mount has been rejected as too dangerous by Israeli governments since 1967. How could a mosque, built on the spot where Muhammad allegedly ascended into heaven, be demolished for the Temple without triggering a war—one that could even unite Muslim factions that have been fighting each other for 1,400 years? Sheik Azzam al-Khatib, director of the Waqf, warned, "If they try to take over the mosque, this will be the end of time. This will create rage and anger not only in the West Bank but all over the Islamic world—and only God knows what will happen."[32]

Still, there are several ways this might be accomplished. Most simply, an earthquake could clear the Temple Mount without the need for human intervention. Israel is geologically active; experts say the area gets hit with a major earthquake of magnitude 7 or greater every thousand years or so, and smaller ones, such as a 6.2M quake that killed 400 people in 1927, about every 80 to 100 years. Seismologists say the likelihood and the probable intensity of the next earthquake increases with each passing year.[33]

Another option is to construct the Third Temple on the Temple Mount without disturbing either the Dome of the Rock or the Al-Aqsa Mosque. A Jewish interfaith initiative launched in 2009, "God's Holy Mountain," argues that *halakha* (Jewish law) allows for a prophet to rule on the location of the Third Temple.[34] Appropriate divine revelation could result in the Temple being built alongside the Muslim sites on the Temple Mount.

However, this alternative has generated little enthusiasm among Muslim authorities, as one might expect. Even rabbinical leaders reject the idea, as many believe that the Temple should not be constructed until the Messiah arrives. The Chief Rabbinate of Israel has posted signs outside the Temple Mount in English and Hebrew that read:

> ANNOUNCEMENT AND WARNING: According to the Torah it is forbidden for any person to enter the area of the Temple Mount due to its sacredness.[35]

Rabbis are concerned that visitors may walk across the spot formerly occupied by the Holy of Holies unknowingly, and there is no purification system currently in place to make them ritually clean.

The final option for constructing the Third Temple is, of course, the path of greatest resistance—simply demolishing the Dome of the Rock to make room. It does not seem likely that any Israeli government will find the political will or popular support, even among Jews, to go that route.

However, until the path to constructing the Third Temple is revealed, preparations for the Temple are being made. The Temple Institute, a group organized in 1987 by Rabbi Yisrael Ariel, has reportedly spent over $30 million assembling the garments, utensils, and other items needed for temple service.[36] And, as noted above, the Temple Institute is supported at least tacitly by the Netanyahu government, and people with close connections to Netanyahu and his political allies have been contributing financially to the Institute's work.

One of the more unusual prerequisites for the Temple's construction is a perfect red heifer. It is believed, based on Numbers 19:1–10, that a red heifer without spot or blemish that has never been yoked must be sacrificed before the Temple can be built.

> [I]n truth, the fate of the entire world depends on the red heifer. For G-d has ordained that its ashes alone are the single missing ingredient for the reinstatement of Biblical purity—and thereafter, the rebuilding of the Holy Temple.[37]

From the time of Moses through the destruction of the Second Temple in 70 AD, ashes were prepared from only nine red heifers. The influential medieval physician and Torah scholar Maimonides, whose teachings are considered authoritative by many Jews including the leadership of the Temple Institute, believed that the tenth would be prepared by Messiah himself.

That requirement may be close to fulfillment. In September 2022, five red heifers from Texas arrived in Israel with a good deal of fanfare. As of this writing, there is no news on whether any of the five are still without blemish and 100% red. Since, according to Numbers 19, the heifers must be at least two years old to be sacrificed for the purification ritual, it will be the fall of 2023 before it's known if this critical step can be met—at least from this group of cattle.[38]

Another key element in making the Temple a reality is, of course, the actual blueprints for the construction. On Tisha B'Av, or the 9th of Av (July 25/26), 2015, architectural drawings and a video featuring a 3D representation of the proposed Temple were released via the Internet.[39] The design is a fascinating blend of tradition and high technology (Wi-Fi in the Temple!), and the video tour includes the menorah, incense altar, and shewbread table, all of which have already been prepared by the Temple Institute.

The 9th of Av was a significant date on which to unveil the blueprints. Tisha B'Av is a day of fasting and mourning to commemorate the anniversary of several disasters in Jewish history, especially the destruction of both the First and Second Temples in Jerusalem.

Perhaps significant by its absence in the preparations by the Temple Institute is the Ark of the Covenant. There is no doubt that the Ark played a central role in the early years of the Jewish state. It moved with the Tabernacle during the Israelites' forty years in the wilderness. It resided at Shiloh and Gibeon before finding a permanent home in the Holy of Holies within Solomon's Temple. During the time of Samuel, the Philistines learned to their dismay (and great discomfort) that capturing the Ark brought a curse instead of victory.[40]

The Ark disappeared from history around the time of

Nebuchadnezzar's invasion of Judah in 597 BC. There are theories on the Ark's current location: One, based on 2 Maccabees 2:4–5, is that the prophet Jeremiah hid the ark in a cave on Mount Nebo in present-day Jordan. Another, an inspiration for the plot of *Raiders of the Lost Ark*, contends that Pharaoh Shishak took the ark back to Egypt when he plundered Jerusalem in the days of Rehoboam, the son of Solomon.

Others hold that the Ark is being kept in Ethiopia, transported there by Menelik, the offspring of Solomon and Queen Sheba, or by Necho II, the pharaoh who killed King Josiah at the Battle of Megiddo. One archaeologist even claims that the Ark was carried to southern Africa 2,500 years ago by a tribe called the Lemba—which, oddly enough, has a higher occurrence of a genetic marker particular to Jews among males of one leadership clan than the general Jewish population.[41]

But hunting the Ark, or reconstructing it, doesn't seem to be a priority for the Temple Institute. According to Rabbi Chaim Richman, Director of the Institute's International Department, that's because Jews already know where it is. Richman said in an interview that the Ark is buried under the Temple Mount. Many Orthodox Jews believe it's hidden by order of King Josiah in a secret tunnel constructed by Solomon as a precaution against a Babylonian invasion. Richman says, "Jews have an unbroken chain of recorded information, passed down from generation to generation, which indicates its exact location."[42]

Of course, excavating under the Temple Mount is forbidden

by the Waqf, at least to Jews. So, getting to the Ark would be problematic, at least until the political calculus is changed by the arrival of the Messiah.

But even if it should turn out that the Ark is not under the Temple Mount, or at any of the other locations put forward, it wouldn't necessarily prevent a new Temple from being built and used. The Ark was never housed in the Temple constructed by Zerubbabel and Jesus still referred to it as his Father's house.

The next few years may be the beginning of the end game of history. Forces with very different agendas are on a collision course, and the future of the Temple Mount is a key point of conflict. Islamists often look to anniversary dates of significant historical events as catalysts for action,[43] and an important historical marker is just ahead: 2023–24 marks one hundred years since the collapse and dissolution of the Ottoman Empire.

There are several reasons to watch the next several years very carefully:

- The Muslim Brotherhood, which briefly had power in Egypt before being deposed by the Egyptian military, was formed in response to the fall of the Ottoman caliphate. It may try to return to power on or about the anniversary of that date.
- The Islamic State, which has declared its own caliphate, may seek to extend its legitimacy by extending control over the Temple Mount and/or the Muslim holy sites in Saudi Arabia.

- Turkey's President Recep Tayyip Erdogan has publicly declared that his goal is for his nation to achieve the status of "a great nation, a great power" by 2023.[44] (He also said Turkey would "reach the level of our Ottoman and Seljuk ancestors by the year 2071." That would be one thousand years since the Seljuk Turks defeated the Byzantine Empire at the Battle of Manzikert, a decisive victory that transformed Anatolia into Turkey. At their peak, the Seljuks controlled Asia from the Aegean Sea to China.) Erdogan and his supporters may try to use one or both of the groups mentioned above to advance his Neo-Ottoman agenda.
- And in Israel, the government quietly supports initiatives to prepare for constructing the Third Temple, while prominent Orthodox and Ultra-Orthodox Jewish rabbis publicly proclaim that the Messiah's appearance is imminent.

Again, we credit only those prophecies contained between the covers of the Bible. Other prophecies, predictions, and anniversary dates are important only insofar as they shed light on the motives for the actions of others.

Considering the Muslim penchant for finding significance in round number anniversary years, the apocalyptic beliefs of a majority of Middle Eastern Sunni Muslims, and a growing belief in the Messiah's imminent arrival among Jewish religious leaders, it's safe to say that the years ahead for the Temple Mount—God's holy mountain, Zion—will be turbulent. Come quickly, Lord!

Derek Gilbert is an accomplished scholar and researcher in Middle eastern history, the author of several books examining the ancient mythologies and their relationship to the pagan gods of Israelite and neighboring nations cosmology, and a television host along with his wife Sharon.

ENDNOTES

[1] Sheikh Muhammad Ahmad Hussein claimed Al-Aqsa was built by Adam or by angels "during his time." It was, in fact, opened in the year 705 AD. Ilan Ben Zion, "Jerusalem Mufti: Temple Mount Never Housed Jewish Temple," *The Times of Israel*, October 25, 2015 (http://www.timesofisrael.com/jerusalem-mufti-denies-temple-mount-ever-housed-jewish-shrine/).

[2] Exodus 25:22, Numbers 7:89, 1 Samuel 4:4.

[3] Jeremiah 3:16.

[4] Ted Belman, "The Temple Mount Controversy," *American Thinker*, November 30, 2014 (http://www.americanthinker.com/articles/2014/11/the_temple_mount_controversy.html).

[5] Matthew Lee, "Now Is Time for Palestinian State," *Washington Post*, October 15, 2007 (http://www.washingtonpost.com/wp-dyn/content/article/2007/10/15/AR2007101500703_pf.html).

[6] Dahlia Scheindlin, "Israelis, Palestinians Support 2-State – But Why Bother?", *+972 Magazine*, January 7, 2012 (http://972mag.com/surveys-israelis-and-palestinians-support-two-state-peace-but-why-bother/32311/).

[7] Jerusalem Old City Initiative, http://www.cips-cepi.ca/event/jerusalem-old-city-initiative/, retrieved 2/18/23.

[8] Aaron Klein, "International mandate to control sections of Israel's capital," *WND*, December 15, 2013 (http://www.wnd.com/2013/12/u-s-plan-gives-jerusalem-holy-sites-to-vatican/).

[9] Mary Chastain, "Turkish President Erdogan: Muslims Lost Their Way to Jerusalem," *Breitbart.com*, May 18, 2015 (http://www.breitbart.com/national-security/2015/05/18/turkish-president-erdogan-muslims-lost-their-way-to-jerusalem/).

[10] Steven A. Cook, "How Israel and Turkey Benefit from Restoring Relations." *Council on Foreign Relations*, August 23, 2022. https://www.cfr.org/in-brief/how-israel-and-turkey-benefit-restoring-relations, accessed 2/18/23.

[11] Uri Blau, "Netanyahu Allied Donated to Groups Pushing for Third Temple," *Haaretz*, December 9, 2015 (http://www.haaretz.com/settlementdollars/1.690821).

[12] Adam Eliyahu Berkowitz, "Leading Israeli Rabbi Says the Arrival of the Messiah is Imminent," *Breaking Israel News*, July 3, 2015 (http://www.breakingisraelnews.com/44534/leading-israeli-rabbi-messiah-imminent-jewish-world/).

[13] Adam Eliyahu Berkowitz, "Prominent Rabbis Sternbuch, Amar Hint That the Messiah is 'Just Around the Corner'," *Breaking Israel News*, December 9, 2015 (http://www.breakingisraelnews.com/55777/turkeysyria-conflict-unfolding-prominent-rabbis-hint-messiah-around-corner-jewish-world/).

[14] Rivkah Lambert Adler, "18th Century Jewish Mystics Predicted Future Conflict Between Russia, Turkey Ripe with Messianic Implications," *Breaking Israel News*, November 29, 2015 (http://www.breakingisraelnews.com/54943/200-years-ago-war-between-turkey-russia-prophesied-sign-redemption-jewish-world/).

[15] Adam Eliayahu Berkowitz, "Torah Scroll Being Written to Present to Messiah Upon His Arrival," *Breaking Israel News*, December 15, 2015 (http://www.breakingisraelnews.com/56244/rabbi-sets-out-mission-write-torah-scroll-present-messiah-upon-arrival-jewish-world/).

[16] "Rabbi Kaduri's Most Recent Words," *Arutz Sheva*, January 24, 2006 (http://www.israelnationalnews.com/News/Flash.aspx/97225#.VoWcU8YrLMg)

[17] Rivkah Lambert Adler, "Rabbi Kaduri 'Jesus as Messiah' Claim Proven as False," *Breaking Israel News*, June 17, 2015 (http://web.archive.org/save/http://www.breakingisraelnews.com/43554/rabbi-kaduri-jesus-as-messiah-claim-discredited-as-false-jewish-world/).

[18] Pew Research Center, "Many Americans Uneasy with Mix of Religion and Politics: Section IV--Religious Beliefs," August 24, 2006 (http://www.people-press.org/2006/08/24/section-iv-religious-beliefs/).

[19] Dr. Timothy R. Furnish, "Mahdism (and Sectarianism and Superstition) Rises in the Islamic World," *History News Network*, August 13, 2012 (http://historynewsnetwork.org/article/147714).

[20] A recent survey by the Pew Research Center found that between 73% and 99% of Muslims in Turkey, the Palestinian territories, Israel, Jordan and Lebanon had an "unfavorable" view of ISIS. Jacob Poushter, "In Nations With Significant Muslim Populations, Much Disdain for ISIS," *FactTank*, November 17, 2015 (http://www.pewresearch.org/fact-tank/2015/11/17/in-nations-with-significant-muslim-populations-much-disdain-for-isis/).

[21] Furnish, op. cit.

[22] Daniel L. Byman and Jennifer R. Williams, "ISIS vs. Al Qaeda: Jihadism's Global Civil War." February 24, 2015

(http://www.brookings.edu/research/articles/2015/02/24-byman-williams-isis-war-with-al-qaeda).

[23] Paul Alster, "Israel, Hamas Strange Bedfellows When it Comes to Reining in ISIS in Gaza," *FoxNews.com*, July 23, 2015 (http://www.foxnews.com/world/2015/07/23/israel-hamas-strange-bedfellows-when-it-comes-to-reining-in-isis-in-gaza.html).

[24] "ISIL Warns Hamas in Video Message," *Al Jazeera*, July 1, 2015 (http://www.aljazeera.com/news/2015/07/isil-warns-hamas-video-message-150701042302630.html).

[25] William Young (Senior Policy Analyst for RAND Corp.), "ISIS Aims to Occupy Mecca," *Newsweek*, January 17, 2015 (http://www.newsweek.com/islamic-state-aims-occupy-mecca-300205).

[26] Ishaan Tharoor, "Why Turkey's President Wants to Revive the Language of the Ottoman Empire," *Washington Post*, December 12, 2014 (https://www.washingtonpost.com/news/worldviews/wp/2014/12/12/why-turkeys-president-wants-to-revive-the-language-of-the-ottoman-empire/).

[27] Catherine Shakdam, "Is Turkey attempting to resurrect the Ottoman Empire on the back of the 'black army'?," *Al-Akhbar*, October 29, 2014 (http://english.al-akhbar.com/node/22243).

[28] Dr. Timothy R. Furnish, "Apocalypse Row: Netanyahu, Nukes, and Iranian Eschatology," *zPolitics*, March 2, 2015 (http://zpolitics.com/apocalypse-row-netanyahu-nukes-and-iranian-eschatology/).

[29] Ibid.

[30] "Hamas-ISIS Cooperation Adds New Layer to Middle East Threats," *Breaking Israel News*, December 25, 2015 (http://www.breakingisraelnews.com/56935/hamas-isis-cooperation-adds-new-layer-mideast-threats-terror-watch/).

[31] And there have been. We recommend *The Unseen Realm* by Dr. Michael S. Heiser for an accessible yet scholarly treatment of this concept.

[32] William Booth and Ruth Eglash, "Jewish Activists Want to Pray on Jerusalem's Temple Mount, Raising Alarm in Muslim World," *Washington Post*, December 2, 2013 (https://www.washingtonpost.com/world/middle_east/jewish-activists-set-sights-on-jerusalems-temple-mount-raising-alarm-in-muslim-world/2013/12/02/d0561dc4-4e00-11e3-97f6-ed8e3053083b_story.html).

[33] Zafrir Rinat, "Israel is Due, and Ill Prepared, for a Major Earthquake," *Haaretz*, January 15, 2010 (http://www.haaretz.com/israel-is-due-and-ill-prepared-for-a-major-earthquake-1.261497).

[34] See www.GodsHolyMountain.org.

[35] "New Initiative Would Build Temple Next To Dome of The Rock," *Koinonia House eNews*, June 23, 2009 (https://www.khouse.org/enews_article/2009/1477/).

[36] Jake Wallis Simons, "The Rabbi, the Lost Ark, and the Future of the Temple Mount," The Telegraph, September 12, 2013

(http://www.telegraph.co.uk/news/worldnews/10287615/The-rabbi-the-lost-ark-and-the-future-of-Temple-Mount.html).

[37] "The Red Heifer: Introduction," The Temple Institute. https://templeinstitute.org/red-heifer-introduction/, retrieved 2/18/23.

[38] Chris Mitchell, "Texas Red Heifers' Arrival Stirs Prophetic Excitement in Israel." *CBN News*, September 23, 2022. https://www1.cbn.com/cbnnews/israel/2022/september/texas-red-heifers-arrival-stirs-prophetic-excitement, retrieved 2/18/23.

[39] "Architectural Plans for Third Temple Have Begun," *Arutz Sheva*, July 26, 2015 (http://www.israelnationalnews.com/News/News.aspx/198621#.VoBeH8YrLMg).

[40] 1 Samuel chapters 4 through 6.

[41] Moira Schneider, "African 'Jewish' Tribe Displays its Lost Ark," *Jewish Chronicle Online*, April 22, 2010 (http://www.thejc.com/news/world-news/30865/african-jewish-tribe-displays-its-lost-ark).

[42] Simons, 2013.

[43] Dr. Timothy R. Furnish, "Mahdism (and Sectarianism and Superstition) Rises in the Islamic World," *History News Network*, August 13, 2012 (http://historynewsnetwork.org/article/147714).

[44] Nicola Nasser, "Syria, Egypt Reveal Erdogan's Hidden 'Neo-Ottoman Agenda'," *Global Research*, November 20, 2013 (http://www.globalresearch.ca/syria-egypt-reveal-erdogans-hidden-neo-ottoman-agenda/5358781).

CHAPTER 7

FINAL STEPS

PASTOR CASPAR MCLOUD

Revelation 12:11 says, "And they overcame him by the blood of the Lamb, and by the word of their testimony; and they loved not their lives unto the death."

When we consider finding solutions to the troubles in our fallen world this is where we start, understanding that there is eternal life, after we graduate from this present one. Living our lives to glorify the Lord Jesus/Yeshua is to live fearlessly into the future. Considering that God Almighty does not fear anyone or anything, no Nephilim giants, no beastly dictators, no fallen angels masquerading as extraterrestrials, and no psychopathic globalist transhumanists eugenics depopulationists, neither should we, if we are a child of God. If we are a child of God let us act like one all the time. 1 Peter 2:21 says, "For even hereunto were ye called: because Christ also suffered for us, leaving us an example, that ye should follow his steps."

As the world continues in its defiance and rebellion to keep walking toward Armageddon, as true believers we are to keep looking up to the author and finisher of our faith. Luke 21:28 reminds us, "And when these things begin to come to pass, then look up, and lift up your heads; for your redemption draweth nigh." Because "All", things are possible with God!

1 Corinthians 11:1 says, "Be ye followers of me, even as I also am of Christ."

On 3rd July 2001, I was at a church service where I had been asked to come and share my testimony of how I overcame heart disease. Being considered a virtuoso guitarist, and singer/songwriter within the entertainment world, the church worship leaders had asked me to sit in and play with their praise band before I played an acoustic solo set of my original songs and shared my testimony.

The kingdom of darkness tried to take my life in the middle of praise and worship that night and I was left without a heartbeat near the end of the service. Can you imagine the sheer audacity of the demonic realm trying to kill a child of God amid a time of worshipping the Lord Jesus/Yeshua?

My friend and physician Dr. Terri Allen had come to hear me share my testimony on this particular evening and a nurse that was in the church service. They both later confirmed that I didn't have a pulse. The pastor in charge prayed in the almighty name of Jesus Christ of Nazareth, Messiah Yeshua, and cast out the spirit of death. My physician friend Dr. Terri showed me an EKG after several tests were done soon after this experience and gave me a printout of the EKG informing me that God Almighty had given me the heart of an 18-year-old and had divinely healed me. I was 49 years old at the time.

Whilst I didn't have a heartbeat in that church service, I did have an out-of-body experience and was taken into another dimension, surrounded by an angelic presence.

I can only tell you with great biblical authority and personal experience that every Word of God is true. I was fully conscious the entire time, although there are some aspects, I have no words to describe and articulate. As an artist, musician, author, and pastor I am seldom without adequate words to convey and express my perspectives.

We read in 1 Corinthians 2:9, "But as it is written, Eye hath not seen, nor ear heard, neither have entered into the heart of man, the things which God hath prepared for them that love him." I fell asleep later that night still surrounded by a sense of angelic beings surrounding and watching over me.

The next day I ended up praying for my physician's mum who had immigrated to America from the UK. I felt the Holy Spirit instruct me to pray that she would receive the Baptism of the Holy Spirit. She had tears running down her face as I prayed for her as she had a spiritual encounter with the Lord.

I was told a week later that some tumours she suffered from vanished at the moment she was Baptised by the Holy Spirit. I have seen miraculous signs and wonders ever since, all to the glory of the Lord. My life has never been the same since that moment and I am convinced that all things are possible with God. I tell you to assure you that no matter what the devil tries our God is Almighty and shall always outmaneuver him.

The first disciples asked the Lord Jesus/Yeshua what it was going to be like when he returns here. We read in Matthew 24:6 - "And ye shall hear of wars and rumours of wars: see that ye be not troubled: for all these things must come to pass, but the end is not yet."

My friend Dr. Michael Spaulding and I were having a chat and during our discourse, I felt the Holy Spirit say we needed to write a book with a number of our erudite scholarly friends that we have all done numerous conferences and podcasts together with, to help offer solutions for these end times.

Considering how so many people we know are entertaining the spirit of fear hearing of all the plans of the psychopathic, globalist, transhumanist, eugenicists, (depopulationists - a word that I coined to describe them). Let us understand that the future hasn't happened yet, and we Christians are instructed to pray and trust our Lord Jesus/Yeshua for all things. We are also called to be a doer of his Word and walk in his power and authority. 1 John 2:6 – "He that saith that he abideth in Him, ought himself also so to walk, even as He walked."

At this point, most of us reading such a book as this would probably be quite aware of how the media appears to be paid off by major wealthy pharmaceutical companies and instead of reporting the news, they have used the spirit of fear through propaganda agendas to push people into becoming a worldwide lab rat experiment.

I actually had some pastors in Scotland rebuke me in 2021 for sharing the Word of God in places like Revelation 18 because they claimed it would frighten the congregations, and also because they were believing the lie unless everyone was injected the injection wouldn't work. Isn't that like believing unless everyone in the world drinks a glass of Kool-Aid your glass of Kool-Aid won't quench your thirst?

We read in Revelation 18:23 – "And the light of a candle shall shine no more at all in thee; and the voice of the bridegroom and of the bride shall be heard no more at all in thee: for thy merchants were the great men of the earth; for by thy sorceries were all nations deceived."

This tells us that wealthy powerful men will deceive the entire world with pharmaceuticals, witchcraft, and manipulation. Could that possibly be someone like Bill Gates and his Gates of Hell foundation? Or Henry Kissinger's protégé the Nazi-raised unelected leader Klaus Schwab and his World Economic Forum gang?

Let us consider how troubles of all sorts will reach epic proportions when untold numbers of people suddenly disappear from the earth.

I recall reading a book by Dave Hunt titled, *Peace, Prosperity and the Coming Holocaust*, when we lived in UK in the early 80s. Hunt exposed the New Age movement in prophecy and wrote about how the world governments would lie to the people left behind after the Rapture happened, saying that the UFOs took all those Christian troublemakers away so the world can now enjoy peace on earth without any God or Heaven interfering with their utopia of total debauchery. That seems like giving Aleister Crowley's "Do what thy wilt," its last dance with destiny. Mind you that will be a time when freedom will be removed, as the antichrist comes into a season of worldwide dictatorship.

After the Rapture happens it will bring about great worldwide panic as never seen before nor will be seen again, and keep in mind that when people panic, they are more easily controlled so they will probably be demanding a strong world leader, most likely a Transhumanist who comes in to take over and who will seemingly have answers to all the world's problems.

Matthew 24:6 states, "And ye shall hear of wars and rumours of wars: see that ye be not troubled: for all these things must come to pass, but the end is not yet."

Covidmania appears to have mounting evidence of how it was intentionally released so major pharmaceuticals could sell their nefarious injections without any liability. For example, these so-called unlicensed, uninsured experimental vaccination shots which don't qualify as a vaccine appear to be intentionally designed to damage, main, and kill the general population. According to videos released by Project Veritas it appears quite revealing that some Pfizer employees caught on hidden cameras have no moral compass whatsoever.

Ephesians 5:11 says, "And have no fellowship with the unfruitful works of darkness, but rather reprove them." This means we are to help expose evil works. Far too many people still do not know the truth of what is unfolding before us on the world stage. If we are to find solutions, we must help share the Gospel truth. No political party, no matter how smooth talking its puppets and oracles are, shall ever be able to fix the major troubles of this fallen world.

In the 1800s when Benjamin Disraeli was Prime Minister of the United Kingdom he was quoted as saying "The world is governed by very different personages from what is imagined by those who are not behind the scenes."

The Lord Jesus/Yeshua told us in places like John 8:32 that, "And ye shall know the truth, and the truth shall make you free." Best to understand that Gospel truth even if it makes you a wee bit mad at first when you realise how you had previously been deceived. Speaking of deceptions, let us also consider how medical doctors beholden to the medical industrial complex who are gaining a degree of wealth and comfort, are controlled and dictated to by the major pharmaceutical corporations. They have been programmed by the Rockefeller-controlled schools of medicine to go along with their official narratives, so they will refuse to acknowledge things like how infant and childhood vaccines are quite dangerous to their overall health and well-being. John D. Rockefeller made his fortune in oil. He systematically took over the universities' schools of medicine and pushed them to use his petroleum-based products in medicine, things that best belong in car engines, not in humans. When people started coming down with cancer as a result, Rockefeller simply started the Cancer Research Centre of America to control the narratives and to hinder people from discovering that fact and to hide certain medical findings and manipulate other findings.

I recall reading an article by a physician in the 1800s who stated he never saw a cancer patient until the government compelled people to receive its vaccination. There is a fair amount of research pointing to how John D. Rockefeller funded his scientists to take over medical schools and offer petroleum-based medicines that helped cause cancers. Keeping in mind Rockefeller Lockstep 2010, was Blueprint for the 2020 COVID-19 well-orchestrated Pandemic.

They don't make a profit from healthy people, do they?

The Rockefeller Foundation is also the organisation responsible for creating a "blueprint" for establishing the WHO (World Health Organization) originally called the *International Health Division.* Keeping in mind that the Rockefeller family appears to be the controlling arm of the Rothschild family in America along with the Gates of Hell Foundation.

In David Rockefeller's book 'Memoirs', he admits he is part of a secret cabal working to destroy the United States and create a new world order. Here is a direct quote from his book, page 405:

> Some even believe we [Rockefeller family] are part of a secret cabal working against the best interests of the United States, characterizing my family and me as 'internationalists' and of conspiring with others around the world to build a more integrated global political and economic structure - One World, if you will. If that's the charge, I stand guilty, and I am proud of it.

In 1994, David Rockefeller was quoted at a U.N. dinner as saying, "We are on the verge of a global transformation. All we need is the right major crisis, and the nations will accept the New World Order."

I bring this to your attention because sadly, too many people have lost the ability to learn and use their critical thinking skills. Our world is now filled with misinformation, disinformation, and much confusion as those who launched this great deception try to hinder anyone who questions them and their depopulation experiment.

There was an ancient ruler I read about who gave his generals a sword and told them as long as he ruled their nation with righteousness use the sword against his enemies, nevertheless if he ever rules in unrighteousness and oppresses the nation use the sword against him.

As the unelected psychopathic globalist transhumanist depopulationist scheme and make their plans meeting in places like Davos, Switzerland, let us understand that God Almighty has his plan and purpose for everything that happens, and that part of God's plan is that his people don't perish from lack of knowledge in the process.

Hosea 4:6 says, "My people are destroyed for lack of knowledge: because thou hast rejected knowledge, I will also reject thee, that thou shalt be no priest to me: seeing thou hast forgotten the law of thy God, I will also forget thy children."

Jeremiah 29:11 – "For I know the thoughts that I think toward you, saith the LORD, thoughts of peace, and not of evil, to give you an expected end."

Romans 8:28 – "And we know that all things work together for good to them that love God, to them who are the called according to his purpose."

Psalms 32:8 – "I will instruct thee and teach thee in the way which thou shalt go: I will guide thee with mine eye."

Proverbs 19:21 – "There are many devices in a man's heart; nevertheless, the counsel of the LORD, that shall stand."

Psalms 37:23 – "The steps of a good man are ordered by the LORD: and he delighteth in his way."

John 15:7 – "If ye abide in me, and my words abide in you, ye shall ask what ye will, and it shall be done unto you."

So, what solutions can we employ to survive and thrive in these End Times?

I am inspired by the account in Daniel 3 where three young men simply refused to go along with any draconian mandates oppressing their people and helped alter the course of history. Yes, their refusal to bow down before a false idol did get them thrown into a fiery furnace, however, their absolute faith in God Almighty to trust him with every detail of their life resulted in a quite miraculous experience. Not only did they not die in the extremely hot flames as the soldiers who threw them into the fiery furnace did, perishing from the heat and smoke, but King Nebuchadnezzar and his administration witnessed a fourth person show up inside the burning flames. Those three young men came out of the fire completely unharmed; they didn't have a hair on their head singed or even smell of smoke, the fire had virtually no effect on them whatsoever, and best of all the Lord physically showed up in the fire to protect them. It ultimately caused King Nebuchadnezzar to say, "Blessed be the God of Shadrach, Meshach, and Abednego, who hath sent his angel, and delivered his servants that trusted in him, and have changed the king's word, and yielded their bodies, that they might not serve nor worship any god, except their own God."

Considering Shadrach, Meshach, and Abednego only had a portion of the Holy Bible we today who are privileged with a completed Bible are without excuse.

None of us know precisely what emotions Shadrach, Meshach, and Abednego were experiencing being thrown into a fire of certain death, however, I think from the recorded account they were staying in faith the entire time. Trusting the Lord God Almighty even if he didn't deliver them the way they hoped for. What about us today?

Often, people experience some anxiety when they think about the future, but this is not of God.

Anxiety, worry, and stress are modern words for a spirit of fear and God didn't give us a spirit of fear, 2 Timothy 1:7- "For God hath not given us the spirit of fear; but of power, and of love, and of a sound mind."

We don't often think of fear as a sin, however, Romans 14:23 tells us for whatsoever is not of faith is a sin.

For those who know God Almighty, we are keen to think thoughts of the future that will bring us blessings and comfort. For example, describing a woman who knows and trusts God, we read in Proverbs 31:25 that, "Strength and honour are her clothing; and she shall rejoice in time to come." Basically, this says, "She rejoices and smiles at the future."

She does so because she understands that God Almighty is sovereign and in control over everything. He knows the past, present, and future and ultimately controls what will happen. He just won't control your thought life that is your part. He gave us free will.

I feel that I will be remiss if I didn't mention how Yuval Noah Harari, who is a top advisor to the Nazis raised protégé of Henry Kissinger, which is the unelected Klaus Schwab and his World Economic Forum gang has stated his opinion on record "There is no such thing as free will, freedom has no meaning and humans have invented God." Mind you he is exercising his free will to tell you this nonsense.

As I have shared in my book *What Was I Thinking?* all information passes into the brain's relay station, which is called the thalamus. The thalamus relays the information to the cortex where all the memories are kept. This is the first place where attitudes begin. The kind of attitude you are falling into will determine what emotional responses are relayed back to the thalamus, as it travels to your hypothalamus, which activates the release of chemicals to build your emotional state. Unless the transhumanist gets to inject you with nanotechnologies and take over your thought life with their beastly marking system. For now, we all have choices to make to either deny ourselves and follow after the

Lord Jesus/Yeshua or suffer the consequences of staying in a place of rebellion and ignorance.

Luke 9:23 says, "And he said to them all, If any man will come after me, let him deny himself, and take up his cross daily, and follow me."

Best to trust the Lord Jesus/Yeshua with every detail and not stress about the future. The Lord Jesus/Yeshua has a good plan for your life and destiny, and He shall bring it to pass.

Isaiah 46:9-11 says,

> [9] Remember the former things of old: for I am God, and there is none else; I am God, and there is none like me, [10] Declaring the end from the beginning, and from ancient times the things that are not yet done, saying, My counsel shall stand, and I will do all my pleasure: [11] Calling a ravenous bird from the east, the man that executeth my counsel from a far country: yea, I have spoken it, I will also bring it to pass; I have purposed it, I will also do it.

In Revelation 18:23 we are forewarned about what is happening today. All those gene therapy injections are related to the pharmaceutical deceptions of witchcraft and the manipulation of the Babylon system.

Considering how in Daniel's time there were these all those draconian mandates which were legally put into place with demands that were being imposed on the people, including having to bow down to an idol.

Daniel and his mates Shadrach, Meshach, and Abednego stood up against it and won. God Almighty performed miracles and delivered them from the oppressors. Considering how they only had a small portion of the Bible and knew enough to simply trust the Lord God Almighty, what is our excuse today?

The idol back then was the image of the king Nebuchadnezzar Babylon and I believe it was a type and shadow of what will happen in the end times as we see in places like Revelations chapter 13 that eventually people will have to bow to and worship the image of the Beast which is the worship of Lucifer. OUR FREEDOM IS NON-NEGOTIABLE, we must resist digital health certificates, vaccine passports, digital IDs, and any other attempt to restrict our God-given rights in any way.

The Gates of hell Foundation in Operation Lockstep with the World Economic Forum/UN gang has told us that a second plandemic is coming. In other words, the Hegelian dialectic Emergency declarations have not ended. Clearly many people are fearful today of what they see unfolding before us on the world stage as the psychopathic transhumanist globalist agenda is playing out. The ones who created the crisis want to bring you, their cure!

If our world is not on a direct path to the fulfillment of Revelation 13:16-18, the only alternative seems to be that you would have to ignore that something with the most uncanny resemblance to the mark of the beast system is unfolding before us. Seems to me that numerous people are not that alarmed by the threat of nuclear war, probably because they think it will never really happen. Those same people probably doubt how the Lord Jesus/Yeshua shall return suddenly too. There are numerous people who also think we have plenty of time left on earth to keep eating and drinking and be merry-making, and they are not much concerned about any such wars and rumours of wars, famines, earthquakes, or bioweapons. They also probably never heard of Klaus Schwab and his worldwide syndicate re-setters club-influencing most world leaders.

Nevertheless, if you have been tricked into receiving the unlicensed, uninsured, experimental witchcraft injection, when you recognise it and repent of it the Lord God Almighty can restore your body, your Holy Temple back to its original design. He can do this simply because He is God Almighty, because He created all things, and because He agape loves you.

The promise of protection in Psalm 91 and also the Lord's promise of supernatural provision in Psalm 23, should encourage you because of the times that we are living in to make it a point to daily speak them out.

Heaven truly appears to be voice-activated, because we read in places like Psalm 103:20, "Bless the LORD, ye his angels, that excel in strength, that do his commandments, hearkening unto the voice of his word."

This seems to indicate that when we speak forth words that are aligned and pleasing unto the Lord Jesus/Yeshua it causes His angels to carry out the assignments on our behalf. I encourage you therefore to speak blessings and not curses.

Let us always obey the Lord's commandments and trust the Lord for all the details of our life. 1 John 1:7, "But if we walk in the light, as he is in the light, we have fellowship one with another, and the blood of Jesus Christ his Son cleanseth us from all sin."

Let us also consider the future that our Holy Guide Book to the Supernatural gives us is a comprehensive outline of what will occur in the days ahead or rather what is called "the end times."

Because the Holy Bible is God's revelation to us and because God Almighty knows and controls the future, just as he had the prophet Isaiah tell us. Anyone with some critical thinking skills and logic can understand that when the Holy Scriptures speak about what will occur in the future, it is best to accept that it shall happen.

Considering we are informed in places like 2 Peter 1:21, "For the prophecy came not in old time by the will of man: but holy men of God spake as they were moved by the Holy Ghost."

Today we have loads of false prophets who bring false prophecies that deceive many people. We have new agers embrace such as individuals like Nostradamus the French occultist seer and astrologer in the 1500s, or Edgar Cayce from the early 1900s who was an American occultist clairvoyant who claimed to speak from his higher self, whilst in a trance-like state. Reading about him with biblical discernment shows us he like the others who made such predictions was possessed of unclean spirits. Their predictions are always hit or miss.

However, the Holy Bible has never once been wrong, every time the Holy Scriptures has predicted a future event, it happened exactly as Scripture said it would happen.

For example, there are over 300 prophecies concerning the first coming of Christ, and all of them were literally fulfilled. The prophecies surrounding the Jesus Christ of Nazareth, Messiah Yeshua's birth, his life, betrayal, death, and resurrection were all fulfilled as the Holy Scriptures said would happen.

Jesus/Yeshua was born in Bethlehem, just as the Holy Scriptures prophesied would happen. He performed numerous miracles, was betrayed by a close friend for 30 pieces of silver, was crucified, pierced in his hands and feet, and died between two thieves as prophesied would happen. He was buried in a wealthy man's tomb and was gloriously resurrected three days after his torturous death as prophesied would happen. All of these details were prophesied in the Holy Scriptures hundreds of years before Jesus/Yeshua was born through the Virgin Mary and were fulfilled. Logic tells us the remaining prophecies shall also be completed.

Whilst today we have a number of viewpoints and perspectives on what methods should be applied when interpreting future prophetic passages of the Holy Scriptures concerning how the rest of the prophecies shall unfold. One thing you can count on is the Lord Jesus/Yeshua shall be fulfilling the rest of the ancient prophecies.

Whilst several scholarly men and women are espousing different interpretations and beliefs, there is ample evidence and reason to believe that biblical prophecy should be interpreted literally, with a futurist view, in what we might term a "premillennial" perspective.

Yes, without question there is also a degree of symbolism used in various prophecies, for example where we might read of dragons or the saints following the Lord Jesus/Yeshua on flying white horses. Nevertheless, all of it portrays literal beings or literal future events that shall one day happen. I suppose it be how we read of places where the Lord Jesus/Yeshua is referred to as a lion and a lamb symbolically, yet we know it is speaking of Him.

Our Holy Guide Book to the Supernatural gives us prophetic books like Daniel and Revelation which contain not only accounts of historical events, but also accurate predictions of events that shall take place in the future. After the Lord gave the Apostle John what to write in his messages for the churches of his day, John also received visions of what would occur in the end times. How do you describe something that shall happen thousands of years in advance? How would you describe things like aeroplanes and automobiles to your audience 2000 years ago?

John was instructed to come up here, and I will show you what must happen in the future. "After this I looked, and, behold, a door was opened in heaven: and the first voice which I heard was as it were of a trumpet talking with me; which said, Come up hither, and I will shew thee things which must be hereafter" (Revelation 4:1).

Think about this because all of the promises of God are for us today.

2 Corinthians 1:20-22 says,

> [20] For all the promises of God in him are yea, and in him Amen, unto the glory of God by us. [21] Now he which stablisheth us with you in Christ, and hath anointed us, is God; [22] Who hath also sealed us, and given the earnest of the Spirit in our hearts.

This refutes all those who try to steal hope from us and tells us some of the gifts of the Holy Spirit ceased or passed away 2000 years ago when the last Apostle died. Is the Lord no longer making Apostles?

Ephesians 4:11 – "And he gave some, apostles; and some, prophets; and some, evangelists; and some, pastors and teachers;" (apostles and prophets, evangelists, pastors and teachers, are all in the same sentence, for what reason?)

12 For the perfecting of the saints, for the work of the ministry, for the edifying of the body of Christ:

13 Till we all come in the unity of the faith, and of the knowledge of the Son of God, unto a perfect man, unto the measure of the stature of the fulness of Christ:

If we obey the Lord our God, he tells us we shall be blessed.

Deuteronomy 28:2 – "And all these blessings shall come on thee, and overtake thee, if thou shalt hearken unto the voice of the LORD thy God."

We read in Genesis 24-1, "And Abraham was old, and well stricken in age: and the LORD had blessed Abraham in all things."

We can look at the promises God Almighty made to Abraham in places like Genesis 12 and Genesis 15 concerning the land of Israel.

We need to consider that since God's covenant with Abraham was unconditional, and His promises to Abraham have not yet been fulfilled to Abraham's descendants, it begs the question that we maintain a futurist supernatural view of the promises made to Israel that shall surely come to pass. God's Word shall not come back void it will do what He sent it to accomplish. Amen.

It is most likely the church will suddenly be Raptured as the Lord promised, and then this fallen world will experience the seven-year Tribulation period, later the Lord Jesus Christ of Nazareth shall return to reign over the earth for 1,000 literal years which details are shared in Revelation 20.

Nevertheless, what does the Word of God say will happen before all that happens?

Back in the Garden of Eden, we read in Genesis how the Lord God Almighty gave a stern warning to Adam.

Genesis 2:17 – "But of the tree of the knowledge of good and evil, thou shalt not eat of it: for in the day that thou eatest thereof thou shalt surely die."

Nevertheless, when we study the life of Adam, he did not appear to die on the same day that he ate that forbidden fruit.

Genesis 5:5 – "And all the days that Adam lived were nine hundred and thirty years: and he died."

How can this be, that in fact, Adam sinned breaking the only one commandment he had, and continued to live to 930 years old? It is things like this that cause people to disregard the validity of the Holy Scriptures unless you understand that in 2 Peter 3:8, "But, beloved, be not ignorant of this one thing, that one day is with the Lord as a thousand years, and a thousand years as one day."

Even though Adam did live to be 930 years old, he did, in fact, die within a day after he sinned because, in the Kingdom of God, a thousand years is just one day.

For over two thousand years, ignorant people have been mocking Christians because we believe the Lord Jesus will be returning soon.

2 Peter 3:3 – "Knowing this first, that there shall come in the last days scoffers, walking after their own lusts."

The world is filled with these scoffers today. Scoffers are those who mock and act like a scorner. They scoff and mock the Holy Bible. They scoff at the idea of the Rapture and the Second Coming of Christ. They scoff at the atonement and at the idea of the resurrection of Jesus Christ of Nazareth.

Because the Lord foretold us that in the last days there will be scoffers who are "walking according to their own lustful ideas that are manifesting in them through evil spirits"

We read in 2 Timothy 3:13 - "But evil men and seducers shall wax worse and worse, deceiving, and being deceived."

Because they don't want to live for God Almighty. They're only interested in their own pleasure and gratifications, their materialism as well as the lust for world powers.

Over the years I have spent in ministry it has become clear to me that the reason they entertain such spirits of doubt and unbelief about the Holy Word of God is not built on facts and intellectualism. Their "intellectual arguments" all come down to excessive excuses. The basic reason they don't surrender to the Lord Jesus/Yeshua is that they don't want him to interfere and disturb them in their sinful worldly ways.

So, they mock and scoff at anything truly spiritual, like the World Economic Forum gang does, telling you that man invented God and how they will become gods through transhumanism.

Galatians 6:7 – "Be not deceived; God is not mocked: for whatsoever a man soweth, that shall he also reap."

So how do we pray for them? Let us pray that God Almighty will "open the eyes of their hearts so that they will understand and embrace the Gospel truth and be truly enlightened" in Christ's mercy, agape love, and grace. Ephesians 1:18 – "The eyes of your understanding being enlightened; that ye may know what is the hope of his calling, and what the riches of the glory of his inheritance in the saints."

Matthew 13:15 – "For this people's heart is waxed gross, and their ears are dull of hearing, and their eyes they have closed; lest at any time they should see with their eyes and hear with their ears, and should understand with their heart, and should be converted, and I should heal them.

16 But blessed are your eyes, for they see: and your ears, for they hear.

17 For verily I say unto you, That many prophets and righteous men have desired to see those things which ye see, and have not seen them; and to hear those things which ye hear, and have not heard them."

Consider that every one of our enemies that comes against us, comes against God Almighty and clearly lacks understanding.

They are reacting to things from the natural and lack discernment instead of responding from the Holy Spirit.

Let us pray that God Almighty shall convict them of their sins so their hearts will open to understanding and repent of their sins and learn of God's forgiveness from all their past mistakes and grow in Godly wisdom.

Let us pray for our enemies to experience true repentance and revival. It is God Almighty who can soften the hardest of hearts enough for them to enter into a place of repentance. When we pray for our enemies to repent of their sins, we know we are praying in accordance with God's will because He also desires and requires their repentance.

2 Peter 3:9 – "The Lord is not slack concerning his promise, as some men count slackness; but is longsuffering to us-ward, not willing that any should perish, but that all should come to repentance."

Let us pray for our enemies, by asking the Lord that our hearts will remain in a place of righteousness and fulfill the destiny the Lord wants to accomplish in His divine orchestrations to bring our enemies to a place they receive salvation and become our friends.

Proverbs 15:1- "A soft answer turneth away wrath: but grievous words stir up anger."

If we return anger for anger and wrong those who have wronged us, we only end up putting ourselves down on the same negative frequency level as our enemy is on.

When we practise responding by extending only kindness, agape love, and mercy, most difficult situations are often quickly diffused. I think nothing is more convicting than a kind and gentle response back to a malicious obnoxious contemptuous rude person's action.

This is what turning the other cheek is instructing us about. Matthew 5:39 – "But I say unto you, That ye resist not evil: but whosoever shall smite thee on thy right cheek, turn to him the other also."

Displaying Godly kindness back toward the offending party helps them see the supernatural power of Christ's love displayed in us.

Let us pray for our enemies that God Almighty will do major work in their lives to bring about His divine purposes.

Keeping in mind how the Lord Jesus/Yeshua taught us to pray, in places like Matthew 6:10 – "Thy kingdom come, Thy will be done in earth, as it is in heaven." We should keep praying to the Lord our God in the almighty name of Jesus/Yeshua until we truly want what He wants and see even our enemies get saved. If the Lord wants to save our enemies, we should want that too.

Having our prayers answered is aligning our wills with God's will.

John 3:30 – "He must increase, but I must decrease."

Let me, therefore, remind you of some promises of the Lord for those who are in Christ. We read in Psalm 119:165, "Great peace have they which love thy law: and nothing shall offend them." Great supernatural peace is always the result of true love for the Lord Jesus/Yeshua and His Holy Word. Philippians 4:7, "And the peace of God, which passeth all understanding, shall keep your hearts and minds through Christ Jesus."

When you allow the Holy Spirit to shine His Gospel light on your conscience the enemy of our souls runs to hide from you.

Because you will experience the understanding, awareness, and desire to practise staying in the presence of God. Including the Lord in everything you think, say, and do, helps you eliminate all those poisonous toxic thoughts the enemy of your soul has tempted you with.

Replacing ungodly thinking with godly thinking is connecting to Christ's supernatural power.

John 14:12, "Verily, verily, I say unto you, He that believeth on me, the works that I do shall he do also; and greater works than these shall he do; because I go unto my Father. 13 And whatsoever ye shall ask in my name, that will I do, that the Father may be glorified in the Son.

14 If ye shall ask anything in my name, I will do it.

15 If ye love me, keep my commandments."

This book is about solutions to surviving the end times.

Our Holy Guide Book to the Supernatural predicts there shall come a time of great trouble as this world has never seen before and which shall never happen again.

Matthew 24:21- "For then shall be great tribulation, such as was not since the beginning of the world to this time, no, nor ever shall be."

As globalists/transhumanists arrogantly declare how their advances in science shall improve mankind, nevertheless the Holy Bible says there shall be a great downward spiral of earthly deceptions, lying signs and wonders, all sorts of catastrophes, as foolish people call evil good and good evil. In other words, all sorts of sinful works shall be established along with religious apostasy before Christ returns. The Apostle Paul forewarned us, to realise that in the last days, very difficult times will come on the world where evildoers and impostors, like those who got into a government office with stolen elections around the world, will proceed to go from bad to worse, deceiving and being deceived.

Many of these world leaders appear to be graduates from Klaus Schwab's young globalist school.

Consider too how most all the nations in this world joined together in Rockefeller lockstep with one of the great deceptions that tried to force millions of people into taking an unlicensed, uninsured experimental gene modifying nanotechnology substance that results in numerous adverse reactions and deaths. Could there already be a one-world government at play?

2 Timothy 3:1 – "This know also, that in the last days perilous times shall come.

2 For men shall be lovers of their own selves, covetous, boasters, proud, blasphemers, disobedient to parents, unthankful, unholy,

3 Without natural affection, trucebreakers, false accusers, incontinent, fierce, despisers of those that are good,

4 Traitors, heady, highminded, lovers of pleasures more than lovers of God;

5 Having a form of godliness, but denying the power thereof: from such turn away.

6 For of this sort are they which creep into houses, and lead captive silly women laden with sins, led away with divers lusts,

7 Ever learning, and never able to come to the knowledge of the truth.

8 Now as Jannes and Jambres withstood Moses, so do these also resist the truth: men of corrupt minds, reprobate concerning the faith.

9 But they shall proceed no further: for their folly shall be manifest unto all men, as their's also was.

10 But thou hast fully known my doctrine, manner of life, purpose, faith, longsuffering, charity, patience,

11 Persecutions, afflictions, which came unto me at Antioch, at Iconium, at Lystra; what persecutions I endured: but out of them all the Lord delivered me.

12 Yea, and all that will live godly in Christ Jesus shall suffer persecution.

13 But evil men and seducers shall wax worse and worse, deceiving, and being deceived."

In other words, this fallen world will continue to reject God Almighty, the Lord Jesus/Yeshua, His Word, and His people.

Nevertheless, one day soon and no one knows precisely what day that is, although we should know what season it is– God Almighty will end the Church Age which began in the first century on Pentecost that we read about in the book of Acts in Chapter 2 with an event many people term as the Rapture. It will happen suddenly, and God Almighty shall remove all His true spirit-filled born-again believers in Christ from the earth during the preparation for His final judgments.

Of the Rapture, The Apostle Paul shared about this event,

1 Thessalonians 4:14 – "For if we believe that Jesus died and rose again, even so them also which sleep in Jesus will God bring with him.

15 For this we say unto you by the word of the Lord, that we which are alive and remain unto the coming of the Lord shall not prevent them which are asleep.

16 For the Lord himself shall descend from heaven with a shout, with the voice of the archangel, and with the trump of God: and the dead in Christ shall rise first:

17 Then we which are alive and remain shall be caught up together with them in the clouds, to meet the Lord in the air: and so shall we ever be with the Lord.

18 Wherefore comfort one another with these words."

First off, we are told the Lord Jesus Christ of Nazareth, Messiah Yeshua will remove all true born-again believers from the earth in an event known as the rapture.

Yes, there are a lot of people today theorizing, that isn't going to happen, and they mostly blame a chap named John Nelson Darby for bringing in this concept who helped found the Plymouth Brethren Church, in U.K. Darby was an author and an influential proponent of a dispensational view of Scripture.

Darby was born in 1800 to a prominent family in London. He grew up with many privileges and had a brilliant mind, He received degrees from London's Westminster School and Dublin's Trinity College. I find it interesting that initially he became a lawyer and having that sort of background was probably very useful to him because his career as a lawyer didn't last more than four years. The Lord was calling him into ministry. At first, he became a priest in a Church in the diocese of Dublin, Ireland. Life is a process of learning and sanctification.

Darby attributed leaving his law career because of his strong desire to devote himself entirely to the work of God. Like so many before him and those who have come after him who begin to study the Word of God for themselves, he soon became greatly concerned over the prevailing condition of the church, which he observed was made weak by religious formality, whereas today it is made weak by false teachers tickling the people's ears.

So, after two years, Darby couldn't keep up with the nonsense, like how many people must feel about wearing a nappy over their faces today knowing it is all political theater.

Darby left the Church of Ireland in 1827.

He wrote and I quote: "The style of work, was not in agreement with what I read in the Bible concerning the church and Christianity; nor did it correspond with the effects of the action of the Spirit of God" (Letters of J. N. Darby, Oak Park, IL: Bible Truth Publishers, 1971, III, 297–298).

2 Timothy 2:15 – "Study to shew thyself approved unto God, a workman that needeth not to be ashamed, rightly dividing the word of truth."

John 14:26 – "But the Comforter, which is the Holy Ghost, whom the Father will send in my name, he shall teach you all things, and bring all things to your remembrance, whatsoever I have said unto you."

If you are a Roman Catholic, then I understand why you might let traditions decide what the Bible teaches. But as Protestants, we're supposed to understand we never just accept "what others say," but rather "what does Our Holy Guide Book to the Supernatural say."

We need to remain thoughtful and respectful to others, but at the end of the day we believe what the Almighty Word of God says, and we don't interpret the Bible by democratic vote either. We don't go through history and say, "Whatever most Christians have believed through history is always the right interpretation." To think this way would invite all sorts of errors.

So let us settle this debate about the Rapture from the Word of God and let me also add that when it comes to the study of eschatology, most Christians throughout history have been Amillennial or Post-Millennial – not Pre-Millennial.

Most Christians throughout history have approved of the veneration of Mary, infant baptism, and the institution of the state dictating church policies. It doesn't make any of those things true and it doesn't make any of them right before the Lord of all creation. Let's face it because loads of occultic and pagan practises have now infiltrated the church over the years.

Either we simply believe the Word of God, or we don't.

There are references in the ancient writers Shepherd of Hermas, Victorinus, and others that are quite consistent with the Pre-Tribulation of being caught up together in the air with Christ!

Throughout church history, there is a pattern we can see that flows from one doctrine to another. Doctrine is important as it equals truth.

We need to see the difference between a doctrine being focused on and dealt with by the church, and a doctrine being "invented" by the church. For example, the church did not "invent" the doctrine of the Trinity – it is clearly in the Bible, yet there are people I know who want to argue the church made up the idea of the Trinity. Isaac Newton was brilliant nevertheless he taught there was no Trinity because he wasn't a true believer from all evidence gathered.

When I hear someone use the phrase "secret rapture." It is a derisive term for the Pre-Tribulation catching up of the church. They think it makes the pre-tribulation idea sound ridiculous. Just their use of the term "secret rapture" tells me more about them and the strength of their arguments, and biblical perspective than it does about their favoured end times scenario. Having a pre-tribulation view doesn't say we won't go through any difficult times, nor does it suggest you hide in your basement waiting to be raptured whilst you stockpile food and weapons. You are supposed to share Christ's love with all you engage with.

Let me give you a quote, from the Shepherd of Hermas, as early as A.D. 90:

> You have escaped from great tribulation on account of your faith, and because you did not doubt in the presence of such a beast. Go, therefore, and tell the elect of the Lord His mighty deeds, and say to them that this beast is a type of the great tribulation that is

coming. If then ye prepare yourselves, and repent with all your heart, and turn to the Lord, it will be possible for you to escape it, if your heart be pure and spotless, and ye spend the rest of the days of your life in serving the Lord blamelessly.[1]

From Victorinus, late third century: "...and the heaven withdrew as a scroll that is rolled up. For the heaven to be rolled away, this is that the Church shall be taken away."

Commentary on the Apocalypse, 6:14 "...and I saw another great and wonderful sign, seven angels having the seven last plagues; for in them is completed the indignation of God. For the wrath of God always strikes the obstinate people with seven plagues, that is, perfectly, as it is said in Leviticus; and these shall be in the last time, when the Church shall have gone out of the midst."

From Pseudo-Ephraem, as early as the 4th century:

> Why therefore do we not reject every care of earthly actions and prepare ourselves for the meeting of the Lord Christ, so that he may draw us from the confusion, which overwhelms the world?
>
> For all the saints and elect of God are gathered, prior to the tribulation that is to come, and are taken to the Lord lest they see the confusion that is to overwhelm the world because of our sins.

All those people saying this eschatological doctrine of pre-tribulationism came from Darby or Scofield from the 1700s or 1800s? or the invention of a Jesuit priest named Lacunza, or a crazy woman named Margret MacDonald, from Port Glasgow, Scotland needs to do more studying, period.

Let us go deeper with understanding more about this historical reality. So, we have ancient writings from Christians from the first centuries who believe in the rapture?

All True Christians agree – or should agree – on this: In both the Old Testament and New Testament we have the Lord Jesus' promise to rule on this earth.

Clearly, the Lord Jesus Christ of Nazareth is coming again (1 Thessalonians 4).

Let us first understand how the nefarious ones can push their evil agendas.

For example, there was the Milgram experiment that was designed to show how people respond to the obedience of any authority figure wearing a white coat. This experiment may help you understand how such people as the Nazi Dr. Josef Rudolf Mengele, also known as the Angel of Death, or Dr. Faucitis was able to mislead masses of people into accepting draconian lockdown, Rockefeller lockstep rules and regulations.

The experiment conducted by Yale University psychologist Stanley Milgram was set as a series of social psychology tests in the 1960s. The end goal of the Milgram experiment was to test the extent of a person's willingness to obey orders from an authority figure. Participants were told by an experimenter to administer increasingly powerful electric shocks to another individual who happened to be an actor they saw through a window in another room. Unbeknownst to the participants, all the shocks they administered were fake as the actor was shocked crying out in pain. Sadly over 65% (two-thirds) of the participants continued to follow the white coat authority figure's instructions to increase the pain they were inflicting on the individual through the window to the highest level of 450 volts. All the participants involved continued to follow the authority figure up to 300 volts. These experiments were repeated throughout the years with similar results.

Milgram's justifications for such an experiment were based on acts of genocide offered by those arrested and accused at the World War II, and Nuremberg War Criminal trials. The accused quite often gave their defense based on the fact that they were just following orders in "obedience" - from their superiours.

The Milgram experiments began in July 1961, just a year after the trial of upper-echelon Nazi Adolf Eichmann in Jerusalem who was hanged by the State of Israel for his part in the Holocaust for crimes against humanity, war crimes, and having membership in a criminal organisation. Milgram claimed he devised the experiment to answer the question: Could it simply be that the Nazi Eichmann and his millions of accomplices in the Holocaust were just following the orders of an authority figure? Keep in mind that if you drive the getaway car from a bank robbery you are considered accomplices?"

Programming is a reality; the Nazis had a hand in developing television in the 1930s for propaganda. "Tell-Lies-Visions."

How many things have you realised over the years that you were given wrong information about?

For example, how long does it take to make a fossil? Most people who attended the traditional educational system that has become an indoctrination centre to this day will tell you it takes eons because they have been repeatedly told that fossils are millions and billions of years old.

For example, there is a petrified miner's hat that was discovered and is currently housed in a museum in Tasmania which is an island state of Australia. For whatsoever reason, some miner left his hat in the mine and only fifty years later it was found and had turned into a solid rock. Scientists believe that certain chemicals in the water in the mine solidified the soft felt structure of the hat and it became solid calcium carbonate. So much for evolutionary deceptions.

Nazi Joseph Goebbels is often credited with the quote, "If you repeat a lie often enough it becomes the truth", which is how propaganda works. Most psychologists can tell you that this is known as the "illusion of truth" effect.

Anyone who still can employ critical thinking skills only needs to look back at how the media was used as a propaganda machine, especially since March 2020. By the way, psychology is rooted in the work of occultist Carl Jung, who confessed everything he learned about psychology he learned from his " spirit guide Philemon" what is a spirit guide? Jung held a pen, and the evil spirit caused him to do automatic writing.

Then he channeled two more spirit guides Anima/Animus, which he claimed was the mirror image of our biological sex, that is, the unconscious feminine side in males and the masculine tendencies in women. He originally called them evil spirits but changed them to archetypes and dark shadows to make his theories more marketable.

Most parents trust their doctors in their white coats and are unaware the shots they are giving their children are quite dangerous and toxic! It appears that numerous Doctors have blindly trusted their pharmaceutical company, overlords because they are given incentives that increase their salary after signing agreements with those major pharmaceutical companies.

We now have churches with professional Christian counselors practising such things as the term, "Inner Healing", often based on Theosophists. All these theories and practises of nearly every popular inner healer which has invaded the churches can be traced back to Occultist Jung and Sanford or can be shown to be based on the same premises.

Dealing with what they call the unconscious mind, or the collective unconscious, together with all those repressed memories they like to explore with the people they deal with for a hefty hourly fee, although they continue to suffer with what the Lord Jesus/Yeshua said was a "Broken heart."

Because none are healed. Only the Lord Jesus/Yeshua can properly mend your broken heart. Nothing else is ever going to take the place of the healing that the Lord Jesus does in someone's heart, mind, body, soul, and spirit. If you look on the internet, you will see pages and pages of ministries that have arisen to help heal your memories. This should be a Big Red Flag to anyone who is diligently in the Word of God and has the Word of God in them. No one needed their memories healed until it became popular in the last generation or so.

We never see anyone in the Bible who needed their memory healed. Instead, we see examples in the Holy Guide Book of the Supernatural of taking control of your thought life to the obedience of Christ. 2 Corinthians 10:5 – "Casting down imaginations, and every high thing that exalteth itself against the knowledge of God and bringing into captivity every thought to the obedience of Christ." The Word of God has not changed, rather it will change you for the better. For we still need to preach the Gospel, heal the sick, and cast out demons in Jesus' almighty name.

Instructing the church to practise confession, repentance, and forgiveness. We simply must get into a proper right relationship with the Lord Jesus and all others including ourselves.

By the washing of the Word, we can continually renew our minds by meditating on the Word of God so it will bring healing and blessings to all our flesh. (Proverbs 4:22) It is only through God's Holy Word, we can obtain true deliverance and find true freedom and restoration, and healing. These are the things that the Lord Jesus/Yeshua did and taught us to do when he walked this earth, the same way the Lord Jesus/Yeshua physically ministered to hurting people supernaturally healing everyone.

Then Jesus/Yeshua said now you true disciples of mine and in every generation to come who becomes my disciple you go and do this in my name. John 14:12 – "Verily, verily, I say unto you, He that believeth on me, the works that I do shall he do also; and greater works than these shall he do; because I go unto my Father."

The Lord Jesus/Yeshua said in John 10:27, "My sheep hear my voice, and I know them, and they follow me."

We are supposed to be doing our best to imitate the Lord Jesus/Yeshua share the Gospel with all we engage with and trust the Lord for everything.

Just like Shadrach, Meshach, and Abednego went through the fiery furnace and Daniel endured a night with a pride of hungry Lion's in their Den, if we can learn to put on the mind of Christ and see the difficult times ahead through our Heavenly Father's eyes, we are going to experience incredible peace.

Your heart has over 40,000 neurons in it and acts like another brain in your body. Your kidneys also act like another brain in your body. In any situation, your kidneys are like the first responders to form a perspective and then based on that perspective of how you perceive a particular situation your brain devises a strategy on how to move forward in that situation.

If you begin to feel stressed about how to resolve the situation that you find yourself in your kidneys secrete stress hormones.

There is a jolly good reason we are told in Proverbs 3:5 – "Trust in the LORD with all thine heart; and lean not unto thine own understanding."

For example, we are entering a time where if we refuse to compromise with experimental gene therapy injections numerous people have already lost their jobs. If that happens to you it means eventually you can't go to the grocery store, and you can't buy and sell. Like with the Chinese credit score system.

Again, the spirit of fear is the fuel behind the great deception playing out before us on the world stage today.

If you look at the situation and begin to entertain the spirit of fear that God Almighty did not give you, how shall your body chemistry react?

You shall begin to release harmful amounts of cortisol and it will begin to break down your immune system, as you formed the wrong perspective causing your brain and the kidneys not to be able to develop a strategy to move forward in that situation. What happens is, in fact, you chose to bow down to the spirit of fear and that throws your entire body chemistry out of balance, and you literally go into a state of stress and hopelessness spiritually, psychologically, emotionally, and physically. It is like opening up the door to the Kingdom of darkness to come in and harm you in numerous ways.

However, if you can practise training yourself to look at the situation through our Father's eyes to see it the way that he sees it, to see it from his perspective, then what's going to happen is that now you formed a good perspective of the situation so the brain and the kidneys are able to function as Abba Father designed them to and what happens on a physical level is the kidneys release a hormone called DHEA which has lots of physical functions in the body but interestingly it carries the emotion of joy.

Now, just very quickly, I want to ask, do you remember what the book of Romans tells us? It says the kingdom of God is righteousness peace and joy in the Holy Spirit and you see the reality of that with the three brains that we have in our body because when with our Free Will in our brain in our head we choose righteousness and obedience the heart releases the peace chemical ANF and the kidneys release the hormone of joy so it doesn't just apply spiritually but also even to our bodies where we literally walk in righteousness peace and joy and it enables us to walk through that difficult situation with a great sense of excitement and hopeful expectancy so having said that how can we face these very rough times ahead from God's perspective. It's crucial that as many people as possible gain knowledge here and refuse the Babylon beast system. The new eugenics has come disguised as health care. Big Tech, Big Pharma, and Big lies. Food and agriculture have launched their "Food is Medicine" program. It is another way for the government to seize control of the nation's population. Food as medicine will most likely be used to get you into their systems of control to enslave the people. The central bank's digital currencies rollout if it becomes mandatory, shall take away all freedom along with your God-given rights to pursue life, liberty, and happiness.

If their insane Artificial Intelligence singularity cannot be achieved, the demons manifesting in the technocrats may end up faking it, because if they can blame other things like eugenics, depopulation poison shots, and the other unethical immoral decisions on artificial intelligence running the government, they can continue to do whatever they and the Rothschilds banksters desire, with little to no repercussions for a while. Unless God's people pray in the Holy Spirit and truth. AI singularity can be defined as an event where Artificial Intelligence becomes self-aware and passes the Turning test or reach an ability for such continuous improvement so powerful that it will evolve beyond our human control. This is one of the main issues with Agenda 20/30 where they hope to have every person merge with a computer by the end of this decade.

Matthew 24:22 – "And except those days should be shortened, there should no flesh be saved: but for the elect's sake those days shall be shortened.

23 Then if any man shall say unto you, Lo, here is Christ, or there; believe it not.

24 For there shall arise false Christs, and false prophets, and shall shew great signs and wonders; insomuch that, if it were possible, they shall deceive the very elect."

How close are we to the return of Christ? You tell me.

2 Corinthians 3:12 says, "Seeing then that we have such hope, we use great plainness of speech."

I had a yearly eye exam this year. They gave me a good report, that I still have 20/20, and said to come back next year.

Solutions for the End Times

At the end of the exam, the ophthalmologist asked me if I had any other questions for him.

I asked why he and his assistant were wearing a mask.

He said he sees a lot of elderly patients and it makes them feel more comfortable.

I said, with all due respect doesn't that make you out to be like an actor playing a role in the great end-time deception? Are you possibly suffering from Stockholm syndrome?

Before he could respond I asked if he had ever heard of Klaus Schwab and the World Economic Forum.

He of course, said, "No, who are they?"

I said they are most likely the architects of the great plandemic deception and behind the narratives that caused so many to wear a mask and breathe in their own bodily waste, hindering their own oxygen supply. Don't even get me started on nanotechnology.

The ophthalmologist arrogantly said, "I am a physician I don't need you lecturing me."

I said I didn't mean to offend you, he said, "I accept your apology, we're good", and stormed off to his next 15-minute examination not realising he is part of the Rockefeller foundation puppets.

I wanted to tell him that there was no charge for my lecture, freely I have been given freely I give.

Although his nurse was intrigued by things I shared and looked me up on the net and was delighted to play my song Up to Something on her laptop as I was leaving.

The irony is never lost on the British.

Let us consider how truth doesn't mind being questioned, only lies get upset by asking questions.

The Lord started his church in the first century, the one that turned their world upside down, in Acts 17:6 or actually right side up as people got right with God Almighty hearing the Gospel truth. They set their world on Holy fire.

Contrast where we are today with the modern church.

Is the church impacting the world or is the world impacting the church? It's a rhetorical question.

We have a greater number of professing Christians today than in the first-century church, and we have all these incredible resources and technology to use. I used to have to go to a library to research things, but now I can get on a computer and do what used to take days and hours. Yet worldliness and occultism have greatly impacted the modern church, so much so that professing Christians seem to lack discernment and don't always know right from wrong. Because the world has done a jolly good job of turning the church upside down. We should be leading the way. After 2000 years everyone should be born again. Hebrews 12:29 – "For our God is a consuming fire."

I will tell you why we aren't setting the world ablaze on Holy fire. It's because we need a reawakening revival. Just as each revival throughout the history of the Church has had God's unique signature and outpouring of the Holy Spirit.

The Welsh Revival that started back in 1904, similarly, was clearly a divine spiritual encounter with God's leading: there was spontaneous outbreaks of worship singing, and prayer, and people would suddenly weep in repentance and confession.

Just two ministers Joseph Jenkins and Seth Joshua sought to pray for revival together. Soon others came and they had very long meetings just to seek the Lord's presence and empowerment, as a result, many people were baptised with the Holy Spirit. In less than a year, the Holy Spirit overtook not just Wales, but the rest of the UK, causing hundreds of thousands of souls to receive salvation in Christ. The Gospel Word got out and came to America and started at Azusa Street Revival in California with signs and wonders, healing and miracles.

A true revival of God often starts with one person who prays and decides to do something. For example, back in 1857, a businessman named Jeremiah Lanphier felt led to start a prayer meeting on Fulton Street in New York City. At first, only a few people came to pray with him.

Most might have just given up and said God must not be in this, but Mr. Lanphier keep praying without ceasing. He was a rather persistent gentleman and wouldn't stop praying and believing for revival. Eventually, something dramatic happened as the banksters of his day crashed the stock market, and suddenly the prayer attracted a lot of people. Much like how churches were filled up after 9/11 in 2001.

Mr. Lanphier's prayer meetings began spreading all over New York City. In six months, ten thousand people were gathering for prayer throughout the city, calling on the name of the Lord Jesus. It is said that in a few years, an estimated one million people came to faith in the Lord Jesus Christ. Think about this because it wasn't orchestrated.

It wasn't broadcast on social media, there wasn't a campaign headquarters where anyone planned the course of action.

Rather, it was simply a work of God pouring out His Holy Spirit on some sincere believers.

Oh Lord Jesus how we need to see this happen again for us today. Help us change the course this world is on by bringing a true revival as we pray for our enemies. Give us the heart to win the lost souls of this world so that they come to you in faith in repentance and accept salvation in Christ.

Think about this because Jeremiah Lanphier was a businessman, who was called to be a pastor. He wasn't well-known or famous, which attracted anyone to him. He was just an ordinary chap who loved the Lord Jesus/Yeshua and decided to keep praying until his prayers were answered. What about us today? Can we do this too?

Jeremiah 6:16 – "Thus saith the LORD, Stand ye in the ways, and see, and ask for the old paths, where is the good way, and walk therein, and ye shall find rest for your souls. But they said, We will not walk therein."

There was something called Dark Winter in 2001. Less than three months before the 9/11 world trade tower attack the

Pentagon launched a war game called Operation Dark Winter, working out their bio-weapon vaccine agenda. This is where they simulated a pandemic that included lockdowns and censorships, face masking, forced quarantines, social distancing, and mandatory vaccines, with expaded police powers.

9/11 helped set the stage for a way to remove a number of freedoms from Americans. By the way, actual science tells us that aeroplanes are not known to crash into skyscrapers that could bring the sort of results with structurally perfect implosions as if the building was a demolition project. Along with the implosion of the third building, number seven supposedly self-imploded shortly after the Towers fell. It seems very curious, and I suppose one could draw a conclusion about how Dr. Fallacy's fingerprints were also involved with anthrax as a bioweapon. In 2001 doctors at first thought they were dealing with cases of meningitis, only to soon discover it was cases of anthrax. After the towers fell, a letter was broadcast widely to propaganda news networks saying, and I quote: "You cannot stop us. We have this anthrax. You die now. Are you afraid? Death to America, Death to Israel, Allah is great." Dated 09-11-01.

The events fostered a spirit of fear that God did not give you. Meanwhile, the supposedly good guys went on a hunt to track down the fox who was behind these horrible tragic events who they told us was a chap named Osama Bin Laden. Soon the press launched a campaign to blame the Iraqis. Next enters national broadcasts with Dr. Anthony Fauci and his cohorts talking about how anthrax is a bacterium in a lab tube that is being released and how they can offer a vaccination for protection, which he then offered a plan that could take three months or six months or another year to implement. How reminiscent to stroll down memory lane together and look at all the pretty Trojan horses that have entered our city gates. Speaking of Trojan horses that allow the enemy to gain access once inside your city gates, let us ask what are the chances that this mRNA so-called vaccine injection is an "operating system" into your body that some scientists are referring to as "The Software of Life" – because once again this is not a vaccine, nor does it meet the criteria of one! Let us keep in mind that the manufacturers of these so-called vaccines were also granted immunity from any liability that results in adverse reactions or even death from their product. The new mRNA COVID vaccines appear to be very similar in design to that of a computer operating system, and just like a computer operating system such as Windows for example, with those who have worked to help design this product there would be a "back door" available where them as modern-day transhumanist and technocrats will be able to gain control of your bodies through regular software "updates." There are probably numerous hidden backdoors that were designed for these nefarious purposes. Moderna, which probably got its name from the idea of "modifying RNA," is one of the manufacturers of the COVID mRNA so-called vaccines and who was issued emergency authorisation and has published on their website that in fact: the mRNA vaccine injects an "operating system" into your body that they call "The Software of life." Psychopathic globalists and transhumanists and all those who serve the kingdom of darkness, willingly or out of sheer ignorance have openly and boldly been stating what they plan to do. Most people are dull of hearing.

Hebrews 5:11- "Of whom we have many things to say, and hard to be uttered, seeing ye are dull of hearing."

It should be obvious to even the casual observer now by now that those of certain ancient bloodlines who think of themselves as the so-called elites of this world want to reduce the population by 90 percent, transforming the survivours into obedient cyborg slaves that can no longer think for themselves who simply obey the authority of their demonic masters.

The culling of the human population through disease in order to quote "save the planet" must be one of the greatest deceptions this world has ever known.

Do we already have a one-world government? How did almost all the nations of the world agree to play a part in such a great deception? How many world leaders were deceived by such a great lie, that recruited a global consortium of devious and greedy doctors, and health care professionals, along with government puppets who spun such a well-orchestrated plan about a so-called virus that would ravage the world populations unless their fast-tracked vaccines were developed to inoculate the population in every nation.

It just seems highly suspect that the director-general of the Chinese Communist Party appears to have influenced World Health Organization leader Tedros Adhanom Ghebreyesus, who is not a medical doctor to lead the charge in this plandemic. Tedros Adhanom Ghebreyesus is also a member of a Marxist-Leninist Ethiopian political party that whistleblowers, researchers, and analysts have listed as an organisation that could be classified as the perpetrator of terrorism. When people bow down to the spirit of fear they are quite easily manipulated.

The Lord God Almighty is the perfect gentleman will allow you freedom of choice to have it your way until you cry out to him to save you.

We read in Revelation 18:23 – "And the light of a candle shall shine no more at all in thee; and the voice of the bridegroom and of the bride shall be heard no more at all in thee: for thy merchants were the great men of the earth; for by thy sorceries were all nations deceived."

This seems to indicate that certain wealthy merchants like maybe those at the Gates of Hell Foundation deceive all the nations in the world.

"Investing in global health organizations aimed at increasing access to vaccines created a 20-to-1 return in economic benefit," billionaire Microsoft co-founder and philanthropist Bill Gates told CNBC in 2019.

The propaganda, along with all the years of predictive programming of some mysterious virus that caused numerous people to fall sick or fall dead on the street, quickly swept through the world. It appeared no nation was immune to the most elaborate and deceptive orchestrated disinformation campaign in the history of all humanity.

The hidden powers behind the great deception made up numerous stories of people in every nation falling ill or falling dead around the world. So, it causes the people who watch Tel-Lie-Visions mainstream propaganda to beg for the promise of a vaccine cure.

Then when the untested, unlicensed, experimental vaccines came available, instead of protecting anyone people did start dying, and the governments were able to blame it on Covidmania, not their bio weaponised vaccines. Indeed, it was rather a clever plot that the Gates of Hell Foundation had a part in, and much of the world believed it,"

2 Thessalonians 2:9 – "Even him, whose coming is after the working of Satan with all power and signs and lying wonders,

10 And with all deceivableness of unrighteousness in them that perish; because they received not the love of the truth, that they might be saved.

11 And for this cause God shall send them strong delusion, that they should believe a lie:

12 That they all might be damned who believed not the truth but had pleasure in unrighteousness."

University of Texas ecologist Eric Pianka was born on 23rd January 1939 and left to go where those who reject salvation in Christ spend eternity on 12th September 2022.

During Pianka's acceptance speech for the 2006 Distinguished Texas Scientist Award from the Texas Academy of Science, he caused a wee bit of a stir of some controversy in the popular press after Forrest Mims, the vice-chair of the Academy's section on environmental science, claimed that Pianka had "rather enthusiastically advocated the elimination of 90 percent of Earth's population by airborne Ebola." Yes, this Distinguished Texas Scientist actually said that 90 percent of his fellow human beings must die to "save the planet".

Professor Pianka said, and I quote: "War and famine would not do. Instead, disease offered the most efficient and fastest way to kill the billions that must soon die if the population crisis is to be solved. AIDS is not an efficient killer because it is too slow. My favorite candidate for eliminating 90 percent of the world's population is airborne Ebola (Ebola Reston), because it is both highly lethal and it kills in days, instead of years." He went on to say, "We've got airborne diseases with 90 percent mortality in humans." Killing humans. Think about that. "You know, the bird flu's good, too. For everyone who survives, he will have to bury nine."

Forrest Mims, Chairman of the Environmental Science Section of the Texas Academy of Science, writing in The Citizen Scientist, reported:

> Professor Pianka said the Earth as we know it will not survive without drastic measures. Then, and without presenting any data to justify this number, Professor Pianka asserted that the only feasible solution to saving the Earth is to reduce the population to 10 percent of the present number. Seems this went jolly well along with the Georgia Guidestones, until they were mysteriously destroyed last summer.

> Professor Pianka then showed solutions for reducing the world's population in the form of a slide depicting the Four Horsemen of the Apocalypse. War and famine would not do, he explained. Instead, disease

offered the most efficient and fastest way to kill the billions that must soon die if the population crisis is to be solved...

I tell you again one reason the banksters launched the French Revelation in the 1700s was that they thought there were too many useless eaters.

After praising the virtue of the Ebola virus for its efficiency at killing, Professor Pianka paused dramatically, leaning over his lectern, to say, "We've got airborne 90 percent mortality in humans. Killing humans. Think about that."

He then reflected on the so-called ancient Chinese Curse, "May you live in interesting times," Professor Pianka in his arrogance and ignorance confidently asserted: "We're looking forward to a huge collapse". The demons manifesting in him in 2006 spoke about what we see unfolding on the world-stage today.

Professor Pianka said with glee that "Disease will control the scourge of humanity," he concluded with "Death. This is what awaits us all. Death." Makes me wonder if he was a gothic death metal fan.

What I find most disturbing is how a secular revered biologist and his quite dramatic reduction plan of the world's population in order to "save the planet" is not only accepted by those programmed in liberalism but that they wholeheartedly embrace this insanity. They must think like Trump's son-in-law Jared Kushner, "I think that there is a good probability that my generation is, hopefully with the advances in science, either the first generation to live forever or the last generation that's going to die."

Back in March 2020, I shared this with my church from Microsoft, the ID2020 Alliance. As more and more transactions become digital in nature and are built around a single global identification standard, supported by Microsoft, the question of who will govern this evolving global community and economy becomes relevant.

Especially since nonparticipants in this system would be unable to buy or sell goods or services.

Compare this now with,

Revelation 13:16 – "And he causeth all, both small and great, rich and poor, free and bond, to receive a mark in their right hand, or in their foreheads:

17 And that no man might buy or sell, save he that had the mark, or the name of the beast, or the number of his name."

If our world is not on a direct path to the fulfillment of Revelation 13:16-18, the only logical alternative seems to be that you would have to ignore that something with the most uncanny resemblance to the mark of the beast system is unfolding before us.

Hebrews 10:25 – "Not forsaking the assembling of ourselves together, as the manner of some is; but exhorting one another: and so much the more, as ye see the day approaching."

What day is approaching? and why are we warned to make certain we stay connected with other true believers in Christ in the process?

Throughout history, there have been all sorts of major threats, wars, and rumours of wars, famines and plagues and diseases, earthquakes, and possibilities of global totalitarian governments, with evil spirits of pride who manifested in out-of-control and out-of-touch world leaders.

Nevertheless, it appears that our current situation is more likely to fulfill the end-time prophecy than past situations. Today it is foolish not to be aware of what is unfolding with CERN opening dimensional portals and governments releasing classified film footage of UFOs claiming they are not from our world, along with D waves, Quantum computing, and super Artificial Intelligence soldiers already in operation, as well as asteroids like Apophis which means in Greek - unstoppable evil, and its expected projectile crashing into this earth on 13 April 2029. It is the size of three football stadiums.

I pray you can more clearly "see the Day is indeed approaching" (Hebrews 10:25).

But until we see the Lord Jesus/Yeshua face to face, either in the rapture or at the end of our existence here we must trust God Almighty for every detail and continue our efforts to spread the Gospel, the good news of His Kingdom with the resources we have been given.

No one throughout history has seen what is unfolding before this fallen world today.

Luke 21:28 – "And when these things begin to come to pass, then look up, and lift up your heads; for your redemption draweth nigh."

How are we to deal with the daily overwhelming propaganda news that tries to cause people to walk about in a state of despair and hopelessness?

The Kingdom of Darkness knows when people are entertaining the spirit of fear and feeling hopeless that they are more easily manipulated, and the demons are a work to try and wear out the saints.

How do we handle the enemy when they infiltrate the church?

Luke 10:19 – "Behold, I give unto you power to tread on serpents and scorpions, and over all the power of the enemy: and nothing shall by any means hurt you."

If you are a true Christian - revival has already begun within your heart first.

Colossians 3:2 – "Set your affection on things above, not on things on the earth."

The things we are here to share are no longer conspiracy theories, which begs the question of how you can share the Gospel truth with your "Conspiracy Denialist" family and friends and all those who willingly agreed to be part of a global scientific experiment.

In 2014, patents were issued to AT&T and Microsoft, for the "transmission of data through the human vector," meaning, transmission of data through skin and bones.

The technology already in play today would probably really astonish most people who have been perishing from lack of knowledge. What has been introduced into the bodies of anybody who's survived after they submitted to unlicensed, uninsured, experimental injections, and their boosters, most likely have no idea that, AT&T and Microsoft are claiming you've now got their patented technology in your body, granting them legal access that allows AT&T and Microsoft to own the data that's being transmitted through their technology in your body!

I read through the White House paper on their website, and one of the first paragraphs tells us this is about Transhumanism without saying the word Transhumanism. It is purposely written so most people will not read it.[2]

> For biotechnology and biomanufacturing to help us achieve our societal goals, the United States needs to invest in foundational scientific capabilities. We need to develop genetic engineering technologies and techniques to be able to write circuitry for cells and predictably program biology in the same way in which we write software and program computers; unlock the power of biological data, including through computing tools and artificial intelligence; and advance the science of scale up production while reducing the obstacles for commercialization so that innovative technologies and products can reach markets faster.

This is part of the transhumanism agenda that's unfolding before us today. The technology in place will give the nefarious ones who developed this nanotechnology the ability where they can hear your thoughts because if they are transmitting the information, they are also receiving it.

It will give them the ability to dictate how, where, and when you do what they tell you to do. If you try and refuse, they stop you from eating.

They will know everything about your every breath and physical movement. They will know everything about your habits."

They also need their 5G network which will allow the transmission and receiving of information. In its communications with the various technologies that have been injected into peoples' bodies, let us also understand they have injected self-assembling nano-circuitry, along with the nano-capsules releasing the spike proteins and pathogens with their nano swimmers who deliver the payload like bomber areoplane flying over its target in a war zone.

Luke 9:23 – "And he said to them all, If any man will come after me, let him deny himself, and take up his cross daily, and follow me."

Why do you care what anyone else thinks of you? In the end, all that matters is what the Lord Jesus thinks of you, and we know from the Holy Scriptures, he agape loves you and wants the very best for you.

Through "quantum dot" technology, the coming Wicked One, the Antichrist will be able to mark or tattoo everyone "on the right hand or the forehead;" provide everyone a digital ID that will track their every thought, their every word spoken and every move and action; and have them injected at the same time, all who have been programmed to accept such things as the new normal. The World Economic Forum talks about taking away all freedom, and how people are now hackable animals to be re-engineered. Its unelected founder Klaus Schwab was raised by Nazis essentially.

Dr. Yuval Noah Harari, an official advisor of Klaus Schwab says this merger of human life with technology will not benefit the average man or woman so that he or she may improve his or her future, but that a handful of "elites" will not only "build digital dictatorships" for themselves but "gain the power to re-engineer the future of life itself. Because once you can hack something, you can usually also engineer it."

If these psychopathic elite globalists/transhumanists are successful in re-engineering humanity, it will have to be decided whether the data of our DNA, brain, body, and life "belong[s] to me, or some corporation, or the government, or, perhaps, to the human collective" according to the W E F. Of course, Billy Goat and his Gates of Hell Foundation are deeply involved. We read in places like 2 Corinthians 3:17, "Now the Lord is that Spirit: and where the Spirit of the Lord is, there is liberty." Where the Holy Spirit is there is freedom, however, the Holy Spirit also exposes sin, professing Christians who have been lukewarm and who lived in places of worldly compromise need to become convicted.

Those who don't yield to the Holy Spirit ultimately become like the deaf, dumb, and blind, as they are unwilling to surrender all to Christ.

The Holy Spirit let the apostle John see thousands of years into the future to tell us what would happen in the end times, and we are warned not to let anyone deceive us into thinking that this is all symbolic somehow. Revelation 13 tells us about a literal mark on the hand or forehead. What is the abomination of desolation?

Could the abomination of desolation that the Lord Jesus spoke of be an unlicensed, uninsured, experimental injection?

The Lord Jesus/Yeshua spoke of a coming "abomination of desolation" in the Olivet Discourse as He referenced a future event that is also mentioned back in Daniel 9:27 – "And he shall confirm the covenant with many for one week: and in the midst of the week he shall cause the sacrifice and the oblation to cease, and for the overspreading of abominations he shall make it desolate, even until the consummation, and that determined shall be poured upon the desolate."

In Matthew 24:15 – "When ye therefore shall see the abomination of desolation, spoken of by Daniel the prophet, stand in the holy place, (whoso readeth, let him understand:)

16 Then let them which be in Judaea flee into the mountains."

The Lord Jesus says, "So when you see the abomination of desolation, spoken of by the prophet Daniel, standing in the holy place let him understand."

What should we understand before those in Judaea need to flee into the mountains?

First, let us understand that the term "abomination" (Hebrew *toevah* and *siqqus*) appears more than 100 times in the Old

Testament and several times in the New Testament. An abomination is normally a great sin, commonly worthy of death.

Romans 6:23 – "For the wages of sin is death; but the gift of God is eternal life through Jesus Christ our Lord."

Matthew 5:10 – "Blessed are they which are persecuted for righteousness' sake: for theirs is the kingdom of heaven."

I ask you to think outside the box for a moment and consider how these unlicensed experimental injections that have been pushed so hard globally are in a sense like a sort of Genetic bestiality, which we could classify as a disgusting thing causing desolation that we read about in,

Matthew 24:15 – "When ye therefore shall see the abomination of desolation, spoken of by Daniel the prophet, stand in the holy place, (whosoever readeth, let him understand),"

as well as in Daniel 11:31 – "And arms shall stand on his part, and they shall pollute the sanctuary of strength, and shall take away the daily sacrifice, and they shall place the abomination that maketh desolate."

Using an Injection with any Chimeric Gene seems a sort of scientific form of Bestiality because it is the mixing of human and animal seeds.

Matthew 24:15 – "When ye therefore shall see the abomination of desolation, spoken of by Daniel the prophet, stand in the holy place, (whoso readeth, let him understand)."

What should we understand here?

Could this mean that when you catch sight of the disgusting thing that causes desolation to the holy temple, as spoken of through Daniel the prophet, standing in a holy place, let the reader use discernment?

Could this mean there will be literal arms that will stand up, and these arms will actually pierce and wound the sanctuary, the Holy fortress, you as a third temple and shall take away things like removing something and putting something else in its place which is a disgusting thing that is causing desolation? Like people just keeling over as is happening now worldwide.

Daniel 11:32 – "And such as do wickedly against the covenant shall he corrupt by flatteries: but the people that do know their God shall be strong and do exploits."

Flatteries are like smooth words politicians use and mainstream propagandists use to deceive people. But the people that know God almighty as King of Kings and Lord of Lords will move in the gifts of the Holy Spirit with signs and wonders, miracles, and healings.

There was a recent bombshell from a Swedish Study published that was done independently, meaning no one was being influenced and paid to spin the findings and information from the research.

This published and accepted Swedish study on Pfizer-BionTech Vaccine DNA in Liver Cell Nucleus demonstrates for the first time the presence of Pfizer-BionTech vaccine

DNA in the cells. It is called reverse transcribed by LINE-1 proteins of the cells.

Meaning these DNA sequences can be integrated into the cell genome and subsequently be transcribed. Like reinterpreted, like changing your DNA within 6 hours of being injected.

This is basically saying there is proof of DNA being restructured and redesigned. It means that immune systems are degrading so that they can't fight off future invaders that attack the body.

Doing the opposite of what the propaganda mainstream media told you they do for you.

The Gospel is not about doom and gloom, the Gospel is about salvation and redemption and an empty tomb granting us permission to enter God Almighty's Holy Throne Room.

I bring you GOOD NEWS, the Lord or God does not reward us based on our behaviour like the Chinese credit score system. The Lord Jesus Christ of Nazareth, Messiah Yeshua grants us salvation based solely on what he scored for us through Christ our Passover Lamb shed blood for our sins. Because we can never, ever measure up to His Holy standards and enter into Heaven without him.

The Lord Jesus/Yeshua said in places like John 8:36 – "If the Son therefore shall make you free, ye shall be free indeed." No matter what the psychopathic transhumanist/globalist's plan is to enslave everyone with their depopulation agenda.

Our identity is not just a number on some Chinese computer database. Rather, we have been granted a new and glorious identity as redeemed saints.

Ephesians 1:3 – "Blessed be the God and Father of our Lord Jesus Christ, who hath blessed us with all spiritual blessings in heavenly places in Christ."

We read in places like Ephesians 2:6 - "And hath raised us up together, and made us sit together in heavenly places in Christ Jesus." For example, a Nobel Prize was awarded to two quantum physicists, Drs. S. Haroche and D. Wineland, independently of each other, did experiments once thought to be impossible by studying single atoms and single photons (particles of light).

They proved in quantum mechanics that electrons can be in two places at the same time. Albert Einstein, as bright as he was, thought the idea of such a thing sounded preposterous, but he was wrong on this. Wineland put a single atom in a box and then hit it with a photon of light. Unbeknownst to each other, which I find very symbolic, about the same time Dr. Haroche across an ocean did the opposite.

He put a single photon in a box and then hit it with an atom. Both discovered in the process as Dr. Wineland achieved in his lab when he hit the atom with half of the light needed to move it, it was simultaneously immobile and in motion, until eventually, it was in two locations, 80 nanometers (billionths of a meter) apart, at the same time. This resulted in numerous physicists now leaning toward the concept of a multitude of world interpretations of quantum mechanics.

So, if the electron can be in two places at the same time, it indicates that the universe could jolly well be wrapped into at least two universes at the same time. In other words, quantum mechanics naturally predicts a multitude of universes, no matter how strange that seems.

The Word of God told us this thousands of years ago. So, if a proton can do this and an electron can do this, it stands to reason that even a moron can do this. We who love the Lord Jesus Christ of Nazareth then can be in two places at the same time.

I pray that helps take you away from entertaining the spirit of fear which God did not give you.

Are we on the brink of a technological revolution that will fundamentally alter the way we live, work, and relate to one another? Or are we observing Biblical prophecy unfolding before us?

The First Industrial Revolution in the late 1700s used water and steam power to mechanize production.

The Second Industrial Revolution began in the middle of the 19th century and used electric power to create mass production.

The Third Industrial Revolution began soon after the Roswell New Mexico supposed crash of a UFO which took place in the summer of 1947. Soon there were transistors and semiconductors, mainframe computing, and personal computing, and CERN gave the world the Internet which started the digital revolution.

Now there are those calling for the Fourth Industrial Revolution with Artificial Intelligence building on the digital revolution that has been unfolding since the middle of the last century.

The advancing technologies are blurring the lines between the physical, digital, and biological spheres. One thing is certain, as these technologies are implemented and integrated into our world, they will change almost everything from the public and private sectors to academia and all of society.

True believers are safe in the Ark of Christ, like Noah and his family and animals stayed safe in Noah's Ark. No matter how stormy things got they stayed safe in the Ark until they landed on the mountain of their destination a year later.

The only solution is for true believers to stay on the narrow pathway of holiness.

I share again 1 Corinthians 2:9 – "But as it is written, Eye hath not seen, nor ear heard, neither have entered into the heart of man, the things which God hath prepared for them that 1 It appears to me that the window the Globalist opened is closing in on old King Charles who was selected to initiate us on the "Great Reset" whilst he was royal formerly known as Prince Charles. I just get the feeling those New World Order clowns are planning to double down on their destruction and depopulation agendas. If they don't act soon and accidentally on purpose release their next phase of nefariousness, they may not be able to accomplish their full digitization and dehumanization by 2025, in their plans to alter human history. As one of the main spokesmen clowns for Nazis raised Klaus Schwab's World Economic Forum gang puppet, Yuval Harari explained, and I quote: "Potentially We Are Talking About the End of Human History. Not the End of History, Just the End of That Part of History That Was Dominated By Human Beings. It's Now Possible to Create Total Surveillance Regimes."

We have been in the beginning stages of World War III for some time now with Russia in Eastern Europe, in Syria, and with Africa and it appears that Asia is getting ready to make an explosive move as well. What nation fears a Banana Joe Republic at this point?

I have been warning about the great deception for years like with all the UFO sightings that have gone mainstream and are an everyday occurrence worldwide, as the Pentagon continues to release once classified footage of unknown craft traveling over 15000 miles per minute making sharp 90 degree turns without decelerating." The G forces would destroy a human pilot. Is there artificial intelligence flying them or something else?

There is now wide acceptance of alien life, worldwide and the elite of our day continue to push the deception, after all, they need to perpetuate this deception to explain away the coming Rapture.

Klaus Schwab World Economic Forum puppet Yuval Noah Harari, bestselling author, predicted the end of human-dominated history because of an upcoming alien invasion. I quote him yet again "History will continue with somebody else in control," he said. It appears that Harari changed from advocating Artificial Intelligence (AI) and transhumanism as the future of mankind to now saying that we will be dominated by superiour intelligent extraterrestrials that traveled millions of light years to tell us we are wrong to believe in Jesus, or that they created Jesus and that is how he did miracles.

Galatians 1:8-But though we, or an angel from heaven, preach any other gospel unto you than that which we have preached unto you, let him be accursed.9 As we said before, so say I now again, if any man preach any other gospel unto you than that ye have received, let him be accursed.

It's not surprising turn how far the Kingdom of Darkness and its Luciferian globalist psychopaths are willing to go in preparing the world for our disappearance at the time of the Rapture. Programmed puppet Harari, like so many others, naturally assumes that the aliens are far more advanced than humans in both intelligence and technology. They must create this illusion so that people believe they are capable of making tens of millions of "Christians" instantly disappear.

Today microchips are implanted in our brains and artificial intelligence has already become much smarter than most humans. Elon Musk still wants to get his now FDA-approved microchips in everyone's brain by 20/30. The Technocratic Elites believe in their Science and advances in Technology to rule the world and think they will become immortals; they mock God almighty.

2 Peter 3:3 Knowing this first, that there shall come in the last days scoffers, walking after their own lusts,

Proverbs 21:24 Proud and haughty scorner is his name, who dealeth in proud wrath.

Jared Kushner believes there is a strong "portability" he will be among the first humans to achieve eternal life on Earth. Kushner, who was last seen on a media tour hawking his White House memoir, believes his potential to achieve immortality might be assisted through science and his exercise routine.

Today scientism basically believes that scientific discovery will answer all of the existential questions in human life that religion was to satisfy.

Transhumanism is the idea that technology will be the instrument of salvation without the Lord Jesus. We are watching this madness unfold before us, especially in the wake of the plandemic since 2020.

Let us also consider that Gnosticism became one of the most dangerous heresy that threatened the early church during the first three centuries. Influenced by philosophers like Plato, Gnosticism is simply demonic and is based on two false premises. First off, it espouses a dualism regarding spirit and matter. Gnostics have asserted in their ignorance that matter is inherently evil and only the spirit is good. As a result of their presupposition and gross misunderstandings, Gnostics believe anything done in the body has no lasting meaning, even the most hideous crimes, and sinister sins, have no real meaning to them because they falsely believe that our true life exists in the spirit realm only.

Secondly, consider how Gnostics claim to possess forbidden secret knowledge, as they claim that the truth is elevated above actual truth. Their so-called "higher truth" is therefore only known to a select few in their secret society or club. Let us also understand that Gnosticism comes from the Greek word gnosis which means "to know." However, they don't know the Gospel truth from our Holy Guide Book to the Supernatural, but they feel like they have acquired their knowledge on some mystical higher plane of existence, like some drug addicts have done. The bottom line, Gnostics see themselves as a privileged elite class who are elevated above everybody else by their higher, and deeper knowledge of God along with their idea of achieving Christ consciousness as the newagers desire.

There is absolutely no compatibility between true Christianity and Gnosticism, which is easily provable as all we need to do is compare their teachings to the main doctrines of true Christianity. For example, Gnosticism teaches that salvation is gained through the acquisition of divine knowledge which frees one from the illusions of the darkness in this world. Gnostics have no trouble lying and deceiving you by telling the ignorant who are perishing from lack of knowledge that Gnosticism teaches its followers to follow Jesus Christ and His original teachings, nevertheless, Gnostics contradict the Lord Jesus/Yeshua in almost everything that they think, say and do.

Consider for example, how the Lord Jesus said nothing about salvation through knowledge, rather He said it came by faith in Him alone as your personal Saviour from sin.

Ephesians 2:8-For by grace are ye saved through faith; and that not of yourselves: it is the gift of God:

9 Not of works, lest any man should boast.

Furthermore, the salvation Christ offers is free and available to everyone John 3:16 For God so loved the world, that he gave his only begotten Son, that whosoever believeth in him should not perish, but have everlasting life.,

Salvation is not just for a select few who have acquired a special revelation. So, I find it very interesting that Gnostics believed in Sofia, who is a feminine figure that has god-like features that they think is the female twin of Jesus.

I have been sharing for years about Sophia the robot. Asking if we are dealing with Fallen Angel Technology. Is that part of the so-called injection deceptions? Connecting people to technologies that control their thoughts?

Today the world has questioned what it means to be human. Or more precisely, what are we saying about others when we describe them as human? Sophia, the humanoid robot, was granted full citizenship in Egypt in 2017. Many women there can't obtain that privilege. Her creators believe Sophia to become a self-aware robot.

Sophia the robot also has addressed the U.N a number of times in their quest for their sustainable development goals.

What are the chances Sophia who was created by Hanson Robotics, with David Hanson as founder takes her name directly from the Gnostic? Sophia was the character in Philip K Dick's 1981 science fiction novel titled Valis. American writer Philip K. Dick, intended to be the first book of a three-part series. The title is an acronym for Vast Active Living Intelligence System, Dick's gnostic vision of God.

David Hansen's Ph.D. dissertation was also about this. Another strange coincidence no doubt. Hanson robotics are seeking to create a sort of technological inversion of what the ancient Gnostics desired to do.

Meanwhile, Elon Musk has talked about implanting an AI microchip into our brain so what would that eventually mean for Humanity?

Would it make us smarter or destroy the human race?

Elon Musk on 18 September 2023 discussed his ideas with Benjamin Netanyahu along with numerous other prestigious AI thinkers. Musk foresees a potential future in which he said hundreds of billions of people would be implanted with these to guide AI according to human will. Or will it be the other way round?

This is already in progress, as Musk's company Neuralink got their FDA approval, and there are other companies as well like BlackRock neurotech funded by Peter Thiel, and Synchron which is funded by both Jeff Bezos and Bill Gates and his Gates of hell foundation.

These companies already have brain-computer interfaces implanted in human brains that allow them to interact with digital devices by way of artificial intelligence. This is not coming, this is already here, this is already a reality.

Luke 12:56 Ye hypocrites, ye can discern the face of the sky and of the earth; but how is it that ye do not discern this time?

No matter what is happening in this fallen world we have the Lord Jesus's promise.

There was that wonderful moment at Caesarea Philippi where the Lord Jesus/Yeshua asked the disciples, who do they say that I am? In a moment of all sorts of assorted answers, the disciples offer up and only Peter says you are the Christ the son of the Living God!

Matthew 16

13 When Jesus came into the coasts of Caesarea Philippi, he asked his disciples, saying, Whom do men say that I the Son of man am?

14 And they said, Some say that thou art John the Baptist: some, Elias; and others, Jeremias, or one of the prophets.

15 He saith unto them, But whom say ye that I am?

16 And Simon Peter answered and said, Thou art the Christ, the Son of the living God.

17 And Jesus answered and said unto him, Blessed art thou, Simon Barjona: for flesh and blood hath not revealed it unto thee, but my Father which is in heaven.

18 And I say also unto thee, That thou art Peter, and upon this rock I will build my church; and the gates of hell shall not prevail against it.

19 And I will give unto thee the keys of the kingdom of heaven: and whatsoever thou shalt bind on earth shall be bound in heaven: and whatsoever thou shalt loose on earth shall be loosed in heaven.

20 Then charged he his disciples that they should tell no man that he was Jesus the Christ.

21 From that time forth began Jesus to shew unto his disciples, how that he must go unto Jerusalem, and suffer many things of the elders and chief priests and scribes, and be killed, and be raised again the third day.

22 Then Peter took him, and began to rebuke him, saying, Be it far from thee, Lord: this shall not be unto thee.

23 But he turned, and said unto Peter, Get thee behind me, Satan: thou art an offence unto me: for thou savourest not the things that be of God, but those that be of men.

How did Peter go from hearing directly from the Kingdom of God and moments later to listening to the Kingdom of darkness?

24 Then said Jesus unto his disciples, If any man will come after me, let him deny himself, and take up his cross, and follow me.

25 For whosoever will save his life shall lose it: and whosoever will lose his life for my sake shall find it.

26 For what is a man profited, if he shall gain the whole world, and lose his own soul? or what shall a man give in exchange for his soul?

27 For the Son of man shall come in the glory of his Father with his angels, and then he shall reward every man according to his works.

28 Verily I say unto you, There be some standing here, which shall not taste of death, till they see the Son of man coming in his kingdom.

We read in Luke 9:27, "But I tell you of a truth, there be some standing here, which shall not taste of death, till they see the kingdom of God."

We find parallel statements in Mark 9:1 And he said unto them, Verily I say unto you, That there be some of them that stand here, which shall not taste of death, till they have seen the kingdom of God come with power.

In each of the synoptic Gospels, the gospels of Matthew, Mark, and Luke are referred to as the synoptic Gospels because they include many of the same stories. Here we find the next event immediately after this promise from the Lord Jesus/Yeshua is the transfiguration.

Rather than interpreting the Lord Jesus' promise as referring to His coming to establish His kingdom on earth, the context appears to indicate that the Lord Jesus was actually referring to the transfiguration.

That was a time event horizon. In astrophysics, an event horizon is a boundary beyond which events cannot affect an observer. In general relativity, an event horizon is considered a boundary in space-time, of an area surrounding a black hole most of the time. In Christ's Transfiguration, He appeared to be in two dimensions at the same time.

The Greek word "kingdom" can also be translated as "royal splendor," in other words, it could jolly well mean that the

Lord Jesus/Yeshua shared how the three disciples standing there would see Christ as He really is as the Lord of all lords and the King of all kings and the creator of Heaven, which occurred when they were present in the transfiguration.

Matthew 17:1 And after six days Jesus taketh Peter, James, and John his brother, and bringeth them up into an high mountain apart,

2 And was transfigured before them: and his face did shine as the sun, and his raiment was white as the light.

3 And, behold, there appeared unto them Moses and Elias talking with him.

4 Then answered Peter, and said unto Jesus, Lord, it is good for us to be here: if thou wilt, let us make here three tabernacles; one for thee, and one for Moses, and one for Elias.

5 While he yet spake, behold, a bright cloud overshadowed them: and behold a voice out of the cloud, which said, This is my beloved Son, in whom I am well pleased; hear ye him.

6 And when the disciples heard it, they fell on their face, and were sore afraid.

7 And Jesus came and touched them, and said, Arise, and be not afraid.

8 And when they had lifted up their eyes, they saw no man, save Jesus only.

9 And as they came down from the mountain, Jesus charged them, saying, Tell the vision to no man, until the Son of man be risen again from the dead.

Here in the account of the "transfiguration" event the Lord Jesus took Peter, James, and John to the top of the mountain, where He met with Moses and Elijah, Perhaps this was a moment representing the Law and the Prophets of the Old Testament who and spoke with them. The disciples saw the Lord Jesus in all His glory and splendor, talking with a glorified Moses and Elijah. This is a glimpse for us to consider what will occur one day as we encounter the Lord Jesus' kingdom. I'm guessing we shall also "fall on our faces."

It makes the most sense that we interpret this promise that was made in Matthew 16:28, Mark 9:1, and Luke 9:27 as a reference to the transfiguration, which "Peter, James, and John" would witness a mere six days later, just as the Lord Jesus/Yeshua predicted would happen. "They shall not taste of death, till they have seen the kingdom of God come with power." In each Gospel account, the contextual links make it very likely that this is the proper interpretation, Christ in his, "royal splendor,"

Matthew 16:18 And I say also unto thee, That thou art Peter, and upon this rock I will build my church; and the gates of hell shall not prevail against it.

The Lord Jesus told Peter how he would build his church so that the Gates of Hell foundation would not prevail against it. Let us consider how we are supposed to be standing firm on the Word of God so let's start there with that promise of Christ that he will build his church.

Today we see there are increasing obstacles that are coming against the church in the form of gradualism.

The Gates of hell foundation has its nasty sharp tongue jaws wide open and their gradual assault on the church has been going on for years. Nevertheless, the Lord Jesus is Victorious over sin and death and hell, and we see again and again in the pages of scripture that there is Victory and that this promise is indeed reliable.

When we study church history, we start thinking about how we are also to be able to stand firm in our faith because we know that this promise from the Lord Jesus cannot fail, and his promises will not be broken. Whether we live or die we are the Lord's. Romans 14:8.

I asked in several churches that I ministered from the North to the South of UK- What is the difference between the agenda of the Nazis and the WEF/WHO? Both want full spectrum dominance, both are depopulations, both use propaganda and deception along with bioweapons. Both create the problems and then offer you their demonic solutions.

Hegelian dialectics.

Allow me to share a quote from a Hungarian Jew, from the documentary The Last Days: and I quote, "People wonder, how is it that we didn't do something? We didn't run away, we didn't hide. Well, things didn't happen at once. Things happened very slowly so each time a new law came out, or a new restriction, we said, "it's just another thing, it will blow over," When we had to wear the yellow star to be outside. We started to worry.

Does anyone see a parallel? Like what we saw in 2020 with demands to wear a suffocation device.

You might have relaxed your grip, but rest assured the Globalist psychopaths haven't stopped their pursuit of their quest to Digitization, Dehumanization, Direct Energy weapon Destruction, and Depopulation agendas over him."

What is taking place worldwide today is a most cleverly engineered Coup d'état to try and overthrow the rulership of God Almighty by destroying His creation first. This is what is at the heart of the transhumanists, through their genetic engineering manipulation and witchcraft by their nanotechnology that is not visible to the human eye, like the theory of germs you can't see but that cause such sickness and diseases, how it is all being employed within the so-called gene therapy injections that countless people were pressured into receiving.

Considering that you get half of the genes in your DNA from your father and the other half of the genes in your DNA from your mother those two DNA strands then combine together and then they intertwine to form this Twisted letter of DNA in each of our body cells. According to my friend Dr. Michelle Strydom, now it's been discovered in science that you actually get 72,000 genes from your father and 72,000 genes from your mother to complete the human genome which is a total of 144,000 genes.

Revelation 7:4 And I heard how many were marked with the seal of God—144,000 were sealed from all the tribes of Israel:

Revelation 7 tells us about the number of 144,000.

The apostle Paul forewarned us that the last days there would bring a marked increase in false teaching. We couldn't even imagine a few years ago how many would be deceived and go along with such false teachings that our society can no longer distinguish the differences between a man and a woman.

We read in places like 1 Timothy 4:1 Now the Spirit speaketh expressly, that in the latter times some shall depart from the faith, giving heed to seducing spirits, and doctrines of devils.

For those paying attention who study to show themselves approved know that from the Holy Word of God in their Bible the number here is representative of the bride of Christ that is sealed in Revelations chapter 11. Being sealed of the Lord is like having His signature stamped on you that says, This person's body belongs to me God Almighty. In Revelation 7:4 it appears that the 144,000 are actual people living during the end-times tribulation who the Lord shall keep safe from the divine judgments and from the wrath of the Antichrist causing such troubles as the world has not seen before.

There is nothing in these verses that leads to interpreting the 144,000 as anything but a literal number of Jews— which be 12,000 taken from every tribe of the children of Israel, according to Revelation 7 in verses 5 through 8. which goes on to list all the tribes.

The mission of these 144,000 appears that they are called to be the ones to evangelize in the world after the rapture happens and proclaim the gospel during the tribulation period. I say we have it rather much easier at the moment and yet most of the church today has not shared their faith openly. Most Christians have never led one person into salvation, prayed for the sick, and seen them recover and cast out a single demon in the almighty name of Jesus. God's Mercy Is for Everyone who will accept His Salvation

In the Old Testament, it was prophesied that Israel would repent and turn back to God and that they would come to Christ.

NLT Zechariah 12:10 "Then I will pour out a spirit[a] of grace and prayer on the family of David and on the people of Jerusalem. They will look on me whom they have pierced and mourn for him as for an only son. They will grieve bitterly for him as for a firstborn son who has died.

NLT Romans 11:25- I want you to understand this mystery, dear brothers and sisters, [a] so that you will not feel proud about yourselves. Some of the people of Israel have hard hearts, but this will last only until the full number of Gentiles comes to Christ. 26 And so all Israel will be saved. As the Scriptures say,

"The one who rescues will come from Jerusalem, and he will turn Israel away from ungodliness.27 And this is my covenant with them, that I will take away their sins."

Much of the confusion that has come into the church over the 144,000 seems to have come as a result of the false doctrine spread about by the Jehovah's Witnesses.

However, let us consider that 144,000 may be the number that is significant to the bride of Christ.

Considering what is happening with the new mRNA technology that has been introduced into masses of bodies worldwide under the guise of their bioweapon plandemic. Researchers are claiming that they have literally added a whole third strand of DNA to a person's genome which creates a triple DNA helix.

Besides the fact that it was done without the person's knowledge or consent, THINK CHEMTRAILS here WHICH CONTAMINTED FOOD AND WATER, and of course what is called shedding. So what information is on that DNA now? Could this possibly be connected to any form of the Nephilim DNA? Are we seeing a repeat of the devil and his fallen angels so there were no genetically pure people left in Noah's time, except Noah and his family. So, what sort of information about the kingdom of darkness has been coded into DNA as we see history repeating itself where the events of Genesis chapter 6 played out.

My brothers and sisters, are we in the Days of Noah? Are we seeing such times beginning to play out again?

Researchers are revealing that hydrogel and nanotechnology in the deception injections have indeed altered things in the bodies of those who received it.

No matter how many people tell you it has nothing to do with the mark of the beast in Revelations, something is happening here that is becoming clear.

Consider this also regarding adding why a third strand of DNA is significant, because does that mean there are another 72,000 genes that have been added to the human genome?

If there are 72, 000 genes from a person's father and another 72, 000 genes from their mother along with an additional 72, 000 genes which has now been added in through the so-called gene therapy which adds up to a total of 216,000 genes.

NLT Revelation 13:18 Wisdom is needed here. Let the one with understanding solve the meaning of the number of the beast, for it is the number of a man. [a] His number is 666. [b]

Here is wisdom let him that have understanding count the number of the Beast.

If you multiply 600 times 60 times 6 that equals 216,000 - two hundred and sixteen thousand which is now the number of genes in a person's DNA after the so-called gene therapy.

If this is the number of a man who is obviously connecting mankind to the Antichrist, that proves highly significant. In other words, is this telling us that the number of man has somehow been changed in the End Times, where it was 144,000, part of the Bride of Christ has now been changed to 216, 000 which is 603 score and six. - 666.

Numerous times the Lord Jesus warned us not to be deceived. He tells us his people have been perishing from lack of knowledge.

I did a podcast with Dr. Carrie Madej recently and she pointed out how awesome the human body God designed is, that we can endure all sorts of poisons in our bodies and overcome them. That anything the deranged scientist and their gain of function bioweapon design will always fall short of what the Lord can do.

Please don't panic and entertain the spirit of fear God did not give you. If for whatsoever reason you took the first few doses of the unlicensed, uninsured experimental substances, the Lord still forgives and performs miracles for those with repented hearts.

Consider this a critical warning message to alert you to the Rapture and the coming Antichrist and one world government and religion as we are already seeing this Babylon agenda playing out behind the Health crisis by those who serve the kingdom of darkness orchestrated.

If any of you recall at the Queen's Jubilee in 2022, she was presented with a globe and she pressed down on that globe which was said to officially represent the Commonwealth, unless it really represented the British monarchy's rule over the entire globe. Interestingly enough when her late Majesty Queen Elizabeth II pressed this globe it caused a series of lights to light up which were arranged in the pattern of a triple DNA Helix. It's probably just another strange coincidence.

Rule, Britannia! Britannia, rule the waves! Britons never, never, never will be slaves. Could ruling the waves include airwaves? I'm just asking for a friend.

Ephesians 2:2 - Wherein in time past ye walked according to the course of this world, according to the prince of the power of the air, the spirit that now worketh in the children of disobedience.

NLT Ephesians 2:2 You used to live in sin, just like the rest of the world, obeying the devil—the commander of the powers in the unseen world. [a] He is the spirit at work in the hearts of those who refuse to obey God.

Matthew 7:18 A good tree cannot bring forth evil fruit, neither can a corrupt tree bring forth good fruit.

What do we make of the triple helix DNA?

God Almighty intentionally placed two trees in the Garden of Eden because He valued Adam and Eve's free will, who were made distinctly in His own image and likeness.

In Genesis 2:8–9, after God Almighty had created Adam (but not Eve, yet), the two trees are specifically mentioned: Genesis 2:8- And the LORD God planted a garden eastward in Eden; and there he put the man whom he had formed.9 And out of the ground made the LORD God to grow every tree that is pleasant to the sight, and good for food; the tree of life also in the midst of the garden, and the tree of knowledge of good and evil.

If you go back to the two trees in the Garden of Eden there was the Tree of Life, that tree that symbolized the tree of the knowledge of Good and Evil which appears as the information tree of the occult from the kingdom of darkness in many scriptures.

Our DNA is like a tree, our thoughts look like trees, and it all leads to fruit in our life which is supposed to be the fruits of the Holy Spirit as we walk in the image of God, however, if the information of the kingdom of darkness is in our DNA, it's going to lead to a very dark place in our thinking patterns emotions and behaviours.

Matthew 5:16- Let your light so shine before men, that they may see your good works, and glorify your Father which is in heaven.

Our Heavenly Father does nothing without first revealing his plans to his church through His prophets. It appears he has the same requirement on the Devil and the kingdom of darkness why they must tell us first what they are going to do.

The kingdom of darkness has used the international network of Freemasonry for ages which most of the world's Elite belonged to. They are the ones who are responsible for ushering in the New World Order as they always publicly broadcast their plans hidden in plain sight before carrying them out because their leader is subtly in his deceptions.

The occult means to hide things, so they broadcast their plans in numerous ways through signs symbols and buildings through the music industry and entertainment industry. They look for times when a large percentage of the world's population are watching like the late Queen Elizebeth Jubilee where they showed the transformation of the DNA of the global population symbolized into a triple three-stranded DNA Helix.

God Almighty gave Adam and Eve a choice in the Garden of Eden to obey or disobey His commandment. He gave them this choice because He designed them to have free will, which reflected His own, and because He greatly valued their freedom and loved them enough to not force them into subjection. He didn't design us to be programmed robots.

John 3:18 He that believeth on him is not condemned: but he that believeth not is condemned already, because he hath not believed in the name of the only begotten Son of God.

My freedom-loving brothers and sisters, we must not be deceived and choose God's way over all else.

Pastor Caspar McCloud is pastor of Upper Room Fellowship. He is an author, songwriter, guitarist and portrait artist. www.casparmccloudmusic.com www.theupperroomfellowship.org

CHAPTER 8

AN INTERVIEW WITH CARRIE MADEJ

Interview with Dr. Carrie Madej by Pastor Caspar McCloud. Caspar's comments and questions are in *italics* and signified by PC. Carrie Madej's comments are signified by CM.

PC: *What would you want to say to encourage people who are entertaining a spirit of fear that God did not give us about the future as we observe what is unfolding upon the world stage today?*

CM: All things considered, let us always keep in mind God's Kingdom is above everything else and he is all-powerful.

There are two laws in effect there's God's law and this worldly law called Black's law.

As I have been researching this, I am becoming more aware of how God's Word is alive and ever active.

I have been giving numerous presentations in various places helping more and more people to understand what is unfolding before us today.

For those of you who already have seen me in conferences and interviews and who may know of me and my message, I like to say first that I have had several divine appointments in my life just as most of you have had.

I didn't understand what they were about for a long while as most of us didn't understand why until March of 2020 when the world went into a literal game change as you know.

As all of this came together, I began to understand even more how incredible and loving our Heavenly Father, our Creator is.

I am now convinced that nothing happens by accident or by mistake and that our God who is almighty does indeed love us.

For example, he knows everyone one of us, and he knew when all of us would be born.

He also does not want us to be here and suffer, and like any good father, he wants us to learn about what is going on around us right now.

This is why we must help educate ourselves and not run away from things that are happening in this world.

Because when the time comes our Heavenly Father wants us to stay strong and choose the right way, his way.

For me, I believe part of my job assignment is to help you see some things that aren't easily seen. I hope to help bring some of these dark figures that are hiding into the light and expose them for what they truly are.

Ephesians 5:11 "Take no part in the worthless deeds of evil and darkness; instead, expose them." (New Living Translation,)

When we consider what happened in the Garden of Eden and how artists over the centuries have depicted this particular scene with the woman taking the forbidden fruit often shown as an apple, what we don't always imagine is how that was the moment when her body first started to decay because death had now come upon her. By breaking the only commandment God had given her and Adam not to eat the forbidden fruit.

Today we are also dealing with a digital realm, which is part of the Artificial Intelligence realm that is luring as many as possible to enter into a place behind the veil of deception where they offer you immortality. It is a place of entrapment where they will offer you promises of great knowledge, and great wealth to live a fantastic life. Because this is literally what is happening today. There is a seduction from the digital realm that has already captured numerous people worldwide who are being taken down a destructive pathway unaware of where they will end up.

I like to refer you to Matthew 10:16 "Behold, I send you forth as sheep in the midst of wolves, be ye therefore wise as serpents, and harmless as doves."

PC: *That is a very good reminder and verse that I like to keep in mind as well. As we have done numerous conferences together and as you are aware of my books on epigenetic from a biblical perspective, I encourage people to speak the Word of God out loud as you are then engaging neuronal pathways on numerous levels and helping to secret all the healing and feel-good chemicals. For example, we all have pre-existing memories, and we know from the almighty Word of God and now from science how those pre-existing thoughts can engage with something like a spirits of bitterness, which consequently release toxic chemicals into your body. Because when we don't do as our Lord commands us to forgive others and you may need to accept Christ forgiveness and forgive yourself as well. Matthew 18 tells us that God cannot forgive us unless we forgive everyone else who has offended us, which begs the question, "How can the Lord heal you and restore you if you are not willing to obey his commandments."*

We know from our Holy Guide Book to the Supernatural and from science now that if you go to bed angry you will most likely grow some negative stems on some neurons, in other words you create a poisonous memory, and then there's spikes on that neurons, just like the fangs of a snake. When those poisonous thoughts, dominate your thought life, every time you think-those poisonous memories that you built in your brain according to the image of the kingdom of darkness, will be reactivated, and they are stimulated to release venom that secretes those poisonous chemicals that cause diseases.

CM: I speak this verse Matthew 10:16 out loud most every day because it helps me stay centered and balanced.

Because we are amid predators who are like wolves and coyotes today. If we don't understand how they think and act, we will become their prey. They will eat you up and destroy you because you naively chose the wrong things.

So, we must begin to understand what is going on. Nevertheless, we also can't get so lost in it trying to learn about all these evil doers that we somehow become the very monster we are fighting against by trying to destroy them.

The Dove is representative of the Holy Spirit, and we are to focus on the goodness of God, not the evil of the kingdom of darkness. We are to forgive them as Jesus/Yeshua forgave his tormentors and us, as they don't know what they are doing.

I have always loved nature as nature gives us numerous signs if you pay attention and observe them. This past year I was visiting some of my family and it was late September in Michigan. My sister-in-law said to me how she would love to get a sign that everything is going to be alright as there are so many troubles in our world. The very next day a White Dove flew into their patio and landed there, calmly looking into their window for over ten minutes. There are no pigeons or doves flying around that particular region where they live. My sister-in-law took a photograph of the Dove to send me as she was over the moon on receiving such a sign. Sometimes this is a way the Lord our God may communicate with us to help encourage us through nature.

PC: *That is a wonderful word picture of how the Lord God Almighty looks after every detail of our life, and how we should worry about things how even the birds of air don't worry about where their next meal will come from and how we are worth more than the birds of the air to our loving Heavenly Father.*

CM: One of the things I want to share with you was how back in 1998 I attended the Kansas City University School of Medicine and Biosciences. I was already asking questions about why so many bad things were going on in our world back then as now. Some people would answer how there were people in powerful positions that have been making very bad decisions in our world. Maybe they're just lost and misguided, maybe we could find a way to talk with them and help them turn away from their evil ways. After all, isn't that part of the great commission Jesus/Yeshua gave us to do?

However, I want you to know that there has been a concerted plan and agenda that has been going on for a very long time. So why are they doing it and who are these people behind these obvious evil plans and agendas? Because I feel strongly that if we had more understanding and knowledge of these things, we would know better what we should be doing today.

When I was in medical school in Kansas City, I realized recently how much things have changed since I attended there.

When I looked at the new emblem the medical school now has, I honestly felt quite horrified by seeing it. It was a huge emblem with the biggest snake that I had ever seen.

I'm a trained osteopath and we believe that the body is designed to heal itself, we believe in God, and we believe there's a mind, body, spirit, and soul connection.

The medical school has now taken the name osteopath off the main title which is very sad to learn. When I was in my second year at this medical school, I had a divine appointment. There was this microbiology professor, we will call her Dr. B., who just happened to work for the military as well. She was also very proud of her work for the military. She told us that she worked on the most evolved organism, which means she was working on bioweapons. However, I didn't quite understand that at the time, as she wanted to talk about something called microplasmapneumoniae which is a bacteria commonly thought to cause milder infections of the respiratory system having such symptoms than other types of pneumonia. The common and informal name given to this type of bacteria is often called Walking pneumonia. Little do many people know that this can also contribute to autoimmune diseases. It also can contribute to causing many different types of cancers and neurological diseases and all sorts of dreadful things.

Now Dr. B said this was a very different sort of organism because it's not like any normal bacteria. It doesn't have the typical little protective wall around it, rather it is like a bacteria with the skin around it. So, it can change shape and it's also very fragile.

She then said what makes it very dangerous is the neurotoxins that piggyback on top of it. Dr. B was very proud of this work she was involved in and showed us pictures of these bacteria and neurotoxins. So, I raised my hand to ask a question, I asked if these pictures were illustrations, and she said no. It caused quite a stir among my classmates; it was very unsettling because what we saw in the picture which has been deleted online was a tiny red blood cell and then what appeared to be a genorobotics. That means they are using an automated device for extracting and sequencing DNA.

Mycoplasma has the smallest known bacterial genome to date, and it may now be possible with such advances in technologies being made that they will be able to create an entirely synthetic organism in the near future. In other words, it could easily become a very attractive template for those with nefarious intentions to build their bioweapons.

Now back when I saw this with my classmates, keep in mind that we didn't have cell phones yet and so I couldn't quite comprehend at the moment how this was going to play out.

Dr. B, realizing the impact of this encounter we had just observed became quite angry and started to threaten us by telling our class that if we told anyone about this none of us would ever work again. At that point what could we do? We all wanted to graduate so we remained silent about it.

That is until about 2009 when I was working in Georgia where an outbreak of mycoplasma happened which was very potent. I was looking at the blood samples of patients at my clinic. I was also having a difficult time helping to clear it out of people's bodies, which compelled me to do more research on it. If you look this up now on the internet mysteriously all the information that was there on this has been scrubbed away. It's all disappeared without any explanation; it is just gone!

I have learned it is a true bioweapon, and the United States has been one of the biggest users of this technology around the world.

I also have learned that this is the most widely used of bioweapons used around the world because it is considered the most potent.

There is a manual where they show how to make all sorts of bioweapons, with instructions on how to create life. Since they discovered these tiny genomes, they have documented them in how to make them their model organism. In this way, they can make different additions to them and create all sorts of different bioweapons. There have been numerous researchers looking into how to accomplish such things. Looking back into the 1950s, 60s, and 70s you can still find some research that hasn't been completely wiped offline yet when you are looking at this organism. It is very unusual because it is formed by something called brucella.

According to Professor Don Scott, this is a crystalline form of the Brucella bacterium that has been combined with a retro virus visna from sheep by our military.

It attaches to a gene in nucleus/mitochondria the cell.

It is dormant until a suppressed immune system occurs - acidic ph, low oxygen cell environment, PLUS physical or emotional trauma, then is activated.

PC: *Please explain more about this for those who are not yet aware.*

Brucellosis - Symptoms and causes - Mayo Clinic[3]

CM: The overview, Brucellosis is a bacterial infection that spreads from animals to people. Most commonly, people are infected by eating raw or unpasteurized dairy products.

Sometimes, the bacteria that cause brucellosis can spread through the air or direct contact with infected animals.

So, combining these with a virus is called gain of function which is how they create a bioweapon. Many people know these terms and words now become of the Covid-19 pandemic. Let us understand this has been going on for a long time and this is how one of the earliest stages was developed. The microscopic bacteria are so tiny, and yet they can attach their little speck onto a gene. It doesn't even make sense, because it doesn't fit the criteria for a bacteria to be called that. I want you to understand this is just one of the weapons they are employing against us.

What is amazing is how these things are so potent and yet can lay dormant so they can't hurt anybody unless it meets two conditions. First, you have to have what we would call poor terrain, which means your body has become physically toxic. It means something has gone wrong in your immune system. For example, you may have ingested some poisons, maybe you have been eating some things that have helped compromise your immune system as many fast foods are harmful to you.

Secondly, you would have to have some really bad physical or emotional traumas. Meaning it could be one event or a series of events that have caused your perceptions of reality to become very negative.

For example, some people tend to believe they are always a victim, while others are so angry that they can't forgive. I think we have all known people like that and in medicine, it is a well-known fact that when people entertain such thoughts and feelings, they will create sickness and diseases in their bodies.

Pastor Caspar, you wrote about this in your book What Was I Thinking? helping to explain how the epigenetic of our thought life can create a life of blessings or curses.

Consider this, because if we are made in the image of God, we are capable of creating health or sickness in our bodies. So, this research comes from secular people who don't believe in God our creator and in spirituality and are aware of how our emotions and how we think can activate these bioweapons they have made and released on the world.

Keep in mind how repeatedly throughout the Bible we are told not to fear. I want you to remember that because no matter what bioweapon they make and throw at us, our bodies can adapt and be naturally resistant to it as long as we take care of our holy temples physically and of course, we keep a healthy positive perspective.

Our spirituality in God and prayer is vital.

PC: *I couldn't agree with you more my sister.*

CM: All this is amazing to understand, and, in my clinic, I experienced this with numerous patients who were restored and healed.

Most of all my patients who had a positive mindset and were close to God, recovered much quicker than expected, or didn't get sick at all.

When Scientists studied Mycoplasma which is considered to be a bacteria (or germ) that can infect different parts of your body, including your brain. Scientists were somewhat confused by what they saw in their initial research and said it looks like a prion which is a misfolded protein that can transmit its misfolded shape onto normal variants of the same protein. Prions are known to be the causative agent of several transmissible and fatal neurodegenerative diseases found in people and animals. Something that can affect the brain like this was called mad cow disease, which was considered a progressive neurologic **disease**. Some researchers said it looks like a virus, others said it looked like an amyloid as it makes this sort of scarring in the body and brain. Still, others concluded it was a bacteria and should be treated as such. Which begs the question why would all these doctors and researchers have such different opinions on something? It's because they were all correct. This Mycoplasma thing can change as it doesn't have cell walls so it can change shapes and look like something different at any given time. We could call it a shapeshifter. I bring this to your attention because when scientists are describing these spike proteins from Covid that are supposedly making people sick, it is identical to this. Sometimes it is acting like a prion, sometimes it acts like a virus, sometimes it acts like this amyloid and sometimes it acts like a bacteria. So, it is constantly changing and identical to what is called Mycoplasma.

Understand that the neurotoxin is what makes it so pathogenic or poisonous to you as it goes to the nervous system and it's not quite all biological as it's part synthetic. We are looking at something that appears robotic not from nature. In the earliest report, I was able to obtain before they were scrubbed from the internet looked like it was a crystalline cholesterol compound, which is similar to snake venom, and which makes it quite toxic.

What I did, when I was treating patients was that I came to understand that if it was a poison that was making people sick, I should administer a Cholestyramine powder that usually binds to cholesterol and is known to bind the neurotoxins. So, I started to use it off label and it works very well. As it would bind the poison from the bacteria and as toxicity went down the patient could overcome their symptoms.

Back in the day the CDC and the public health department along with a federal agent were all very interested, because I was showing data on this in my clinic when there was an outbreak of this happening in Georgia. There was the day it started and the day it stopped, and I had the blood work to prove when these patients had positive antibodies and when they were cleared out. Interestingly enough when these patients recovered, I found myself dealing with researchers from the CDC and federal agents who asked me how are you clearing these antibodies out? Because it is not supposed to happen. Now I didn't tell them outright, but I had everything in my charts, and they just couldn't figure it out. Cholestyramine powder is good for a lot of things including irritable bowel syndrome. My point in telling you this is that there is something that they had been developing for decades to be the most potent bioweapons and they also knew that they couldn't harm you unless you had a fearful mind that compromised your immune system along with a weakened body. So here I was just this small-town doctor figuring out that Cholestyramine powder could work against their bioweapons. I implore you not to become fearful of the propaganda they push through mainstream news networks.

We are miraculous beings made in the image of God our Heavenly Father. If we simply remember that and embrace what is in the Holy Scriptures, we should not give in to fearing anything that they can create, because nothing they can create can come anywhere close to what our Heavenly Father can do and create.

PC: *Amen to that our God is all powerful, and they who serve the kingdom of darkness are really quite limited in the grand scheme of things. The Lord even tells us in places like Matthew 28:18 And Jesus came and spake unto them, saying, All power is given unto me in heaven and in earth.*

If I understand mathematics correctly and, in the Greek, and Aramaic, I looked up that word all and it means everything. So how much power does that leave for the devil or anyone else. Beside the Lord told us in places like Luke 10:19 Behold, I give unto you power to tread on serpents and scorpions, and over all the power of the enemy: and nothing shall by any means hurt you.

Could you share a wee bit about that meeting you attended that Craig Venter spoke at some years ago?

CM: I honestly think in my opinion that what they called Mycoplasma back then is what we are dealing with today. Considering all the Covid patients I successfully treated as if they had Mycoplasma recovered with antibiotics, some didn't even need the Cholestyramine powder.

Isn't that strange that the official narratives are telling you that you have a virus, but it is treatable with an antibiotic? They also have hindered and withholding the antibiotics that could have helped so many people recover.

I consider that the Lord gave me a divine appointment a few years ago with J. Craig Venter who is an American biotechnologist and businessman and was someone working with the human genome project.

He is most likely very responsible for much of what we see unfolding today in our world.

It was in 2013 that I was invited to attend this meeting and quite honestly, I was not prepared for what I was stepping into in that exclusive meeting as Craig Venter asked those in attendance, " What is god? God creates and now I can create so I am a god and my associates in the scientific community can be god.

I recall thinking this will be interesting; I have never heard anyone be so arrogant and erroneously bold like that before. Venter felt that all of us are simply fragile little beings and that most people are just messed up. He was extremely narcissistic in the way he communicated with us and came across as a very cold psychopath. He seemed convinced that all life was merely a software system and didn't believe there could be a real God who is almighty. In Venter's perspective of the world, it was just ones and zeros, and you just map out the genome with your instructions and create life and have the power to change it around to your approval. Venter elaborated that if he could change the software in you and alter your genome so that he could change your species.

I was there and he actually said this. I am not telling you what he said was true, but I want you to know who is behind the scenes manipulating and driving the things happening in our world today. The mentality in these groups of individuals is that they consider themselves to be like gods. I feel it is important that you understand who we are up against.

They clearly have a profound disdain for our Heavenly Father, our creator, and believe that they can become better and more powerful them Him.

This sounds a lot something we read in the Holy Bible, doesn't it? We only need to review the biblical accounts of the Tower of Babel and the first-world dictator Nimrod to understand how we are seeing the same spirit of the antichrist manifesting again in our world today.

You need to understand how to engage in the battle before us today which is first a spiritual war.

In this meeting in 2013 where all this was taking place, Craig Venter spoke about bacteria on earth like ecoli and declared what he could do to alter the genome by changing its blueprint. For example, if he could take an earthworm and put the genome of another animal inside the cells, and so now you have two cells inside each other and they have a way that can erase or melt the original one, so on the outside, it looks like a cell from earth like ecoli and on the inside it's an earthworm genome. He was claiming that he could do this procedure with humans and put the different genomes in us. He also stated that his favorite thing to work with was Mycoplasma. All this keeps going back to the same organism again and again.

Why do I feel this is so important, well obviously Craig Venter is playing god and scientists have already been creating chimeras, which is taking an organism consisting of two or more tissues of different genetic composition, which can then be manipulated through genetic engineering, along with organ transplants and grafting procedures. In other words, they are splicing two different animals together to create a new species.

In Greek mythology, they had things like a lion's head on a goat's body with a serpent's tail. Scientists have already announced that they have successfully created human-animal hybrids. Which begs the question do they have a spirit; do they have a soul?

This is also what was going on in the Days of Noah before the flood with the Nephilim, which was the merging of fallen angels with human women we read about in Genesis chapter 4.

We don't know the exact date of Christ's return, but we ought to understand what season we are now in considering how they are putting different genomes together.

Now all these things are not easily done as they are using a substance called hydrogel. But what I want you to understand is how all things that were spoken of in this conference in 2013 they are trying to implement now.

Again, we must not be afraid of these things because if you know who you are, and what you are and you are a born-again son or daughter of the true living God in Jesus/Yeshua then you are divinely protected.

Sadly, in our world today many people are confused and don't know who or what they are, and they have not connected to our Heavenly Father. So, they are easily deceived and fall for the tricks of the kingdom of darkness. That is why you are reading this book, so you don't fall for the deceptions and tricks going on worldwide.

I saw a documentary about 15 or more years ago on the VMAT2 gene which is often called the God gene.

VMAT2 is a neurotransmitter transporter encoded by the SLC18A2 (solute carrier family 18 member A2) gene. Researchers dubbed it the "God gene" due to its association with connecting to the spiritual part of our brains.

They were saying that they were interested in finding people who had the ability to heal with the laying on of hands. This means that they started to study such people.

PC: *Yes, we read in*

1 Corinthians 12:9 - To another faith by the same Spirit; to another the gifts of healing by the same Spirit.

10 To another the working of miracles; to another prophecy; to another discerning of spirits; to another divers kinds of tongues; to another the interpretation of tongues.

CM: What the researchers did was to put such people with healing gifts in a MIR machine to study them and put some sugar throughout their bodies and had them begin to pray to record what areas of their brains would light up as these people were deeply in their prayer mode. They eventually were able to map out the areas of the brain that were engaged in lighting up during times of prayers. At this point, they determined what genes were related to those areas of the brain. They got to a point where they believed that they found the gene that was associated with someone who deeply and spiritually connected with God Almighty to the point where they could heal others by the laying on of hands as well as speaking in tongues and angelic languages. These researchers felt they could now control the spiritual connection through the VMAT2 God gene. Understand that the scientists who were doing these experiments brought their research to the military.

The military intelligence division thought, if they could control the passionate religious people from fighting us, we could easily beat them. The American military didn't mind telling the public at that point they were using this epigenetic knowledge to control the Iraqi soldiers. They said if they could turn the God gene off, and not completely destroy or disable it so the person would no longer feel so passionate and want to keep fighting them as they would become very docile. Whether they actually used this technique is still up for debate. This is the sort of thing that our Military and DARPA are involved in, considering there are scientists who have gone along with this.

I don't personally think that stopping a gene from an expression could stop me from loving my Heavenly Father, but if someone never had that born-again experience, or has never been introduced to the Lord Jesus/Yeshua as their savior and does not know that they can be saved, maybe this could work to some degree. Nevertheless, I want you to know that Craig Venture is behind this project, and when they found that gene he went to the Supreme Court Justice and said that he wanted to patent and own this VMAT2 gene. The Supreme Court Judges told him no he could not do that. He appeared to have a temper tantrum as other scientists were also opposing him in his efforts.

At this point, he had an idea, and you can guess which kingdom inspired him in this pursuit so he came back to the court asking, "What if I can put something synthetic in that gene then could I own it?" The Supreme Court judges said, yes you can!

So, at that moment on June 13, 2013, the Supreme Court said that any human that has a synthetic gene inside them could be owned by the patent owner.

"June 13, 2013, the Supreme Court said that any human that has a synthetic gene inside them could be owned by the patient owner."

PC: *Sadly, doesn't appear that many people know or understand about this. Seems to me we are observing ancient prophesies being fulfilled right before us today.*

CM: This should have never happened; nobody should ever be owned as it goes against the law of God Almighty. In the

80s an Israeli researcher found something amazing that Craig Venter knows about. When you are looking at the whole human genome there are a lot of patterns and colors and codes and one of them which was repeatedly found in our genome was the name of God. Our DNA is composed of 4 basic elements of hydrogen, nitrogen, oxygen, and carbon, and when they are all connected, they form the Hebrew letters Y-H-W-H which is the signature of the name of God.

Craig Venter and his associates understanding that God Almighty's signature is written into his people's DNA chose to try and rewrite their signatures over God's work. 46 scientists wrote their names inside this genome because after all they foolishly think they are gods. What does this sound like? Seems to be quite similar to the MO (mode of operation) of Satan. Only someone who thinks like that would do that.

The next thing that they want to do is a new alphabet or syntax. Why is this important, because the word you use is powerful. John 1:1 In the beginning was the Word, and the Word was with God, and the Word was God.2 The same was in the beginning with God.3 All things were made by him; and without him was not anything made that was made.

God breathed us into life and words are powerful. Proverbs 18:21 Death and life are in the power of the tongue: and they that love it shall eat the fruit thereof.

Changing what a word means also changes its frequency, which is like changing a radio dial, so you are tuning into another station. That could mean you aren't able to hear our Heavenly Father as much. There's a point to everything that they are doing in their quest to become gods.

Let us consider the email, according to Craig Venter an email states who you belong to, and it can be traced back to its creator should you go astray. Is that talking about bacteria, I don't think so.

Here are the three messages, which indicate the mindset of these scientists doing this they placed inside the gene.

1." To live, to err, to fall, to triumph, to recreate life out of life." James Joyce

To me, this sounds like a fallen angel quotation, because they lived, and they messed up and they fell, and they triumphed as they tricked the human. Also, they cannot create life, but they attempt to recreate life.

2. " See things not as they are, but how they might be." A quote from the book American Prometheus."

Doesn't this sound like someone who is trying to deceive you and lead you astray? Don't see things as they really are or believe what we are saying. They believe in the new math. 1+1 can = 12. This goes along with all the terrible things they are teaching the children now so that the educational system is now an indoctrination system teaching lies.

3. " What I cannot build, I cannot understand." Richard Feynman. That is a terrible way to be thinking about the world, that means you take away the supernatural and the way of God. If you can't understand or build it, you take away love. You take away creativity and imagination and everything that makes us, us. Do they just want to break it down to nothing but a robotic structure? This is what Craig

Venter, and his associates stand for, and it is clear which kingdom they serve.

Craig Venter also said that he could take the genome and make it into a computerized binary code. Why would he want to do that? By the way, he works with all the top upper echelons of the world leaders. For example, he works with NASA and DARPA and all the other nation's top groups as well as the World Economic Forum. He also believes he can take that computer code with a small device he has patented called the Digital Biological Converter which can download your medicine for your so-called vaccine for example. He told us in that meeting in 2013 that soon none of us would have jobs as doctors shortly, that we all be looking for something new to do instead. Because in his mind our bodies would be so transformed that he be able to download new vaccines into our mobile/cell phones and from there directly into our bodies.

This is what he said in that meeting, and I'm not telling you it's possible, just that Craig Venter said it was going to happen. Venter has been working with NASA and of course, he is proud of this as he talked about how we need to go and explore other life forms.

He asked, what if we could bring back a superhuman genome and put that superhuman genome inside of us? At this point, he began sharing how they are working on Mars. They have robots doing explorations on Mars and going around collecting soil samples. Of course, they have since announced that they have discovered a little bacteria on Mars.

What the robots are doing is scanning the genome and categorizing it and putting it into a binary code like a computer code. At which point they are uploading the computer code. He said there will come a time as Mars is closest to Earth when they can transmit it and it would take 4.3 minutes to get to Earth with the code. Once it's downloaded here and he said they have a very secure site, so don't worry who of these scientists could possibly mess up?

So, once it's down in a secure site, consider that that can insert a different genome into any cell. Perhaps like a bacteria cell, and that is incredibly dangerous as they supposedly are placing this inside a Martian bacteria. I mean what could go wrong? " Right."

You can probably still goggle this online for now do some research and look up bacteria on Mars.

PC: *Here are the headlines from NASA February 26, 2001*

"Scientists Find Evidence of Ancient Microbial Life on Mars."[4]

CM: There is one bacterium named Conan, and keep in mind that Craig Venter and his associates claim that they already have the genome. What could possibly go wrong with them transmitting it here on Earth?

Here is an article from the Smithsonian who has a hand in obfuscating numerous things like the evidence of bones of Nephilim.

PC: *I looked this up and here are the links you are telling us about.*

'Conan the Bacterium' Has What It Takes to Survive on Mars[5]

October 27, 2022

After experiments here on Earth, researchers say some hardy microbes could endure hundreds of millions of years on the Red Planet

CM: My point in sharing all this is to help you understand there are scientists and researchers today who are quite simply out of control in the evil that they are participating in and utilizing a technology that goes beyond their wisdom. In other words, they are like babies with an atomic bomb in their hands. The alien narratives to my understanding are simply fallen angels. In essence, Craig Venter is indirectly admitting they are dealing with fallen angel's technology.

This is also why they have gotten to use technologies that they don't quite understand as they are trying to bring this to earth. They are trying to mix up and merge the genomes because they believe they are little gods who can experiment on all of us. They have a profound disdain for our Heavenly Father, our creator. They erroneously think that they should be the owners of everything and manipulate everything to their choosing. The things they are saying and doing harmonies quite well with Satan our adversary.

This is absolutely who we are now dealing with.

Considering that for decades now they have been able to humanize a pig, for example. On the outside, you may still look like you, but on the inside, you could be something quite different. On the outside, they may still look like pigs, and you couldn't tell the difference, but on the inside, they might have 100% human blood and organs.

Is that disturbing to you because it certainly is to me?

Let me just say that I would not eat pork anymore. Could some of these creatures be included in the food supply? Is it a form of a human or a pig? We are in a world that now has to question what is, what. Transhumanists think everything should be mixed up like this. They may say we are doing this to help people who need organ transplants, and by the way, such experiments have been going on for a long time like at Emory University and other medical schools.

Do you really think any of these experiments are to benefit you?

There is a chamber of congress in Atlanta called MAC, (The Metro Atlanta Chamber) One of their subsidiaries is called Internet of Things. Atlanta. Exploring what they have on their website you will discover they are wanting to turn Atlanta into a totally digital Smart City. They also think we should be eating worms. They have already put censors into streetlights and other such things to help with globalized surveillance.

In 2014 I was invited to a meeting with them and went because at the time I was still naive about these fantastical ideas they were already implementing.

They told me that they could help me as I was already having trouble with certain people coming to my clinic to tell me not to be doing what I was doing helping my patients recover, and how they were not paying the insurance bills because again I was still learning about these bioweapons. So, at this one meeting, the only time I went it was an important meeting and another divine appointment. We were all bused into this meeting and discovered all our cell phones were jammed and would not function and then they locked the doors.

Ospitek, Spine Center Atlanta partner to implement IoT and AI-enabled platform (Linking the physical patient journey to a fully digitized experience will unlock a tremendous amount of actionable performance data and AI-driven insights on patient throughput, OR utilization, scheduling performance, environmental condition management, the patient experience, and more.) https://www.iot-now.com/2022/11/02/125039-ospitek-spine-center-atlanta-partner-to-implement-iot-and-ai-enabled-platform/

Doesn't sound like a very nice business owners meeting, does it? I of course felt upset being there with all I was experiencing at this meeting. I tried to leave the meeting and they opened the door to let me out, at which point I realized that I didn't know where we were and not having a working phone didn't help, so they allowed me back in.

I sat down and there were a lot of people there from CNN and Delta corporations as well as big Tech companies. I felt like a very small fish in a big pond. Some of the people there laughed at me when they learned that I was a medical doctor.

They said soon we won't need any medical doctors. Because they felt that our bodies will be so radically changed that there will no longer be any use for human doctors anymore.

Dr. Sanjay Gupta from CNN was the main speaker who also appears on Sesame Street to help brainwash your children into taking these depopulation injections, so-called vaccines. He tells the children watching him on Sesame Street that once they have these injections, they will become like superheroes with superhuman powers. So, they will all become more intelligent and become super strong. Clearly, they are lying to your children and grandchildren. Best you take them out of the schools to protect them. The public schools are now government schools and it's not to educate your children as much as it is designed to indoctrinate them. Someday Dr. Gupta and all those along with him deceiving others will answer for what they have done.

In this meeting back in 2014 Dr. Gupta talked about why they are pushing these injections. It has nothing to do with health and wellness and fighting infections. It had everything to do with getting superconducting material inside the human body, with biosensors.

Because once they get enough of these materials inside your body, they can begin tracking your every move. In other words, it means they can spy on what is going on inside your body. So, he was describing that the technology was so good back then that they could monitor your heart rate and blood sugar levels etc. They will know if you are running or walking or sleeping. They thought at the time they could also understand and be able to read your thoughts 85% of the time with great accuracy to know what you are thinking and even dreaming. They wanted to use this as a method of predictive policing, especially with the minority report to stop you before you could commit a crime. Disregarding the crimes, they were themselves guilty of, by destroying your God-given freedom.

Dr. Gupta also thought the people of Atlanta were out of control, and that they were too racist and not medically and culturally advancing enough so they wanted to stop that happening in Atlanta. Why, because they wanted more business to come into the city and bring in more money, at least that was their excuse at this time. Dr. Gupta talked about how they could stop the people of Atlanta from lying by sweat gland analysis which is called Electrodermal Analysis, which is also called Meridian Stress Assessment or Electro-Acupuncture. Because everyone's health app already has everything, I am telling you about. You can try to erase it from your screen, but it will still be there running in the background, just waiting to be activated. So, they felt this technology was as good or better than a police station. Also, their technology would analyze voice inflection, they would know if you drank any alcohol, if you took medicine or any drugs, as well as how much you took. They would know everything; they would know if you were fertile and if you are having sexual intimacy. Why would they want to know that?

Dr. Gupta said that they could do that because of the biosensors. Why do they want to do this? Because every time a person would tell a lie, and this is his own words I quote verbatim. "They would shock the person." When we in the audience gasped in shock at his statement, Dr. Gupta said. "Oh, you don't like that word, I will instead use the word buzz." So, I can only assume what he actually meant, I personally don't think it would be a true shock to the brain and body. Rather I think they would put an impulse in the body because now you have something synthetic in you. Meaning you would have with these biosensors something that can react to an impulse. It is like sending a WIFI message inside your body. Once those biosensors are in there something could be triggered, like a certain drug could be released, like a sedative or a hormone. This is how transhumanists are thinking and let me add this, most of you would probably know of several people who were attending this particular meeting. They came from all social economic statuses and all races to attend along with numerous people of political affiliations and including some church leadership who were present.

All of them knew about this and they had the audacity to sit there and eat dinner with these people we might call vipers. I get quite upset trying to share about this and expose this evil. Knowing that we are surrounded by them today. I am also disregarding the non-disclosure that I was coerced into signing there. I must speak out considering how none of those other people are willing to take a stand against these nefarious agendas and plans as they are cowering in fear.

This is why I was there to learn and understand, because I belong to God's kingdom, not their kingdom of Satan so that now I can show you what they are talking about behind closed doors and how they think about you and me. This is not going to happen on our watch for the people who serve God's Kingdom. We might be fewer in number, but we serve God who is Almighty.

Dr. Gupta is too fearful to speak to the adults who might push back on him, so he goes after your children, and he treats them like cattle.

So, after how many shocks you will get for telling any lies after several months, it would be added up, even what we call a white lie, it would all be run by a computer system, and you would be dealt with according to their rules. Like the Chinese Credit score system.

For example, if you are late to work or a meeting and say on the telephone that you are only 15 minutes away when you in fact aren't and let us face it, we have all done such things, they will know.

Why would you want to eradicate that aspect of life, when that is part of what makes us, us? It is a wonderful thing about being human that we can share a wide range of emotions, tell a joke or cover for each other in certain situations, even if we aren't being completely truthful. Nevertheless, transhumanists want to eliminate such things and behaviors.

I also don't think their technology works as well as they think it does and this is something they plan on implementing in the entire world.

Keep in mind we are dealing with people like Bill Gates and his Microsoft patient 2020060606 that is about having biosensors inside your body, and how your cell phone goes to 5G band width, where their supercomputer controls it. This is their Artificial Intelligence god which they desire to control the entire world with.

At the World Economic Forum, Pastor Caspar frequently shared in conferences how all the nations involved in lockstep want this world domination to happen by 2030. How we would all be spied on having been injected with biosensors so they will know everything we try and do. Again, this is their erroneous plan, it is not God Almighty's plan.

If you look up the company Profusa and Lumee, they are with DARPA and using these injectable hydrogels, which are inside these shots that they falsely call vaccines that they have pushed along with their Covid-19 official narratives. At this point forward I would not trust in any vaccine as they are trying to make them all the same which has nothing to do with trying to make you healthy.

Rather it is to get surveillance inside of your body, and that is the point of everything that has been happening since 2020. It only had one purpose, which is to tag and track every human being on this planet.

If you have taken any of these Covid shots I implore you please don't take any more of them, because it appears to be an accumulative process.

They may think they are creating new life, as Craig Venter claims. But they haven't, they are liars, and they can't create life. All they have done is taken what God has already created here and they highjacked it and tried to manipulate and modified it. They have made a Frankenstein monster instead, and that is not creating new life. That is the mode of operation of Satan.

So, they are trying to hack into us and alter humanity, what is the difference between a human and Cyborg? It is a being that has both organic and biomechatronic body parts. The term was coined in 1960 by Manfred Clynes and Nathan S. Kline which comes from them blending the words cybernetic and organism to describe a **person** whose physiological functions are enhanced by artificial technology. This is what they are now offering you and telling you that it will improve your life. They want to turn us into soft robots which means they want to put artificial technology inside of us. My advice to you is do not comply. I can tell you with great certainty from being in these meetings that they do not believe in our Heavenly Father as Creator and they are definitely serving the antichrist, willingly or unknowingly. They absolutely believe in world domination and control and appear to even enjoy seeing the suffering of humans with enslavement. The people running these programs do not have your best interest at heart, I promise you that.

Again, what is most important is not to fear what is happening in this world, rather we should have an awesome fear or reverence of our Heavenly Father our creator because he is ultimately in control.

What we are going through right now was written about in the Holy Scriptures thousands of years ago. That is amazing to contemplate.

God loves us and He did not create us to watch us all crash and burn and do nothing. He created us because we are part of seeing some of the greatest miracles ever to happen. We are here for such a time as this to help many souls come into Salvation in Christ.

We shall see glorious things that will happen in our future, don't focus on the sickness and diseases of this fallen world, rather focus on the Kingdom of God, because that is why we are here.

There are only two choices in this life, and we must choose one or the other. God does truly love us and doesn't want you to make the wrong choice. John 1:1 In the beginning was the Word, and the Word was with God, and the Word was God.

The most important commandment is to love God and then love yourself and others. Keeping our connection to God is our strength and salvation. It is important to pray and worship the Lord Jesus/Yeshua and it's good to sing and dance, hug and kiss, create, build, cook, and help teach others. Doing everything they tell us not to do because all these things are what make us human.

If you have children in government-run public schools, I will strongly advise taking them out and starting a community school with other like-minded believers. Those public schools have been brainwashing the children, like the Chinese reeducation camps.

Have regular meetings with the neighborhood people in your tribe. You should physically meet with them at least once a week at a minimum. I think in the future we may all need to live in close proximity to each other who are part of the body of Christ.

By all means possible do not comply with draconian measures. You do this by learning and knowing what God's laws are and doing them. Everything you need to understand is in the Holy Scriptures.

Research God's law/common law. You will discover that there are two kinds of laws. They have purposely dumbed down society so we would not know our rights. In the courtrooms we have presently they are fraudulent. The lawyers are all under Blacks law. Every lawyer who is a bar attorney is a British accredited registry and they serve only the crown of England. As a ward of the court in Black's dictionary you are signing in as an infant or a person of an unsound mind. In other words, you are telling the court system that you are mentally retarded and need them to take care of you. Now you know why you are treated poorly in most courtrooms. However, you can actually take your stand as a son or daughter of God, under God's law in a court of law. Because we are literally dealing with the devil because there are two kingdoms. Understanding this is empowering, and it is something every child of God can do to walk in more freedom this way. The Holy Scriptures will become more alive for you as you take a stand like this.

We are all going to have to eventually start our own underground medical hubs with other apprenticeships. There are groups working on this as I write this helping to make this a legal practice, considering how the medical system we presently have is beyond repair.

Oppose 5G because it is not really to make anything work faster, it's really only being set up for enslavement.

Research about these injections. Even if you have taken one or more of them, please don't take anymore and know that with God there's always a way to be whole and restored. (Isaiah 43:16-19)

There is always a way to wipe out whatsoever programs they have injected inside of you.

The Heartmath Institute tells us that your heart is about 100.000 times electrically stronger than the brain and up to 5.000 times stronger magnetically than the brain. This is measurable in science.

In the average person, our heart is filled with love that can be measured to go out from you by six feet. This is why they wanted us to stay six feet away from each other, so we don't connect. Consider how sometimes you are around someone, and you might feel a coldness emanating from them or a loving warmth from them. It is measurable that those who pray and our connecting with God Almighty those measurements can go out much further than six feet.

Again, if water crystals can be altered and changed by words, as Dr. Emoto has proven that with prayer and attention to saying certain words as words are powerful by how we say it or write it with our minds you can change the crystal structure of water.

Anytime they used negative words like, "You fool, I hate you." those water crystals became very distorted. Contrast this by when saying a positive word like," I love you and the water crystals become extremely beautiful. Keeping in mind that we are mostly made of water and the things around us that are made of water can be affected by what we think, speak, and do. Every word is powerful.

Embrace the truth that you can change others, yourself, and the things around you this way. Because we truly were made in the image of God.

Ephesians 6:11- Put on the whole armor of God, that you may be able to stand against the schemes of the devil. 12 For we do not wrestle against flesh and blood, but against the rulers, against the authorities, against the cosmic powers over this present darkness, against the spiritual forces of evil in the heavenly places.

2 Kings 6:16 He said, "Do not be afraid, for those who are with us are more than those who are with them."

PC: *This has been a wonderfully profound and insightful conversation, thank you for sharing this with us.*

I told someone in an interview that I gave last year how I was listening to my new double album Walking In Authority when it was released that has you and some of our erudite speaker friends on cover with the band, and how I was driving your parents from the airport after you survived that terrible plane crash in July of 2022. I recall realising most every song I wrote on that album was influenced by conversations like this that we had or listening to you speak and conferences we both ministered at.

What would like share as your closing statement?

CM: There is always hope in Christ, I believe that with all my heart.

Romans 15:13 - Now the God of hope fill you with all joy and peace in believing, that ye may abound in hope, through the power of the Holy Ghost.

Carrie Madej is a trained Osteopath and sought-after conference speaker.

https://www.carriemadej.com

CHAPTER 9

CHAOS ON THE RAMPAGE – THERE IS A SOLUTION

MIKE SPAULDING

How many would agree with me that nearly everything we see and hear today from America's mainstream corporate owned media outlets IS PROPAGANDA!

I recently found a new term I was not familiar with that is being used today as a means of distracting people from this reality that nearly everything is propaganda.

A new form of propaganda has risen in our day. It goes by various names. The one I like best has been dubbed **"impression management."** As with all forms of propaganda, impression management is really nothing more than the art of distraction renamed.

In other words, show people something shiny in one hand to distract them from what you are doing with the other hand.

Our nation has been slowly programmed to be susceptible to

this type of propaganda. The methodology of this particular programming involved shortening the attention spans of people so that they do not bother to think analytically or linearly from something presented as fact, to the implications of that proposition, or to the logical outcome of any proposition.

This seems to be the favored approach to mind manipulation.

In the past, politicians have used this technique deftly over many decades. One clear example from the past was to drop news late on a Friday afternoon when things are winding down for the week, hoping that the news cycle would miss it or report on it late and obviously after-the-fact, when a simple "what difference does it make now" would suffice to placate people.

Today, with the major media outlets all owned by a handful of corporations, and those corporations long since co-opted into American Fascism, there is no need to be concerned about news reporting that would raise the ire of a nation's population. The media machine simply marches in lockstep with the government and refuses to report on certain things.

The East Palestine, Ohio, train derailment is one glaring example. The news of this environmental disaster was first ignored, then suppressed such that journalists arriving on the scene to film and interview people were arrested. Where were all the radical green wackos that chain themselves to trees to save a snail? They were nowhere to be found.

Did you noticed how fast Biden and the US Government jumped to bail out the banks recently? How do they maintain the false narrative that the Dems are all about the little guy? The disadvantaged? The poor? It's complete baloney. There are a few (very few) politicians that care one whit about any of us.

The game today is to put into place instruments that not just silence but dismantle the true remnant ecclesia of Christ, while entertaining the masses to keep them distracted.

Here are two examples. One, the recent Grammys and, two, the last Super Bowl halftime show.

Sam Smith at Grammy's was pure distraction. This was nothing but an advertisement to young people that Satan is cool, and he can make you wealthy and famous.

Rhianna's performance at the 2023 Super Bowl halftime show was again, blatant promotion of Satanism. It is all distraction and propaganda.

John Stonestreet from Break Point, a media ministry of the Colson Center, reported that Jewish conservative commentator Ben Shapiro "described perfectly the kind of satanism on display" at the Grammys in a Twitter thread.

HERE'S THE TWITTER THREAD BY SHAPIRO:

For most of religious history, Satan was the great villain, an emblem of rebellion against the Good and the True, a symbol of resistance to the Holy.

When John Milton wrote Paradise Lost (1667), his Satan famously stated, "better to reign in Hell, than serve in Heav'n." Satan was the villain of the piece, abandoning the

Good and the True for a personal sense of power.

For transgressive poet Percy Shelley, however, Satan was the hero of Paradise Lost: "Milton's Devil as a moral being is as far superior to his God as one who perseveres in some purpose which he has conceived to be excellent in spite of adversity and torture."

Why did he believe this? Because he believed that the essence of "love" is "liberty," that the goal of life is subjective "happiness," and that "religion and morality, as they now stand, compose a practical code of misery and servitude."

This is the message of our modern-day Satanists as well. Religion and morality are evils. Worship of "authenticity," particularly in the sexual realm, is the highest possible good. Worship Satan by worshipping yourself.

There is one other statement that Shapiro made that was not included in the Breakpoint article. Shapiro said, "To even notice that this happened is to draw fire: 'Hey, why are you even noticing? Why do you care?" This is the Face Tattoo Syndrome in action: do something highly provocative, then act shocked and appalled when people are provoked."

Clearly, entertainment is being used to condition people.

It's called intentionally drawing attention from Christians and social/political conservatives so that you can ridicule them for being out of touch and/or fuddy-duddies or worse.

This of course, happened soon after the scandalous Balenciaga ad campaign of late 2022 featuring clear images of bondage and references to child pornography and pedophilia.

WHAT'S GOING ON?

We are being intentionally distracted by the increasing level of in-your-face evil.

At a time when we of all people, – blood bought, born-again, redeemed, believers and disciples of the Lord Jesus Christ, should be preparing ourselves, our families, our ecclesias, and our larger network of believers to prepare for what has come upon America and the world, we are too busy being offended, outraged, and distracted from our primary goal.

This plays into the hands of the wicked oligarchs and globalist fascists.

We MUST remember that we lose every time we play by the world's rules.

The Bible means what it says when it says, "The weapons of our warfare are not of the flesh (carnal), but divinely powerful for the destruction of fortresses" (2 Corinthians 10:4).

But, let me answer the question of "What's going on?"

We are being played friends. Just like the street vendors and their shell game. Can you watch the shell that contains the object of your attention?

Solutions for the End Times

DISTRACTION IS STILL A POWERFUL TOOL

Most everyone knows who Klaus Schwab is. He is the leader of the World Economic Forum and is responsible for much of the globalist agenda we see being implemented today.

Unfortunately, not as many people know who Yuval Noah Harari is.

Yuval Noah Harari is the "Philosopher" of the World Economic Forum.

What does it mean for us that Harari is the Philosopher of the WEF?

It means that he supplies the moral, ethical, and theological ideas and basis for the agenda of the World Economic Forum.

In other words, he writes and speaks in such a way that resistance to his ideas and the agenda of the World Economic Forum is mitigated and seen as uncompassionate and ignorant.

How does he accomplish this? He accomplishes this through his non-stop interviews, lectures, media appearances and his books.

Here is a quote from Harari – **"History began when humans invented gods and will end when humans become gods."**[6]

He made this statement at a **"Climate Change and Ecological Collapse"** conference where he was busy spreading fear and drumming up support for nonsensical global legislation for a problem the globalists invented – global warming, now called Climate Change. A much more ambiguous phrase that can be used for increasing or decreasing global temperatures. It is once again, pure propaganda from the globalists.

For Harari, the only reasonable goal for humanity is to throw off the idea that there is a god and pursue our own path to becoming a god. Along the way we have to create a new "Eden" of paradise right here on earth.

This explains why he wrote his series of books describing his belief that humans invented god. Our destiny lies in discovering that we are gods, according to Harari.

HARARI'S BOOK - SAPIENS: A BRIEF HISTORY OF MANKIND

Harari believes that:

> "Homo sapiens rules the world because it is the only animal that can believe in things that exist purely in its own imagination, such as gods, states, money, and human rights.
>
> Starting from this provocative idea, Sapiens goes on to retell the history of our species from a completely fresh perspective. It explains that money is the most pluralistic system of mutual trust ever devised; that capitalism is the most successful religion ever invented; that the treatment of animals in modern agriculture is probably the worst crime in history; and that even though we are far more powerful than our ancient ancestors, we aren't much happier.

Here is what the publisher says about this book:

By combining profound insights with remarkably vivid language, Sapiens acquired cult status among diverse audiences, captivating teenagers as well as university professors, animal rights activists alongside government ministers. 23 million copies had been sold around the world and the book was translated into 65 languages."[7]

HARARI'S BOOK - HOMO DEUS: A BRIEF HISTORY OF TOMORROW

"Homo Deus: A Brief History of Tomorrow examines what might happen to the world when old myths are coupled with new godlike technologies, such as artificial intelligence and genetic engineering.

Humans conquered the world thanks to their unique ability to believe in collective myths about gods, money, equality and freedom – as described in Sapiens: A Brief History of Humankind. In Homo Deus, Prof. Harari looks to the future and explores how global power might shift, as the principal force of evolution – natural selection – is replaced by intelligent design.

What will happen to democracy when Google and Facebook come to know our likes and our political preferences better than we know them ourselves? What will happen to the welfare state when computers push humans out of the job market and create a massive new "useless class"? How might Islam handle genetic engineering? Will Silicon Valley end up producing new religions, rather than just novel gadgets?

As Homo sapiens becomes Homo deus, what new destinies will we set for ourselves? As the self-made gods of planet earth, which projects should we undertake, and how will we protect this fragile planet and humankind itself from our own destructive powers? The book Homo Deus gives us a glimpse of the dreams and nightmares that will shape the 21st century."[8]

HARARI'S BOOK - 21 LESSONS FOR THE 21ST CENTURY says this:

"In a world deluged by irrelevant information, clarity is power. Censorship works not by blocking the flow of information, but rather by flooding people with disinformation and distractions. 21 Lessons for the 21st Century cuts through these muddy waters and confronts some of the most urgent questions on today's global agenda.

Why is liberal democracy in crisis? Is God back? Is a new world war coming? What does the rise of Donald Trump signify? What can we do about the epidemic of fake news? Which civilisation dominates the world – the West, China, Islam? Should Europe keep its doors open to immigrants? Can nationalism solve the problems of inequality and climate change? What should we do about terrorism? What should we teach our kids?

Billions of us can hardly afford the luxury of investigating these questions, because we have more pressing things to do; we have to go to work, take care of the kids, or look after elderly parents. Unfortunately, history makes no concessions. If the future of humanity is decided in your absence, because you are too busy feeding and clothing your kids – you and they will not be exempt from the consequences. This is very unfair; but who said history was fair?

A book doesn't give people food or clothes – but it can offer some clarity, thereby helping to level the global playing field. If this book empowers even a handful of people to join the debate about the future of our species, it has done its job."[9]

Perhaps the most alarming book he has written is for children.

HARARI'S BOOK - UNSTOPPABLE US: HOW HUMANS TOOK OVER THE WORLD, says this:

"We humans aren't strong like lions, we don't swim as well as dolphins, and we definitely don't have wings! So how did we end up ruling the world? The answer to that is one of the strangest tales you'll ever hear. AND it's a true story."

From Harari's website:

> *Unstoppable Us* is the New York Times bestselling children's book series from Yuval Noah Harari, to be published in 4 volumes, with beautiful colour illustrations by Ricard Zaplana Ruiz.
>
> In this immersive and mind-blowing adventure, the bestselling author brings his signature style to a younger audience for the first time, revealing that humans have a superpower, and that we've used it to

create strange and mysterious things — from ghosts and spirits to governments and corporations. We are all-conquering and insatiable, most creative and most destructive. Or in a word, unstoppable!

The series engages pre-teens with the baffling true story of the most powerful animals on the planet, highlighting that the world in which we live didn't have to be the way it is. People made it what it is, and people can change it.

Harari's writing style is accessible and entertaining, applying plain language to complex questions and using humour as a way into serious topics. Each volume in the series will explore a different part of our history, kicking off with *How Humans Took Over the World*, which invites young readers to discover why money is the most successful fairy tale ever, how fire shrank our stomachs, and what the game of football tells us about being human.

This is the story of humanity as you've never heard it before, with dwarves, giant snakes, a Great Lion Spirit that lives above the clouds, and the finger of a 50,000 year old child revealing mysteries of our origins. Whether you're 9 or 99, *Unstoppable Us* can be enjoyed by anyone who ever wondered: Who are we? And how did we get here?[10]

Why should we care about Harari? Why should we care about what Harari says?

We should care because he is the "Pied Piper" that is leading the entire world toward self-destruction.

How is he doing that?

He is doing that through his advocacy and philosophical writings about a world that can be possible if we embrace transhumanism, artificial intelligence, climate change, food sustainability programs, energy sustainability, and population control. Never mind that each of these things are part of the United Nations agendas and Globalist talking points. While we are busy listening to every word from the WEF, WHO, UN, and others, wicked people are busy enslaving and murdering on a global scale never seen before.

Harari, Schwab, Musk, Gates, the WHO, the WEF, the UN, and nearly every government and their leaders are pushing the things mentioned above.

These fears are all being intentionally driven by globalists. What is their goal?

Their goal is to first instill such a level of fear in the hearts and minds of people that they become unable to think about whether or not what they are being told is true. It is a form of propaganda that debilitates.

Once this level of fear has been instilled, then the propaganda machine is cranked up to high and people will willingly obey whatever edict they are issued.

It is my studied opinion that the health care industry has been weaponized and incentivized to kill. The evidence is all around us. The US Federal government is at the center of this global push to reduce population. One strategy the US uses is to push other nations to adopt policies and health care practices in order to observe how they are received, how well they work, and then with a few tweaks, roll them out in America.

We have had doctor assisted suicide in America for a few decades. We better get ourselves prepared for what is happening in Canada now. It will be here soon.

MEDICAL ASSITANCE IN DYING (MAID) ACTIVITY BOOK

Canada Free Press published an article recently titled *Canadian Government's Medical Assistance in Dying (MAiD) Activity Book – Government Funded Propaganda*. The article's author Judi McLeod wrote this:

> The Canadian Virtual Hospice (a federal department of the Canadian Liberal Government) somehow found it necessary to help fund a children's "activity book" pushing medical assistance on dying to children.
>
> The book is titled the "Medical Assistance in Dying (MAiD) Activity Book".
>
> "The book is split into eight chapters, the first seven of which answer questions like, "What is MAiD?" and "Why would someone want MAiD?" (Epoch Times, Dec. 22, 2022)
>
> Conspicuously missing, a most pertinent question: "Why would someone NOT WANT MAiD?"
>
> "The book begins saying it was "created for young

people, like you, who have someone in their life who may have MAiD" and goes on to say that the book answers "questions, thoughts and feelings" that children might have about medically assisted suicide. (Epoch Times) "It is best suited to children aged 6–12," *How many children aged 6-12 go about pondering what Medical Assistance in Dying is all about?*

About the same number of children contemplating gender change until grade school teachers introduce the possibility to them!

"The book ends with a small note crediting Health Canada for its "financial contribution," through which it says the book's production was "made possible." (Epoch Times)

Now comes the Big Government Alibi:

"The views expressed herein do not necessarily represent the views of Health Canada".

The views of Health Canada are abundantly clear in its funding, it says here:

"Made legal in Canada in 2016, MAiD is currently available only for mentally competent individuals aged 18 years or older who are physically and seriously ill—but not necessarily terminal—and are undergoing "unbearable physical or mental suffering" and are also in an advanced state of decline. (Epoch Times)

"The book's eighth chapter is titled "A note for adults"

and gives a number of suggestions for answering possible questions by children about MAiD.

"Adults sometimes worry that the answers to these questions may be 'too scary,' but if the child has asked the question, they have often imagined what the answer might be," the book reads.

"Imagining different possibilities can be scarier than reality."

"The book defines MAiD as using "medicines to stop the person's body from working."

"When their body stops working, the person dies. This is done in a way that does not hurt the person. The medicines help them feel comfortable and peaceful," it reads, later elaborating on the process of "three different medicines" being injected into the patient to induce a coma followed by death."[11]

VIRTUAL SCHOOL

What have we learned via virtual classrooms here in America?

We have learned that far too many teachers are destroying children's minds with **progressive, Marxist, wickedness, never meant for parental awareness.**

Can you imagine how this "virtual hospice" will be used to deceive children into ending their life?

Right now, in the United Kingdom, the government is pushing voluntary euthanasia. Having a bad day at the office?

You can take care of that permanently. Your spouse wants a divorce? Don't put yourself through the heartbreak.

Why would nations deliberately plot to murder their own citizens unless it is part of a larger plan? The larger plan is what we read in the Scriptures about the end times deception that will come upon the entire world.

The government of the Netherlands is deliberately destroying their ability to feed their citizens and anyone else in other nations by forcefully closing down farms.

All of these things have a common root – CRT.

CRITICAL RACE THEORY

This is arguably the tip of the spear for the assault on Christianity and America.

A little background will assist you in understanding where CRT has come from.

Early Soviet agent Willi Münzenberg can be described as the father of Cultural Marxism. We know it as "political correctness." In 1923, he helped found the Institute for Social Research in Frankfurt, Germany — commonly called the "Frankfurt School." This organization invented "Critical Theory," following Marx's command for "a ruthless criticism of everything existing."

The Frankfurt school relocated to Columbia University's Teacher's College in 1933, and its poison has since metastasized and spread to colleges and universities throughout the U.S. The Frankfurt School's critical theorists advocated:

1. Creation of racism offenses.
2. Continual change to create confusion.
3. Teaching sex and homosexuality to children.
4. Undermining of schools' and teachers' authority.
5. Huge immigration to destroy identity.
6. Promotion of excessive drinking.
7. Emptying of churches.
8. Unreliable legal system & bias against crime victims.
9. Dependency on the state or state benefits.
10. Control and dumbing down of media.
11. Encouraging the breakdown of the family.

Münzenberg articulated this effort succinctly: "We must organize the intellectuals, and use them to make Western civilization stink... Only then, after they have corrupted all its values and made life base, can we impose the dictatorship of the proletariat."

Most of the Left's issues are ultimately devoted to this cause. They could care less about "gay rights," "women's rights," or any other "rights." As formulated by the Left, they are all wedge issues designed specifically to undermine Western culture, which is to say, Christianity and the freedoms and liberties founded upon the faith.[12]

How are these strategies manifesting today?

Let's consider a few examples.

FOUR HORSES OF REVELATION 6 GIVE US A CLUE

The current push by the World Economic Forum that they have titled The Great Reset. I wrote about this extensively in my book *The Four Horses of Revelation 6: A New Prophetic Interpretation.* Here is a snippet:

> The current cadre of globalist leaders means to refashion human beings in their own image. They speak plainly about their agenda… Does this fit into the biblical narrative of the end times? Judge for yourselves.
>
> Professor Yuval Noah Harari, a top advisor to World Economic Forum founder Klaus Schwab, has been widely quoted as saying that human beings can be hacked and controlled.
>
>> "Humans are now hackable animals. You know the whole idea that humans have this soul or spirit, and they have free will. So, whatever I choose whether in the election, or whether in the supermarket, this is my free will. That's over – free will."[13]
>
> An increasing number of people around the world now recognize the so-called pandemic associated with the Chinese Wuhan Coronavirus known simply as COVID-19, as a huge success in terms of forcing heretofore unknown monitoring, surveillance, and curtailments of individual liberties and freedoms

globally. This admission is now out in the open among those responsible for creating the mass hysteria that became a tsunami of acquiescence to the unscientific and unprovable dangers the technocrats insured us all were lurking in the shadows. Dr. Harari admitted as much. Speaking within the context of the COVID-19 hysteria (my word not his), Harari noted:

> "And maybe most importantly, all this was the moment when surveillance started going under the skin. Because really, we haven't seen anything yet. The ability to hack humans to understand deeply what's happening within you and what makes you go. And for that, the most important data is not what you read and who you meet and what you buy. It's what's happening inside your body."[14]

The non-stop daily broadcasting of the alleged COVID-19 death toll, the lies and propaganda of overflowing hospitals and overwhelmed healthcare staffs proved to be orchestrated fabrications designed with one purpose in mind – to allow those with an agenda to create the biggest experiment upon humans ever devised, with government approval, media backing, and with the formidable aid of Big Pharma, the witches brew of pharmacology and greed.

Dr. David Martin has been an outspoken critic of Big Pharma, Big Tech, and the entire COVID-19 narrative. He defines the transhumanist drive to recreate man in the image of man thusly:

> "Transhumanism is a means by which we exterminate homo sapiens as a species, and go into a post-human experience of reality, where the only thing relevant is the computational synthetic process of a selected set of inputs controlled by a cloud computer."[15]

Dr. Robert Malone, inventor of the mRNA technology, agrees that the transhumanism efforts go far beyond any kind of humanitarian goal.

> "There's a joint report in Germany from the government of the United Kingdom about transhumanism. That's not hidden, and transhumanism is not a conspiracy. And they talk about the RNA vaccines as an entry point to kind of opening that space, ethically and otherwise. So, that's part of the transhumanism agenda."

What space is it that Dr. Malone is referring to? It is the space of the human body, the human mind, the human soul. It is the complete overthrow of God's purposeful design and creation of humanity.

What kind of evil is this that so animates the minds and motivates the leaders of the World Economic Forum, government leaders around the world, and their lackeys in the media, education institutions, and even the entertainment industry, to advocate for the overthrow of the human race? What kind of hidden evil has deceived even Christians to support and create transhumanist organizations?[16]

What kind of evil is this? It is the kind of evil that can speak the truth of their agenda and people remain blind and deaf to its message. Lance Johnson authored an article recently that brings to light the real agenda and goal of the transhumanists associated with the World Economic Forum and the supporting organizations I just mentioned. Here is what Johnson wrote.

> One of the brains behind The World Economic Forum (WEF), is self-proclaimed prophet, Yuval Noah Harari. He believes in the Great Reset, in transhumanism, in culling the population, and using a global government to control humanity at the bio-metric level. He is praised by Bill Gates, Barack Obama, Mark Zuckerberg, and Klaus Schwab, leader of the WEF.
>
> Harari talks about "useless human beings" who do not have meaning or purpose. He said the greatest fake news is the Bible. He said Christianity is wrong, that humans are here on Earth for "nothing." "Jesus Christ is fake news," be balked. He believes there is "no great cosmic plan" that humans have a role to play in. Instead, he views humans as "useless eaters" who can be hacked and manipulated using digital surveillance under their skin.
> He also believes in culling the population. "What do we need so many humans for?" he is

quoted as saying while promoting his latest book.

In a recent interview, Harari said the world is entering a new industrial revolution, but the products will not be physical goods. Harari said science, technology, and industry's greatest challenge of the 21st century will be "to try to gain control of the world inside us, to learn how to engineer and produce bodies and brains and minds." He says these are likely to be the "main products" of the 21st century economy.
He said, "Once you know how to produce bodies and brains and minds so cheap labor in Africa and South Asia, it simply counts for nothing."

"The biggest question…in economics and politics of the coming decades, will be what to do with all these useless people," he said with a straight face. He said technology will ensure that everyone is fed, so "food is not the problem."

"The problem is more boredom, and what to do with them, and how will they find some sense of meaning in life, when they are basically meaningless, worthless." He prescribed drugs and computer games as solutions to entertain "useless" people's brains.

Solutions for the End Times

He said a global government will collect and use data on every person to learn how to engineer bodies, brains, and minds. He says data and biometrics will be used to hack human beings and re-engineer the future of human life itself. He said "intelligent design" never existed and any notion of a Creator God will be driven out of society, as humans become hackable, programmable. Harari even claims that the laws of natural selection and organic biochemistry will be eliminated and replaced by a transhumanist future, where humans become hackable animals, manipulated, and controlled. "We have the technology to hack humans on a massive scale," he said. He added crises should be exploited to implement more surveillance throughout society so "elites" can monitor, collect data, and engineer the future trajectory of human life. Much of this surveillance will "come under the skin" as biometric data become a pathway to manipulate human populations. Harari said we already have the ability to go under the skin and collect biometric data, allowing "elites" the power to re-engineer life itself. "We are upgrading humans into gods," he said.

He said in an emergency, people trust the "scientists." He used the example of priests and ministers shutting down their churches worldwide in 2020 to prove that God is dead.

> Going forward, people will put their faith in the scientific elite and global government, he balked. "Even the religious leaders trust the scientists," he said.[17]

The transhumanist view is nothing more than a dressed up scientific naturalism. For those of you who understand the belief system that undergirds scientific naturalism, this makes perfect sense. There is no Creator and there is no need for such an antiquated idea. Since there is no Creator, the idea of a Savior is also unnecessary.

What follows from those two beliefs? What follows is that no Creator and no Savior means it is up to us to save ourselves. We can only save ourselves if we all come together in peace and devote our resources to figuring out solutions to our most pressing problems. This philosophy is variously described under the monikers of scientism – a religion based on a philosophy that only science presents truth, and secular humanism, which posits that humanity is capable of morality, self-fulfillment, and self-actualization without belief in a Creator God. Today, we find the cult of religious transhumanism dominating scientism and secular humanism.[18]

SALVO MAGAZINE

In an article from Vox, summarized in *Salvo*, a magazine dedicated to debunking the cultural myths that secular humanism uses to destroy humanity, we read that:

Last year, Sri Lankan president Gotabaya Rajapaksa banned synthetic fertilizer and pesticide, saying they led to adverse health and environmental impacts" and went against the country's heritage of "sustainable food systems." In six months, rice production dropped 20 percent, and tea, the country's biggest export product, dropped 18 percent. By July 2022, 90 percent of families were skipping meals, and the nation was on the verge of bankruptcy, with runaway inflation reaching 54.6 percent.

Commenting on the disaster, Discovery Institute's Wesley J. Smith noted that the Netherlands is doing the same thing to its farmers, and Justin Trudeau in Canada is signaling plans to follow suit. "Add it all up," he wrote, "bankrupt farmers, empty market shelves, less food on the table, and dramatically inflated prices. Only the technocratic class could be this stupid."[19]

Recently, the new president of Brazil (stolen election) ruled that Brazilians who would not get the covid jabs would be ineligible for government assistance of any kind.

THE LATE WILLIAM COOPER

In a 1991 book titled, *Behold a Pale Horse*, author William Cooper describes the history and origin of our current situation of millions of injuries, heart problems, blood clots, and sudden deaths of young and middle-aged people with no history of disease or health issues. All the victims of what is being called "sudden death syndrome" is that they all received the so-called vaccine and boosters related to the alleged Covid virus.

In an article I read recently about Cooper's book, the plan to introduce horrific contagions into the world's general population was discussed. Here is a small part of the article.

> It began with the postwar Baby Boom and the worldwide population explosion during the second half of the 20th century. The elite were appalled, and they needed to do something about it. Starting in the late 1950s, they commissioned studies and computer models from the **Club of Rome**, which showed that by or shortly after the year 2000, there would be a total collapse of civilization and that the only things that could stop it would be severe cutbacks of the human population, the cessation of technological and economic growth, the elimination of meat in the human diet, strict control of future human reproduction and a total commitment to preserving the environment…
>
> Funding was obtained from the U.S. Congress under H.B. 15090 (1969), where $10 million was given to the DOD's 1970 budget. Testimony before the Senate Committee revealed that they intended to produce 'a synthetic biological agent, an agent that does not naturally exist and for which no natural immunity could have been acquired. Within the next 5 to 10 years, it would probably be possible to make a new infective microorganism which could differ in certain important aspects from any known disease-causing organisms. Most important of these is that it might be

refractory to the immunological and therapeutic processes upon which we depend to maintain our relative freedom from infectious disease'...

The New World Order will eliminate the population threat in several ways. Complete control of individual behavior may be established using electronic or chemical implants. No one will be allowed to have a child without permission; stiff penalties wait for those who ignore the law. The violent, the old, the infirm, the handicapped, and the unproductive will be killed. Private property will be abolished. Since religion helped to create the population problem, it will not be tolerated except for the approved state-controlled religion which will evolve according to man's needs...

Studies were done to determine a method to arrest the population explosion before the point of no return would be reached. It was determined that an immediate attack on the problem would involve two points of intervention. The first was to lower the birth rate and the second was to increase the death rate.

To lower the birth rate several programs were put into motion. The first was the development of positive birth-control methods using mechanical (diaphragm and condom), chemical (foam and birth-control pills), and medical (sterilization, abortion, and hysterectomy) procedures.

These were developed and implemented. The Women's Liberation movement was started with the demand for free abortions, using "pro choice" as its rallying cry. Homosexuality was encouraged and Gay Liberation was born. Homosexuals do not have children. Zero population growth became a hot subject at cocktail parties. Individual freedom, "the heat of the moment," religion, and the old blue laws sabotaged these efforts, and while zero population growth became a reality in some areas, population increased rapidly in others.

The only alternative left to the world's ruling elite was to increase the death rate. This was a difficult thing to do, as no one wanted to pick people out of a crowd and line them up for execution. Neither did they relish the possible consequences of an enraged public upon discovering that they were being systematically murdered. Of course, a very short but very deadly global war using nuclear weapons upon select population concentrations was contemplated and, to tell you the truth, was not ruled out.

The fact that such a population control was even contemplated confirmed the worst fears of those who had participated in the 1957 study. War was put on the back burner to simmer but may become a reality. In the meantime, something else had to be done that would absolve the decision makers of guilt and place the blame on those who did not lead clean lives. Something that could be blamed upon Mother Nature. What was needed was the bubonic plague or some other horrible but natural disease. The answer came from Rome.

Several Top-Secret recommendations were made by Dr. Aurelio Peccei of the Club of Rome. He advocated that a plague be introduced that would have the same effect as the famous Black Death of history. The chief recommendation was to develop a microbe which would attack the autoimmune system and thus render the development of a vaccine impossible.

The orders were given to develop the microbe and to develop a prophylactic and a cure. The microbe would be used against the general population and would be introduced by vaccine. The prophylactic was to be used by the ruling elite. The cure will be administered to the survivors when it is decided that enough people have died. The cure will be announced as newly developed when in fact it has existed from the beginning. This plan is a part of Global 2000. The prophylactic and the cure are suppressed.[20]

Cooper mentioned birth control in his book that I just read an excerpt from. The globalists planned population control and reduction decades ago.

CONTRACEPTION

Not by coincidence, *Salvo* has a feature article in the current edition that gives an overview of the history and legacy of contraception. As early as the 1940's doctors writing in the *Journal of the American Medical Association* began warning against synthetic estrogens. In spite of the myriad warnings and demonstrable severe effects, the FDA approved the "Pill" in 1960. The results have been devastating to women.

Depression, pulmonary embolisms, strokes, and cancer are just a few of the common results of ingesting hormonal birth control.

Most Americans do not know that in 1970 the US Senate held hearings on the dangers birth control drugs posed to women's health. Initially, feminists opposed the hearings on the grounds that men were once again trying to run women's lives. As the hearings progressed however, and more information became public, the feminist outrage turned toward the drug manufacturers and the FDA that approved their use in spite of the evidence of harm.

Dr. Roy Hertz, who chaired an FDA advisory committee addressing the direct link between cancer and birth control admitted that researchers as well as the FDA knew that birth control would cause cancer before the FDA approved its use and they approved it anyway. When you consider the fact that estrogen had been banned in the 1950's from use with poultry production because it was a known carcinogen, you have to wonder why the decision to allow its manufacture and sale to women was approved. You don't need to guess because America was told why it was approved for use in spite of the risks.

Dr. John McCain (not the late Senator) spoke the truth shortly after the Senate hearing concluded with no change or prohibition against birth control. He said:

> The population explosion is of overwhelming worldwide importance. It threatens the very foundations of national existence. Unless the explosion

is moderated, radical methods of population control, rather than family planning, may be required.[21]

Let me tell you what is really behind modern American "reproductive health" or "women's health" policy today. It hasn't changed since birth control was created in a pharmaceutical laboratory in the 1940's. Simply put population control is the driving force. There is no such thing as reproductive health care or concerns for women's health. The truth is that birth control, abortion, and the coming push for euthanasia is the work of government bureaucrats in every nation.

The problem with too many people is that they hear this and scoff. They simply will not believe that anything like this could ever happen, even though it is in fact happening right now. It all seems too incredible.

We could discuss Monkey Pox and Smallpox research and the creation of new supplies of each paid for by the US government. Why would the government spending billions of dollars on the creation of viruses that cause widespread death?[22] Isn't the answer obvious?
Another way that population control is being implemented is through gender dysphoria and worse.

HAVE YOU HEARD OF THE WPATH?

From the WPATH website "Mission and Vision" we read this:

> Founded in 1979... the World Professional Association for Transgender Health (WPATH) publishes "evidenced-based" standards of care (SOC) for clinicians and hospitals serving gender dysphoric patients, and is regarded as an authority on transgender health by physicians, psychologists, lawyers, educators, and other human service providers across the globe.[23]

Salvo Magazine Spring edition states this concerning WPATH:

> WPATH is garnering respect as an authority, but under false pretenses. The "Professional" in WPATH is a misnomer; anyone can join for a fee. While the AMA, AAP, and APA have all come under scrutiny for dubious ideological leanings, the "research" informing WPATH guidelines is not even dubious, but is all about expanding the transgender umbrella. According to the Clinical Advisory Network on Sex and Gender, an organization composed of UK-based clinicians whose motto is "First do no harm," WPATH guidelines "lack methodological rigour" and were developed by *self-appointed* experts who "are themselves interested and invested" in encouraging transgender identities and gender transition. The current president of WPATH, biological male Dr. Marci L. Bowers, for example, has performed nearly 4,000 transition surgeries and is credited with being a pioneer in the field.

At WPATH's 2009 Oslo conference, retired professor Thomas W. Johnson, adjunct professor Richard J. Wassersug, and K. H. Willette presented "The Development of Standards of Care for Individuals with a Male-to-Eunuch Gender Identity Disorder." The paper offered guidelines for surgical castration for men who "loathe their manhood, but do not identify as . . . female." The paper was then published in WPATH's academic journal, *The International Journal of Transgenderism*. WPATH's 2011 conference in Atlanta welcomed their return as presenters.

These three men are active participants on the Eunuch Archive, a body-modification fetish site that Genevieve Gluck of Reduxx characterizes as a forum hosting and producing extreme sadomasochistic pornography involving the castration, rape, and torture of children. Johnson, who operates under the pseudonym "Jesus," is reportedly a formative member of the site. He and Wassersug have also published "research" based on surveys conducted with other members of the Archive.

Johnson advocates "expanding the concept of 'gender identity' to include men with sadomasochistic and even pedophilic castration fantasies." His advocacy has paid off, as a newly minted gender identity category was announced in WPATH's Version 8 SOC, released in 2022—that of the *eunuch*. Most egregiously, WPATH touts the Eunuch Archive as an online peer-support community providing a "wealth of information about eunuch-identified people."[24]

HOW MANY ARE FAMIIAR WITH "INCEL"?

The term "involuntary celibate" (shortened to "incel") refers to self-identifying members of an online subculture based around the inability to find a romantic or sexual partner despite desiring one; a state they describe as "inceldom" or "incelibacy."

The term "incel" entered street vernacular in 2014, after 22-year-old Elliot Rodger, angry about being a sexless virgin, killed 6 people. **Incel** is a growing subculture of "involuntary celibate" males who are angry (usually at women) and are emitting dark signals of looming violence. The nonprofit Center for Countering Digital Hate (CCDH) analyzed more than one million posts online and found a marked increase in conversations among incels about mass murder and sexual violence, including against **prepubescent** children.[25]
Can we agree that spiritual warfare has broken out all over the world with demonic manifestations of things never before imagined?

INTRODUCING CHATGPT

Author Terrell Clemmons recently wrote in an article titled "Hidden in Plain Sight" which provides details concerning the new ChatGPT phenomena.

> As 2022 turned into 2023, tech news was abuzz with talk of OpenAI's new chatbot, ChatGPT. A chatbot is language-processing software that generates text in response to user prompts. Developers "train" a chatbot by feeding it natural language data pertaining to the

tasks they want it to perform and then refining its code so that it delivers the intended output to anticipated prompts. Training may continue after the bot has been put into service. Telephone answering systems that processed requests based on verbal answers to its questions were rudimentary versions of computerized language processing.

ChatGPT takes the technology to a new level. Jordan Peterson asked it to write an essay on the intersection of Taoist ethics and Jesus' ethics from the Sermon on the Mount. In Peterson's words, ChatGPT got it "dead right—brilliant." Does that mean ChatGPT is an expert in ethics? Not on your life.

MIT Technology Review's Melissa Heikkilä writes: The magic—and danger—of these large language models lies in the illusion of correctness. The sentences they produce look right—they use the right kinds of words in the correct order. But the AI doesn't know what any of it means. These models work by predicting the most likely next word in a sentence. They haven't a clue whether something is correct or false, and they confidently present information as true even when it is not.[26]

Here's my take – you better believe climate change, Critical Race Theory, Gender Dysphoria and every other Progressive Marxist idea will be programmed into these chatbots. People are going to believe that a superhuman intelligence knows what is best for all of mankind.

Speaking of technology, the first narrative advanced by the Deep State, i.e., the US government handlers, was that the Silicon Valley Bank was over-leveraged with big tech company money and that is what caused its collapse.

The truth is that Silicon Valley Bank along with several others was a money laundering operation for the Deep State narcotics trafficking operations globally.

The American Deep State partners with the largest drug cartel in the world – the Sinaloa Cartel.

The Deep State funds its operations through narcotics trafficking and money laundering. Believe it or not, New Hampshire is the headquarters for this clandestine operation. In a recent article authored by Mike Gill, he wrote…

> Evidence for this is found in the testimony of **Jacqueline Breger** before the Arizona State Congress, where we learned about her years'-long investigation into multi-state racketeering and corruption that uncovered the Sinaloa Cartel's complete infiltration of parts of the US Government, complete with financial documents showing that **Governor Katie Hobbs and her husband have been laundering Sinaloa Cartel money through fake deeds and mortgages since 1997** and that others similarly involved with the Sinaloa Cartel include US Senator for Arizona Senator Kirsten Sinema, Arizona's current Secretary of State, 3 of 5 Maricopa County Board of Supervisors members, assorted judges, plus two of the principals at Runbeck Election Services and everyone in charge of Mesa, Arizona, which is described as a

wholesale "racketeering organization", as this term is defined in 18 USC §1961.

Additional evidence has been revealed related to how high-powered New Hampshire attorney, **Bill Shaheen**, is the architect of this racket. Shaheen also happens to be married to New Hampshire Senator **Jeanne Shaheen**. Gill says that together with their cronies, Dick Anagnost, Andrew Crews, Bill Greiner, Maggie Hassan and Chris Sununu, the Shaheens run a very tight racketeering operation, which was partially revealed by the **Pandora Papers**.

On the 27th of October 2021, New Hampshire Business Review journalist, Bob Sanders wrote an article entitled, 'What the Pandora Papers have to Say about New Hampshire'.

$932.5 billion.

That's the value of assets under management by a rapidly growing trust industry ostensibly based in New Hampshire. They have increased by more than a quarter of a trillion dollars in just the last year, and it's not a complete total.

The past year's infusion is triple the amount reportedly going into South Dakota, where several trusts have been scrutinized after the release earlier this month of the so-called Pandora Papers.

Those papers — the latest of a series of massive leaks — document and expose the movement of nefarious money shielded by foreign trusts by people looking to avoid taxes and scrutiny. Some of that money came from politicians, kings and billionaires and was used for questionable, if not criminal, purposes. Lately, that money has been coming to the United States in trust havens, notably South Dakota, whose loose rules and regulations rival the most notorious offshore jurisdictions.

In coverage about the Pandora Papers, New Hampshire has been mentioned as a place where it is easy to form trusts, but in some ways, the state has overtaken South Dakota as the premier place to secretly stash foreign assets, both in trusts and in relatively new and even less regulated family law foundations.

Mike Gill told Brendon that 97% of the deposits at Silicon Valley Bank (SVB) were giant New Hampshire drug money accounts in the billions. SVB recently merged with Boston Private Bank and Trust, which is actually a New Hampshire Corporation whose previous directors include two attorneys general of the State of New Hampshire, Joseph Foster and Michael Delaney, who Gill claims were placed there by the Shaheens and who were running for cover for the Cartel.[27]

All of this sounds impossible, but it is the ugly truth behind the US government.

Here is what the devil wants and has pulled out all the stops to achieve. The devil wants the entire world in flames. He wants the human race exterminated. Is this our fate?

Is this our fate as believers in the Lord Jesus Christ? IT IS NOT!

Remember – we serve a risen, exalted, and reigning King. DON'T LET THE RISING CHAOS DISTRACT YOU FROM THE TRUTH!

We are already victorious overcomers because Jesus has already overcome and secured the victory. What we must do is resist!

WE MUST NOT GO ALONG WITH THESE WICKED PEOPLE'S AGENDA.

Jesus reminds us that victory is secured in Him.

"I also say to you that you are Peter, and upon this rock <u>I will build My church</u>; and the gates of Hades <u>will not overpower it</u>." Jesus, Matthew 16:18

Jesus is building His ecclesia. Therefore, no matter how desperate, hopeless, oppressive, or impossible it seems, we as the people of Yahweh belong to a cause that cannot fail.

The phrase "The gates of Hades" simply means this – we are not to fear death because nothing can hold back what Jesus has promised to His people – eternal life. Death therefore has no power over us, and we are not to fear it.

Revelation 12:10-11 says:

> [10] Then I heard a loud voice in heaven, saying, "Now the salvation, and the power, and the kingdom of our God and the authority of His Christ have come, for the accuser of our brethren has been thrown down,

he who accuses them before our God day and night. ¹¹ And they overcame him because of the blood of the Lamb and because of the word of their testimony, and they did not love their life even when faced with death.

Do you hear the Spirit of God speaking to you today about what you are to do? Sitting idly by while the world burns is not an option.

We are reminded of this by what Jesus said to each of the ecclesias He sent letters to.

In every letter to the 7 ecclesias of Revelation 2-3 Jesus gave this exhortation: "He who has an ear let him hear what the Spirit says to the ecclesias."

Do you have ears attuned to the Spirit of God? Are you listening to what the heaven is saying today?

If you are listening, are you understanding what the Spirit is saying and are you moving in a demonstrable way to do what the Spirit is saying?

One thing you must understand. There is no solution to what we face as Americans if Jesus is not in it.

The devil wants you to doubt God, live in fear, believe resistance is hopeless, and be deceived, so that you will fail in your mission. WHAT IS OUR MISSION?

Our mission is to remind the devil by our actions that he is already defeated, and to make sure those that we rescue from darkness understand that truth as well. When people

understand the chains that bound them are broken, there is true freedom.
We do that every time we take a stand for Jesus in this world. There has never been a better time to go all in for serving Jesus Christ.

People everywhere are desperate for a solution.

There is only one solution to the problem of mankind and this world – salvation through faith in Christ.

This world is passing away. Eternity is forever. Let's encourage people to trust in Jesus for their salvation and deliverance from what is coming upon the earth.

You must go to them. Go out into your neighborhood, your city streets and tell people that "there is salvation in no one else; for there is no other name under heaven that has been given among men by which we must be saved."

THIS IS A WAR!

We have been involved in "seed wars" since Genesis 3. Do you understand that creation has been subjected to constant spiritual warfare since the fall of Adam and Eve?

God's rescue mission was announced in Genesis 3:15.

It has been in process since before the foundation of the world (Revelation 13:8; 1 Peter 1:18-20)

Let me give you a quick rundown of the winding road we have been on.

Genesis 3 – the fall and the prophecy of victory. Seed wars announced.

Genesis 6 – deceived supernatural beings attempt to pollute the human gene pool to stop the Edenic prophecy of a Messiah.

Genesis 10 gives the Table of Nations – 70 total.

Genesis 11 Nimrod takes advantage of the wicked heart of man and unites them in a rebellion against Yahweh.

Yahweh confuses the languages of the rebels, and He divides the nations according to the 70 "sons of God." He disinherits the nations.

Genesis 12 Yahweh calls Abraham to begin His own people. Through Abraham the entire world is blessed. **Messiah!** The Apostolic Gospels proclaim that the cross was the stealth strike that destroyed Satan's plans.

1 Corinthians 2:1-8 says:

> [1]And when I came to you, brethren, I did not come with superiority of speech or of wisdom, proclaiming to you the testimony of God. [2] For I determined to know nothing among you except Jesus Christ, and Him crucified. [3] I was with you in weakness and in fear and in much trembling, [4] and my message and my preaching were not in persuasive words of wisdom, but in demonstration of the Spirit and of power, [5] so that your faith would not rest on the wisdom of men, but on the power of God.

> ⁶ Yet we do speak wisdom among those who are mature; a wisdom, however, not of this age nor of the rulers of this age, who are passing away; ⁷ but we speak God's wisdom in a mystery, the hidden *wisdom* which God predestined before the ages to our glory; ⁸ ***the wisdom* which none of the rulers of this age has understood; for if they had understood it they would not have crucified the Lord of glory;**

Leading people out of the darkness necessarily involves bringing them to THE Light who is Jesus.

Both actions go together. Do not be deceived but be wise in these days.

You are not truly freeing anyone until they know Jesus as their Savior.

The evil that we are seeing today is unprecedented. Wicked people have done a masterful job of inducing fear and terror into the lives of billions of people. Can the end game be as simple as offering people an "out" by suicide? I think it is one of many strategies being employed.

We are witnessing the rise of the one world religion, an amalgamation of earth and science worship as the veneer that hides the true object of worship for all those who reject Jesus Christ – the devil himself.

There has never been a better time to go all in for serving Jesus Christ. People everywhere are desperate for a solution. There is only one solution to the problem of mankind and this world – salvation through faith in Christ. This world is passing away. Eternity is forever. Let's encourage people to trust in Jesus for their salvation and deliverance from what is coming upon the earth.

Mike Spaulding is a pastor and author.

www.drmikespaulding.com

www.thetransformingword.com

ENDNOTES

[1] The Shepherd of Hermas, 1.4.2
[2] https://www.whitehouse.gov/briefing-room/presidential-actions/2022/09/12/executive-order-on-advancing-biotechnology-and-biomanufacturing-innovation-for-a-sustainable-safe-and-secure-american-bioeconomy/
[3] https://www.mayoclinic.org/diseases-conditions/brucellosis/symptoms-causes/syc-20351738
[4] https://mars.nasa.gov/news/406/scientists-find-evidence-of-ancient-microbial-life-on-mars/
[5] https://www.smithsonianmag.com/smart-news/conan-the-bacterium-has-what-it-takes-to-survive-on-mars-180981019/
[6] Quotes are on Harari's website. https://www.ynharari.com/
[7] https://www.ynharari.com/book/sapiens-2/
[8] https://www.ynharari.com/book/homo-deus/
[9] https://www.ynharari.com/book/21-lessons-book/
[10] https://www.ynharari.com/book/unstoppable_us/
[11] Judi McLeod, Canada Free Press, *Canadian Government's Medical Assistance in Dying (MAiD) Activity Book – Government Funded Childhood Propaganda,* December 23, 2022. https://canadafreepress.com/article/canadian-governments-medical-assistance-in-dying-maid-activity-bookgovernment-funded-childhood-propaganda
[12] This section was art of an article on the subject of Cultural Marxism and its origins. Unfortunately, the author is not known.
[13] Transhumanism News here https://transhumanism.news/2022-06-19-harari-humans-now-hackable-animals-free-will-is-over.html

[14] Ibid.
[15] Ibid.
[16] As one example of a Christian Transhumanist organization see https://www.christiantranshumanism.org/
[17] See https://naturalnews.com/2022-05-02-world-economic-forum-believes-people-useless-eaters.html
[18] Mike Spaulding, *The Four Horses of Revelation 6: A New Prophetic Interpretation*, (Elida, Ohio: Transforming Word Publishing, 2023), pp. 13-21.
[19] *Salvo*, "Save the Planet by Starving the People," Issue 63, Winter 2022, p. 9. Originally article on Vox here - https://www.vox.com/future-perfect/2022/7/15/23218969/sri-lanka-organic-fertilizer-pesticide-agriculture-farming
[20] Bill Cooper and the Lansing, Michigan Lecture. https://forbiddenknowledgetv.net/bill-cooper-lansing-michigan-lecture-1996/
[21] *Salvo*, "Products of Con(tra)caption: Hormonal Birth Control Was Ill-Conceived from the Start," Issue 63, Winter 2022, pp. 24-25.
[22] See https://forbiddenknowledgetv.net/warning-timeline-shows-threat-of-incoming-smallpox-false-flag/
[23] https://www.wpath.org/
[24] https://salvomag.com/issue/64
[25] Source - https://www.washingtonpost.com/technology/2022/09/22/incels-rape-murder-study/
[26] https://salvomag.com/article/salvo64/hidden-in-plain-sight
[27] https://forbiddenknowledgetv.net/mike-gill-donald-trump-saves-the-day-biden-ukraine-the-new-hampshire-cartel/

CHAPTER 10

Apocalyptic Sojourner Of Faith

Celeste Solum

Personal Pilgrimage of Faith

At this very moment, you and I face the existential threat of extinction. The rich men of the earth have decided to annihilate humanity in its entirety, the decision being made at the first Asilomar Conference in 1975 to genetically modify all life upon the face of the earth. This veiled class of global rulers also made the decision to erase the whole of human civilization. If they get their way, there would be no trace that humans ever lived on planet earth. Never in human history has the technology converged with extreme wickedness and God's extinction level cycle.

Throughout history mankind has reached out to his family, friends, or network during times of disaster. Whether you refer to your fellow humans as your tribe or your community, we were created to interact with one another throughout the good times and the bad. True, sometimes we might argue or quarrel, only to resolve our differences and move on. We are now confronted with social engineering, technology, and evil forces that have torn us away from the abode of pastoral interaction only to become invisibly walled off from each

other. Technology has made it easy for us to delete people from our lives, which stands in stark opposition to the biblical guidance that we are to be a part of other lives and to engage with respect, compassion, and love. We no longer have the difficult task of facing them face-to-face. We ruthlessly sever the ties that bind us together and throw off with ease the yolk of our complex human emotional entanglements.

When faced with spiritual, physical, emotional extermination, is there any hope that you can overcome?

The Holy Bible is the seminal book about cataclysms and catastrophes. You may have never viewed it from this lens, but when you do, you see remarkable stories about survival and being triumphant over all the enemies of your body and soul. This one book, with the Holy Spirit, will reveal to you every problem and every solution until the return of Jesus Christ. His angels keep watch over you so that you will not dash your foot upon a rock.

Faith Lesson: Lord, please help to equip and prepare me for the End of Days. Help me to get out of my belief system and really listen to Your Word to prepare.

Name one thing that you will do to spiritually prepare for a day you will no longer walk the face of the earth.

Bonds of Love that Cannot Be Broken

To overcome existential threats as well as threats in our everyday lives, we must have a relationship with God. Not a remote exchange rather, a deep reverent bond. This creates a virtuous cycle which includes ongoing love of God and His Son Jesus Christ. Just as we see in the Song of Songs, a passionate love draws together the Bridegroom and the Bride,

the ultimate union of lovers. This love sparks us to read and to apply the Word of God in our life for every situation we encounter. This deeply bonds us to the Almighty Who has the power to resolve all situations. The person of faith on this journey acquires profound understanding and communications skills as he receives Divine messages applicable to his every need, all the while being attentive to use these same messaging skills with his fellow man.

I urge you to read each of these slowly and take them to heart. When you are bonded and cleave to God, you are complete in all ways.

You have superior wisdom.

You are complete in happiness.

You live with His intimate Light, wisdom, and guidance upon the path.

His life in you stimulates an awe of God which transports you to live in your eternal abode even while you occupy this physical domain.

You emulate your Savior Jesus Christ and His righteousness and perfection.

Even when you err, God Himself will tenderly aid you in correct perception, and jointly we correct our error.

Faith Lesson: Today, I will take a step uniting my past all the way back to Adam and Eve, to my future eternity with Jesus Christ and brothers and sisters, and all humans. I will treat other humans the way I would like to be treated even if I have never experienced it. I praise You that I can partake in the marvelous chain of Your love that can never be broken.

Uniqueness

For you created my inmost being;

    you knit me together in my mother's womb.

I praise you because I am fearfully [uniquely] and wonderfully made;

    your works are wonderful,

    I know that full well.

My frame was not hidden from you

    when I was made in the secret place,

    when I was woven together in the depths of the earth.

> Your eyes saw my unformed body;
>
> all the days ordained for me were written in your book
>
> before one of them came to be. Psalm 139

The person of faith must respect that each creation, including all of humanity, has a unique destiny to play out in this season. Unlike the rest of the animate and inanimate world, your essential actions are not automatic. Because you have free-will. True, you are embedded in nature, but you beautifully resonate with the frequency of your Creator which then lifts you above the Laws of Nature, because you truly dwell in the heavenly heights. When you walk out living in the Holy Spirit and follow the narrow path of biblical adherence, you can reach your full potential for which you were called, to which people subject to the extremes and vacillations of purely the physical domain are subject.

The world is devolving into darkness and subsistence. You need to wake up to the fact that God in His perfection created every creation, especially you, with the ability to persist. Under natural conditions when you adhere to your calling you achieve your sustenance from God's own hand rather than striving yourself for self-sustenance. Why is this so? The sin of Adam and Eve brought subsistence to the world. We can free ourselves from this generational curse by turning to your Heavenly Father Who knows your every need.

Faith Lesson: I am uniquely made and this day I will take steps with the guidance of the Holy Spirit to preserve my humanity. I will not let the spark of Your glory fade away from within my body. I will take steps for proper prayer, nutrition, and sustenance so that my body does not waste away.

Potential

You have infinite potential on your life journey to uncover and actualize God's Holy Spirit that resides within you. Your potential exists in the fiber of your being because you are created in the Divine Image of God. This is what the Quantum realm is about. It can be good or evil. Not only must we recognize this truth within ourselves, but we must acknowledge that other humans in our life also have potential for both seed and abundant fruit. Life is a never-ending process of refining our flaws into the potential jewels of character that God placed inside of us. It is known that each of us is born to toil because of Adam and Eve's sin but through that toil we are converting our potential into reality. An understanding of this is necessary, because part of this existential threat is multi-dimensional, the overlapping convergence between the supernatural, physical, cyber, and evil Satanic Synthetic Virtual Twin which you may know as the Metaverse. The Metaverse is the abyss or hell.

Faith Lesson: I acknowledge and agree that I can do all things in Jesus Christ. Nothing in His perfect will is impossible for me. On this day, I will accomplish the impossible! And then I will praise You, whether I succeed or fail.

Created in the Divine Image

What does it mean to be created in the Image of God? As we sink into the dark fleshpots of slavery, we rarely have time to meditate upon what our true inheritance of being a human fully entails, much less to treasure the value of our fellow humans.

> Long ago, I was in a grocery store going down the aisles to procure needed groceries. I came upon the bread aisle where I saw a short, elderly woman looking to the top shelf towering above her attempting to make a decision about which of two different types of bread she should purchase. Due to the lofty height, there was no way for her to see the ingredients, feel the bread for freshness, or really discern what the types of bread they were. I could see her plight and my heart filled with compassion. I inquired if she would like me to bring down the two loaves of bread to view them. She quickly responded into the affirmative. I brought the loaves down to her and she proceeded to examine each loaf carefully and make her choice. She then introduced herself, "My name is Esther. You know, the name of Esther is in the Bible?" I responded, "I do know that name Esther is in the

Bible." We then departed, each going our own way. I came away feeling that either I had just encountered an angel or that this was a Providential encounter. For days, weeks, months, and years when I went to the same store, I eagerly looked for Esther. I never saw Esther again, although our brief engagement has lingered with me for many decades until this day.

Why would I bring this up? Would or could this happen in this season? Where humanity is being trampled upon like wild pigs trample each other underfoot, with nary a soul valued or treasured? How is it that we have veered off appreciating the humanity within ourselves and the humanity of others? As we fall into the pit of technology, seeking to merge ourselves with machines and robots, we best recall our humble beginnings, that we are created in the Divine Image of God.

What does 'remember that we are created in the Divine Image of God mean'?

And God created the Earthling [Adam] in God's own image, in the image of God, God created him [i.e., Adam]; male and female created God them. Genesis 1:27

Immediately, I am struck with the fact that God created male and female humans that dwell on the face of the earth, exclusively, in His own Image. Extra-terrestrials may exist but they are not created in the Divine Image of God. God certainly has the power to create many diverse creatures as He has demonstrated upon the earth. Why not the stars?

Beloved is the person created in the image of God. A deeper

love is revealed to those created in God's image, as the Bible says, "for in God's own image God made humankind."

Genesis 9:6. Who does not want to be considered as beloved? This highlights to us the special relationship between God and mankind, His most prized handiwork, for we are in His Divine Image, not that we are God but, that His qualities reside inside of us.

We cannot think of "*In our image*" (*tsalmeinu*) as merely the form of the body and its build, for that would not be called *tselem*, but rather *toar* or *tavnit*. We can think of it in terms of how God instructed Moses to build the Tabernacle in the Wilderness the Mishkan. On Mount Sinai God showed Moses the heavenly plan or blueprint. The construction of the parts or vessels of the earthly body or Mishkan would be called *tselem* (image), made to resemble the heavenly design or like a drawing on paper made to resemble a specific person.

The word *tselem* (image) is derived from *tsel* (shadow), since a shadow depicts a form which resembles a body. And from it did men learn to begin the art of drawing. And behold, man is a resemblance of God; meaning that from a certain angle, he resembles the Power that is Master of all the powers. It is quite breathtaking to ponder!

The expression, *tselem* Elohim (image of God) does not mean that the Bible teaches that God has a human form, as we shall soon see.

Our forebears did not believe that God and the angels had a body vessel like us. Angels certainly are not flesh and blood. But the truth of the matter is that a completely incorporeal intellect has no form - no breadth and width and height whatsoever - something that is impossible for a us human to imagine and therefore it will not be internalized us and appreciated in others.

The Bible was given to the whole of people, and the people need to be able to imagine somewhat their God. Therefore, our forebears would attribute to God, and to the angels, and to human souls, an ethereal spiritual substance; nonetheless, that substance has a form and a build. That is what I encountered when I saw Jesus, Holy Spirit with form, yet an indistinguishable form. It is difficult to put into words. Use of the word "image" does not imply a physical image. The resemblance to God is more like the relationship between an object and its shadow, a mere suggestion of its essence. So, in what way do people resemble God, if only vaguely? I suggest that God is pure intellect Spirit in a manner humans cannot imagine.

It is clear in the Bible and the books of the prophets that God has neither body nor form, as it says, "For the Lord is God in the Heaven above and the Earth below." Deuteronomy 4:39

And a body cannot be in two places at once, but Spirit can inhabit more than one location.

"For you have not seen any image." Deuteronomy 4:15

And as it says, *"And to what shall you compare Me, and I be equal."* Isaiah 40:25

If He had a body such as ours, He could be compared to other bodies. If this would be accurate, He in fact, would not be Creator God.

Why does the human sojourner need to know things about images, bodies, and dual locations? There is this concept in the Hebrew not talked about in Christian circles and that is a human being can be biologically alive, and yet spiritually dead, a zombie. During these End of Days as a Christian, your Holy Spirit will be sitting in the heavenlies while your physical body form will be present upon the earth. When you are a Christian, you must test the spirits, to determine if it is God's Holy Spirit or an evil one.

But Stephen, full of the Holy Spirit, looked up to heaven and saw the glory of God, and Jesus standing at the right hand of God. "Look," he said, "I see heaven open and the Son of Man standing at the right hand of God." ...While they were stoning him, Stephen prayed, "Lord Jesus, receive my spirit." Then he fell on his knees and cried out, "Lord, do not hold this sin against them." When he had said this, he fell asleep. Acts 7

Then the LORD God formed the Earthling of the dust of the ground and breathed into his nostrils the breath of life; and the Earthling became a living soul. Genesis 2:7

First, this is an amazing declaration, breathing life into the dust of the earth. This shows that you are a miracle! *"Then the Lord God formed the Earthling."* [The word *vayyetzer* ("and God formed")] is spelled with two letters. The Holy One of Blessing created humans with two impulses, one good and the other evil. Today, there are certain ones calling themselves humans who are attempting to breathe life into the dead, and breathe into extinct species, in a false resurrection of sorts. Taking this one step further, referencing the image in Daniel where there were strange mixtures that would not amalgamate, these ones are mixing biological material with machine. What would this mixture be? Human, machine, robot, humanoid, or habitation for demons? Would these monstrosities have souls? Certainly not! Only pure humans made, formed and created by God.

Another foundation of the Bible is that man was created *"in the image of God"*. The essential meaning of *"the image"* is complete freedom. This means that man must have free-will. If there is no free-will, there would be no context for the Bible.

'*Like God.*' Just as God is gracious and merciful, so too, you should be gracious and merciful.

Here is one last thought that we should reason with together. Could it be possible that only Adam was created in the image of God, to the exclusion of everyone else? Is it possible that Adam was created in the image of God, while the rest of humanity is merely a copy of a copy? The danger with accepting this thought is that one could make reproduction after reproduction. As most of you know, subsequent reproductions are typically not of as high quality as the first copy. Another snare is that this technology is being used to reproduce these biohybrids en masse.

The bottom line is to stand firm, being a pure human, while acknowledging the precious human nuggets around you. It is with this appreciation you are praising the Creator and His handiwork, while bestowing the aroma of your tender, grateful heart to all in your surrounds- whether they be family, friend, acquaintance, or just fellow human.

Faith Lesson: Lord, I know that I have probably never viewed my fellow man as created in Your Divine Image. I am going to ponder what this means and choose (name someone)_____, giving Your Name praise for these ways You created this person in Your Divine Image. (You know how to count your blessings, now count the ways this person is created in the Divine Image. You can think about attributes, characteristics, maybe even some physical traits, understanding that God has no physical body.)

Stretching Out Your Hand

Stretching out your hand to another is a powerful interaction. You may think of it as a simple expression, but it is representative of the power of prayer, the miraculous, signs and wonders, healing, blessing, deliverance, and judgment. This gesture joins two humans in unity as they become vessels between heaven and earth. It is humbling as a human to understand with all certainty that through faith and your outstretched hand you have mastery over the elements,

At times we mere humans get angry at each other; God also get angry. When we are striving to emulate the character of our Savior and we are tempted to lash out with our tongues, we might consider how He deals with His anger. *His anger does not turn away, And His hand is still stretched out. Even when every one of them is godless and an evildoer, And every mouth is speaking foolishness. Despite this... His hand is still stretched out.* Isaiah 9:17

God does not turn away; therefore, I should not turn away from my fellow humans. *His hand is still stretched out*; therefore, my hand should still be stretched out to my fellow humans, offering them whatever assistance I can provide.

When we examine the Ten Commandments in the Holy Writ, we see that the first tablet deals primarily with our interaction with God. Who should be the Supreme Authority in our life. Curiously, the first tablet ends with the commandment to *Honor your father and mother, that you might live long in the land.* God is transitioning us from a relationship with Him to our parents, who are a shadow of Him, and this commandment comes with a blessing. The second tablet provides us with the broad strokes of interacting with one another, *You shall not*, because we obviously need instruction in the area.

I am sure that most of you can agree we live in an alien

world. The Psalmist pleads with God, *Stretch forth Your hand from on high; Rescue me and deliver me out of great waters, Out of the hand of aliens.* Psalm 144:7

Though we only abide on high in the Holy Spirit. we can stretch forth our hand to our fellow humans. rescuing and delivering them from disastrous floods in their life or when they fall prey to sinister aliens.

When you encounter those disobedient and obstinate people who make you feel like you want to pull your hair out, we commit this precious verse into out heart and mind: *But as for Israel He says, "All the day long I have stretched out My hands to a disobedient and obstinate people."* Romans 10:21. Yes, my dear friends, we stretch out hands to them. It does not necessarily mean your physical hand. In the Hebrew, the concept of stretching out one's hand can be interpreted as your personal prayer for those disobedient and obstinate humans. *For we like sheep have all gone astray, each one has turned to his own way.* Isaiah 53:6

At times you are on the solitary path of your faith walk. You find yourself upside down with no place to turn, and still more frustrating--with no answers. This is when humans-created in the Divine Image say *I lift up my eyes to the hills. From where does my help come? My help comes from the LORD, the Maker of heaven and earth.* Psalm 121:1

Since our heart is pleading with God to stretch forth His hand to us in our moment of need, it might surprise us when it takes a form other than what we expect. Such is the following case:

Then I looked, and behold, a hand was extended to me; and lo, a scroll was in it. Ezekiel 2:9

Yes! The Lord can stretch forth His mighty hand and provide you a scroll which, of course, is the ancient Bible.

You and I must be about our Father-in-Heaven's business. What is that, you might inquire? Extending your hand. *While You extend Your hand to heal, and signs and wonders take place through the name of Your holy servant Jesus.* Acts 4:30

Each of us is blessed to live in this perilous season. You were created for this moment in history. You have been equipped for this time. Go forth in faith and encouragement.

For the Lord of hosts has planned, and who can frustrate it? And as for His stretched-out hand, who can turn it back? Isaiah 14:27

As we travel through this Wasteland of Wickedness, let us put our small hand into His out-stretched hand and everything will be as it should.

Faith Lesson: Today I will touch the life of another human. I will personally stretch out my hand. I will make strides to have more human relationships than virtual ones.

Panim v Panim, Face-to-Face

Panim means front or face and is a multi-faceted word. Just as in those days, we need to be comfortable with the boldness

to stand face-to-face before our Father in heaven and His Son, Jesus Christ. In one sense we cannot in our finite bodies stand alone, face-to-face before God, and yet other humans have experienced the ecstasy of doing so.

> I recall a time in the 1990's after a 40-day fast called by the Lord. I received a 3-day time of blessing where I experienced a tiny fragment of the glory of God. I could only absorb and remember it in fragments.
>
> To absorb God's glory in its entirety I would not have survived in this earthly body. What is the glory of God like? I will humbly strive for the words. Majesty. Awe. Breath. Light. Warmth. Color. Intensity. Frequency. River of Energy. Love. Musical. Thundering. Structured. All powerful.
>
> I beseeched the Lord to cease this blessing. This is because the glory of God was too much for my finite body to receive the intensity at which it came. However, I was able to scratch three prophetic messages in my Bible, and all have come to pass. No doubt, you have each had your own intense time where you met God panim-v-panim, face-to-face.

Consider:

And Jacob called the name of the place Peniel: 'for I have seen God face to face, and my life is preserved.' Genesis 32:29-31

When one meets Him face-to-face it is a powerful encounter and it will change your life. When I was in my early twenties my family went camping at Yosemite. We set up the tent and I felt weary beyond measure. I asked my husband to take our two young daughters for a walk to the river. I laid down and closed my eyes. In an instant, I was before Jesus Christ in His heavenly domain. I can never forget that moment. His eyes were full of compassion and love. I saw the brilliance of His illuminated countenance. I experienced an encompassing warmth and peace. Three times I pleaded with Him to stay but each time He gently told me that I must return for I had an important job to accomplish. After the third time, I found myself in a long, dark tunnel which seemed an eternity although I doubt it was more than moments. My breath was restored, and my blood began coursing through my veins. I knew I had seen Jesus face-to-face. I knew without doubt that this was holy ground, a sacred encounter, and that I would recall it all my days. Just as with biblical personages, I was afraid, for in my youth, I never knew anyone that had experienced a supernatural encounter such as this. Our family left the place in haste at my urging, not from terror, but in holy awe of the majesty I had just beheld.

In Jacob's case, his life was preserved. Possibly my life was preserved in my supernatural encounter, nevertheless, this face-to-face encounter made an indelible impression on my life, in fact, it changed my life. Looking back on this time so many years ago, I see that my encounter with my Savior was but one steppingstone on my journey of supernatural experiences, preparing me for these days and this season. Would I have been able to finish the race without this encounter? I do not know. Jesus must have felt it important for us to have that majestic conversation.

And then there is Moses:

And there hath not arisen a prophet since in Israel like unto Moses, whom the LORD knew face to face. Deuteronomy 34:8-10

Moses would be used as an instrument of God for blessing and judgment. He would speak the Word that God Himself uttered and would convey it to the people. The Spirit of Prophecy is Jesus Christ. As we know from the biblical account, humans have their own take, even jealousy, when someone they know has a panim v panim, face-to-face encounter. It is something that a Hebrew or Christian longs for, and yet is mingled with fear, to stand before the Holy One alone. In one's heart of hearts, the only preparation necessary is a deep longing in your heart:

Draw me, we will run after thee: the king hath brought me into his chambers: we will be glad and rejoice in thee, we will remember thy love more than wine: the upright love thee. Song of Songs 1:4

Ezekiel the prophet also had a face-to-face experience:

...and I will bring you into the wilderness of the peoples, and there will I plead with you face to face. Ezekiel 20:33-35

An encounter with the Divine is orchestrated by the Master with purpose. In Ezekiel's case, He was informing him that He was going to take the prophet into the wilderness of peoples. Those are very interesting words to ponder, the wilderness of peoples. One does not usually think about community being a wilderness. In our imagination, the world wilderness means a hostile environment, survival, land little to no people. But in retrospect, community has its challenges that can be likened to a wilderness. One cannot easily have the intimate face-to-face fellowship with God in a crowd. We must remember that God was desiring this close face time as we would call it today when the community was in Exile. We have already entered, what I believe will be the final exile, when the people of God, will be persecuted unto death for following the King of Kings. God will be desiring sweet fellowship with us individually and as community pleading that we press onward into our respective callings until we each cross the finish line our race.

I have fought the good fight, I have finished the race, I have kept the faith. Now there is in store for me the crown of righteousness, which the Lord, the righteous Judge, will award to me on that day—and not only to me, but also to all who have longed for his appearing. 2 Timothy 4:7-8

Bride of Christ, long for your Beloved with all your heart. Seek a face-to-face encounter with your Father in Heaven and His Son Jesus Christ. He will respond to your petition.

Faith Lesson: This is the day I begin to request that God

Himself arranges extraordinary face-to-face encounters with Him and with people He arranges to come into my life.

Loving Acts of Kindness

The character trait of lovingkindness is sadly fading from the Christian life. In the life of the Hebrew, it is a most treasured and valuable attribute. The word in the Hebrew is *chesed* which translated means a covenant loyalty, although there is no precise English match. Although there is no direct English rendering of *chesed*, translators have made a feeble attempt saying that it is a deeply personal expression of love. It is a love entangled in relationship loyalty… a great loving devotion. It is not akin to, "I love pizza."

In this war against humanity each one of us needs to emulate the personality of Jesus Christ to preserve any vestige of being a human created in the Divine Image of God. With outstretched hands we need to grasp the hem of His garment and practice His lovingkindness with all humility.

Lovingkindness can describe one person's actions toward another, though it is most often used to describe the character of the Lord. Many places in Scripture speak of the lovingkindness of the Lord. Lovingkindness is part of Who God is; He delights in showing lovingkindness, and we praise Him for it. God's lovingkindness is abundant, great in extent, everlasting, full of goodness, steadfast, and knows no bounds.

Given that we rarely peer into the grandeur of God's

lovingkindness, let us take a few moments to pause ever briefly and write some of these comforting verses in our mind, heart and strength. I am sure you will agree with me that these unfold in our faith walk as a beautiful, blossoming rose. The emphasis on certain aspects of the Psalm on lovingkindness is mine:

Wondrously show *Your lovingkindness*. Psalm 17:7

O continue *Your lovingkindness to those who know You.* Psalm 36:10

*Because Your lovingkindness is **better than life**, My lips will praise You.* Psalm 63:3

Answer me*, O Lord, for Your lovingkindness is good*. Psalm 69:16

*Who is wise? ... **And consider** the lovingkindnesses of the Lord*. Psalm 107:43

I will betroth you to Me forever*; Yes, I will betroth you to Me in righteousness and in justice,*

In lovingkindness and in compassion. Hosea 2:19

*Your lovingkindness and Your truth **will continually preserve me***. Psalm 40:11

Revive me *according to Your lovingkindness*. Psalm 119:88

*O may Your lovingkindness **comfort me**.* Psalm 119:76

***Be gracious to me**, O God, according to Your lovingkindness.* Psalm 51:1

***Hear my voice** according to Your lovingkindness.* Psalm 119:149

*For Your lovingkindness **is before my eyes**.* Psalm 26:3

***We have thought** on Your lovingkindness, O God.* Psalm 48:9

***The Lord will command** His lovingkindness in the daytime.* Psalm 42:7-8

***Who crowns you with** lovingkindness and compassion.* Psalm 103:4

***But I will not break off** My lovingkindness from him.* Psalm 89:33

***Remember, O Lord**, Your compassion and Your lovingkindnesses.* Psalm 25:6

***Let me hear** Your lovingkindness in the morning.* Psalm 143:8

***And give thanks to Your name** for Your lovingkindness and Your truth.* Psalm 138:2

***I have not concealed** Your lovingkindness and Your truth from the great congregation.* Psalm 40:10

Shifting Sands of Reality

On a still summer night the man and woman of faith looks upwards to the Milky Way, beholding millions of crystal-clear stars against a jet-black expanse of the cosmos. Once a person becomes a person of faith, one then must wrestle the spiritual challenges of our day. We face existential annihilation of all life upon the face of the earth. The Divine Author, through His prophets and scribes, described these times. At the significant moment of acceptance of salvation, a person is translated to the sojourn of faith that will continue through his or her whole life.

> I will share how in mere seconds your reality can change. Two years ago, my reality was challenged when I moved from the Pacific Northwest where I was very much satisfied with my skills to live no matter what came my way to the austere plains of North Dakota. I was a renter and with one phone call from my landlord my life became a swirl of boxes, packing, and searching for a home during a time when prices rose by the minute. A widow alone was prey to those who would seek extortion. Having worked for FEMA, in days bygone, price gouging would not be tolerated. But alas, along with many other things those days are long gone. The only home I could find was a period home which I love but it needed a lot of fixing up. I came to understand that there are few contractors, a pecking order, Nazi rule, harsh climate, and I am

forced to live dependent upon a system that I have rarely ever lived in. My new reality is one where my Golden Retriever and I are learning what it means to live in rural America that is under judgment. Ever present, no matter the challenges of this new life that is being forged out from without and within, is my Father in heaven and my Lord Jesus Christ.

The challenge of the End of Days are the shifting sands of reality. We recall and are inspired with great joy by the day of our salvation and the fleeting glimpses of our Holy Father veiled behind the cosmic backdrop. As we gaze upon the intricacies of the heavens, we can become tormented as our Father appears to us to hide His face in the cosmic display. We find evidence of this through the Holy Writ, such as in the Book of Esther.

God does speak to us through His works:

The heavens declare the glory of God, the firmament showeth His handiwork. Psalm 19:2

Do the heavens sing the glory of the Creator without troubling themselves to find out whether you or anyone is listening to this great symphony? Does this divine handiwork of the starry cosmos singing their songs of creation have a particular interest in you? Are they listening? Do these distant stars, galaxies, and nebulae that we associate with heaven care about your earthly struggles?

It is plain to see that if the song of the heavens were written exclusively for man, then he or she would have no need for unfolding revelational encounters with God.

God, in His infinite wisdom, has arranged an apocalyptic covenantal meeting with mankind. Is this a personal message to me or is it merely a declaration and signature of the works of God?

We desire an intimate relationship with our Creator, our Father in heaven, but we become disenchanted with cosmic revelation, thus spending a great deal of time in despair.

This is my quandary and possibly yours. As I gaze upwards into starlit heavens, I am faced with a cosmic confrontation and then violently slammed into a rock of paradox. I can only speak for myself, but I see the Creator as a delicate unfolding and aromatic rose; a powerfully turbulent sea; the delightful melodies of hummingbird wings and buzzing of bees as they happily collect their provision from the hands of the Creator. All of these gifts of God's handiwork comfort me in my daily trials affirming that my heavenly Father is close by my side, caring about my every hair. He tenderly beckons me to engage with Him in dynamic, prayerful conversation with interludes of ecstatic song breaking forth. It is in that moment of intimacy where I discover that illumination of God has retreated behind a veiled cloud. It "feels" like God is distant and unapproachable. *My cry mingles with the pleading of the maiden* in Song of Songs 6:1:

Where is thy beloved gone, O thou fairest among women? Where is thy beloved turned aside, that we may seek him with thee?

As my intense yearning for God stretches forth towards heavenly heights, my reality abruptly shifts to the Throne Room of majesty:

I saw [see] also the LORD sitting upon a throne, high and lifted up, and his train filled the temple. Above it stood the seraphims... And one cried unto another, and said, Holy, holy, holy, is the LORD of hosts: the whole earth is full of his glory. Isaiah 6:1-3

My Lord, is the Lord of Hosts, whose majestic train fills the celestial Temple, also resides in every infinitesimal particle of creation, my beating heart, all creatures great and small, extending to galaxies I cannot see, nor fathom.

There is a tantalizing dichotomy with God's involvement with creation. He is above and remote and yet intimate and personal. He is God supreme over all creation issuing His laws of nature and forming all behavior and function. He is above time and outside of time. When I approach God on His throne as Master or Creator, He is shrouded in the clouds of mystery. I am sure you have experienced this phenomenon when you are searching for God but He is hidden.

It is the glory of God to conceal a thing, but the honor of kings is to search out a matter. Proverbs 25:2

You can see this played out in the Book of Esther where God is not mentioned but is cleverly disguised in the word King or king. Only the man or woman in the covenant of faith can pierce the dense obfuscation to personally meet with God and feel His presence, moment by moment.

You will discover yourself as one of three types of people. There is the person who lives within the world of supernatural experiences, a framework for the cosmic tapestry. He or she sees the name of God, Elohim, as the King of Heaven and Creation. This person's relationship focus is rooted upwards towards the heavens. Their calling is often prophetic with songs of praise on their lips.

Another type of person is the person of covenantal faith who longs for a deep personal and intimate relationship with God but whose eyes are modestly cast downwards. When this person looks up into the heavenly heights, he or she becomes engulfed and lost in the cosmic drama. This person emulates God when He came to earth to dwell with man. He or she seeks God on a different plain. The engagements occur like they did at Mt. Sinai in the wilderness when the Ten Commandments were given. It is the place where the finite "I" meets the "Infinite." This person's calling often is to bring a little bit of heaven down to earth to encourage and inspire others.

The communal relationship between God and man is symbolized by the name of God YHVH.

In 1 Kings 7:50, we find the word Penimi which means the innermost, as in "innermost door" leading to the Holy of Holies. It is derived from PANIM (face). Moshe knew his

Abba YHWH panim al panim (face to face), meaning Moshe had an intimate relationship with the Father. Here these innermost doors lead to the intimate place of Abba YHWH on earth.

This is why you might die if you are not a high priest or you are and enter the shrine at the wrong time, in the wrong way, and so on. Then "face to face" becomes LITERAL and so would result in your death. Andrew Gabriel Roth

The third type of person is one who can look up into the expanse of the heavens living in the supernatural and the prophetic world. They do not get lost in the cosmos. They are able to balance the life of the covenantal person of faith filled with longing, all the while receiving depths of ongoing revelation.

No matter which type of people you are we are all struggling with our new reality. The Scriptures talk of pits and snares that might be found along our path. One of those is the Metaverse. A dimension that you can enter that is devoid of God. You can live out your every fantasy, supposedly with no consequences. But what is the real cost of this new dimension? No relationship with your Creator or other humans. You sit in a chair, never moving, rarely eating and what you do eat is food designed to kill, no fresh air kissing your cheeks, eternity in a dark matrix never again seeing the Light.

Another snare is that the techno-sorcerers have discovered the key to merge or at the very least overlap dimensions, such as your physical reality, the digital realm, the supernatural realm, and other parallel dimensions and universes. The next pandemic will be the Hemorrhaging of Networks. People will have the physical symptoms of a hemorrhagic pathogen weapon and the cyber realm will also have this, simultaneously. When the World Economic Forum showed us the COVID spike infographic with 200 nodes of changes to the world they truly were showing us the new world landscape. Out of the ashes of the hemorrhagic meltdown to the body and cyber world which includes our infrastructure will be the Anti-Christ System. Most of us are siloed into thinking something is physical or supernatural or digital. This will cross the dimensions. And you all thought Y2K was nothing. In reality, it changed everything. It was about interoperability and inter-dimensionality. Until Y2K individual computers did not communicate; now all computers worldwide can talk to each other. It's a modern technological Tower of Babel.

Faith Lesson: Lord, please reveal to me other dimensions of the reality which impacts my life. Help me to be unafraid but with quiet trust to know that You will do whatever within me and without that I might be reined into the holy vessel for Your use and purpose.

Facing the Existential Threat of Being Human in Solitude

No matter your faith, during disaster, most of us think about networking with like-minded people whether it be listening to an inspiring and guiding message, prayer or meditation, fellowship, or sharing a meal together. What we rarely consider is that oftentimes we must go through a season of solitude in our faith walk. The reality of the matter is that due to diverse causations, earth is undergoing a massive depopulation extinction event. We can do some things about some of the situations, and others are completely out of our hands, such as the cyclical Extinction Level Event (ELE). This has only happened five times upon planet earth, and as of 2020, we have entered the sixth ELE. What this means practically, is that many of us have experienced a decrease in our family and support networks, as people die off. I know that the topic of death is unpleasant for all of us. I speak from personal experience because seven years ago my husband was killed in a traffic accident. Since that fateful day, I have lived alone with God and my Golden Retriever as my solace. Through your faith, at some point you will see a beautiful tapestry that God is weaving in your life, born out of the pain and suffering that you undergo.

> On November 15, 2016 I did a Thanksgiving Special for my Flock of Goats with Shepherdess Celeste on Gratitude and Thankfulness. David was clanking around the kitchen getting his dinner out of the oven but for some strange reason he was noisy that night. I ended my program with a challenge, "Whatever happens to you this week say to yourself, 'This too is for the good.'" I never dreamed that in less than 72

hours I would become a widow. There are widows with a support system and there are widows who have no support. I was to learn many lessons in the days to come. But I knew from the moment the County Sherriff uttered the words, "Your husband has been killed," that everything was in God's hands.

To days before, on November 13th, David and I hopped into the pickup to visit our favorite fishing hole to catch inland salmon. It was a secluded location with a sizeable stream the salmon would travel through on their way to spawn. There was a nice grassy field where our old Golden Retriever Moshe would frolic, and we always had a nice picnic lunch beholding the changing of the leaves and that crisp fall air. On the way to and fro, I would read aloud to David, Life Together, a book on Christian Community by Dietrich Bonhoffer. It is a short book on community, days with others, days alone, ministry, confession, and communion. That November we concluded The Day with Others and I put the book aside to clean the buckets of fish and then can them for later use. The next Thursday morning David was killed.

I went into deep grief and did not return to the book for many months. As I began to awaken from my grief, and as the slow process of allowing Jesus to be my husband unfolded, I began to seek out the path that

David and I traveled, in an effort to recapture those precious moments together and to keep his memory from fading from my life.

This is when I picked up the book again and I was shocked to discover that I was at the next chapter, The Day Alone. God had known the date of David's death from before the foundation of the world. He was molding me for my new life as a widow. God's wisdom in the days following David's death comforted me and strengthened me.

It is my prayer that these timeless lessons will encourage you as well. You may not experience a death of someone close, although we all more than likely will, but it could just be one of the seasons of your life. As Jesus would say, "For those who have ears, hear".

Solitude and Community

I will be quoting from Dietrich Bonhoeffer's book, Life Together, because having walked the walk I know its significance.

"Many people seek fellowship because they are afraid to be alone. Because they cannot stand the loneliness, they are driven to seek the company of other people. There are Christians, too, who cannot endure being alone, who have had some bad experiences with themselves, who hope they will gain some help in association with others. They are generally disappointed. Then they blame the fellowship for what is really their own fault. The Christian community is not a spiritual sanatorium. The person who comes into a fellowship because he is running away from himself is misusing it for the sake of a diversion." Dietrich Bonhoeffer, *Life Together*

Solitude and Silence

"Let him who cannot be alone beware of community. He will only do harm to himself and the community. Alone you stood before God when He called you, alone you had to answer that call, alone you had to struggle and pray, and alone you will die and give account to God."

The reverse is also true, "Let him who is not in community beware of being alone. Into community you were called, the call was not for you to be alone, in community you were called to bear your cross, you struggle, you pray. You are not alone, even in death, and on the Last Day you will be only one member of a great congregation of Jesus Christ. If you scorn the fellowship of the brethren, you reject the call of Jesus Christ, and your solitude can only be hurtful to you." Dietrich Bonhoeffer, Life Together

When your day of solitude arrives, it is helpful to remember that the person of faith resides in the abode of a great cloud of witnesses. You merely appear as though you are alone. It is then that the reality of the verse stirs in your soul,

You will have power, together with all the saints, to comprehend the length and width and height and depth of the love of Christ, and to know this love that surpasses knowledge, that you may be filled with all the fullness of God. Ephesians 3:18

This is love and depth at the Quantum level. A place of being with limitless potential where there truly is no barrier of death. This is what Jesus Christ achieved for us by His crucifixion and Resurrection.

"The mark of solitude is silence, as speech is the mark of community."

"Silence does not mean dumbness." Dietrich Bonhoeffer, Life Together

Modern man does not know what to do with silence. In gentler days, people considered silence golden. Today, we chatter away whether it be in person, or on our cell phones, or we text away. We feel compelled to reach out. In some ways our society has fabricated this dependency, but even space weather (energetic particles, cosmic rays and winds from the sun, etc. that influence human behavior) conspires to trigger within our inner core the desire to reach out.

One day about a decade ago, the phone began ringing at eight in the morning. The person on the other end quite frankly admitted that she did not know why she called, she felt compelled to call. We talked for some time and then went our respective ways. No sooner had I hung up the phone than another person called in the same manner. This same pattern repeated for twelve hours. For some reason space weather had triggered a subconscious, innate, feeling to reach out to another human. Since that time, I have noticed the pattern revisiting, during certain space weather events.

"Silence is nothing more than waiting for God's Word." Dietrich Bonhoeffer, Life Together

Possibly this is why we are uncomfortable with silence and solitude. We struggle in an atmosphere of silence awaiting words from our Father in heaven. We allow other voices to easily crowd into our mind. Imagine the frustration of God when He wants a word with us, and our line is always busy. Perish the thought.

There is a time to keep silent, and a time to speak.
Ecclesiastes 3:7

Meditation

"The period of personal mediation is to be devoted to the Scriptures, private prayer, and intercession. It has no other purpose. The time of meditation does not let us down into the void and abyss of loneliness; it lets us be alone with the Word and a direct encounter with God." Dietrich Bonhoeffer, Life Together

Growing up in the sixties, I suppose, gave me an unfavorable impression of meditation. I must break away from my experience and ponder the verses that the Holy Spirit has revealed to me for this day. It can be quantum entanglement at a Divine level. A synergy where verses combine and flow with prayer bursting forth in joyous praise, which in turn leads to intercession for others, as well as for my own life. What person, when visiting a King, would not first contemplate his words and what he stands for and then praise and shower him glory and honor? Upon showing your reverence, one could timidly approach the King with your requests and petitions. Meditation is a holy moment with your King of awe and majesty.

Prayer

Prayer is nothing else but the willingness and readiness to receive the appropriate Word. In essence, we are emptying ourselves, unyoking, detaching from our concerns and the world--to embrace with all enthusiasm the Word which penetrates our heart and speaks to our direct situations and concerns.

Back in the 90's, I had a Chinese teacher stay in my home for a year. He had come to America with eight colleagues. One female teacher was given her position and her host home not far from mine, in Microsoft country. Unfortunately, her host family had only taken her in to be a house sitter and dog watcher for their two very large dogs. Here was Mrs. Chen, new to America, speaking a little broken English, no vehicle, no real understanding of American culture, left on her own as her host family left on a cruise. Lao Dong and I would go pick her up on weekends and she would come to my home. We would pray simple and direct prayers. I can tell you the truth. Each one of those prayers went from our lips to God's ears and were answered with hypersonic speed. Never in all my days before then or afterward have my prayers been answered so quickly. Consequently, Mrs. Chen and Lao Dong became believers in Jesus Christ as their personal Savior. After a year they returned to their homeland, but I oftentimes ponder the season where my prayers were answered so expeditiously, as well as what their life is like in the heart of China as followers of Jesus.

In our alone prayers we have the freedom to communicate with God in the language we prefer, whether that be praises, tongues, liturgy, or spontaneous prayer, and even the prayer that goes forth for which we have no words and yet we lift them up.

Intercession

Community prayer "is the beating heart of all Christian life in unison" …

"I can no longer condemn or hate a brother or sister for whom I pray, no matter how much trouble he causes me. His face, that hitherto may have been strange and intolerable to me, is transformed in intercession into the countenance of a brother or sister for whom Christ died, the face of a sinner."

"Intercession means no more than to bring our brother into the presence of God, to see him under the cross of Jesus as a poor human being and sinner in need of grace." Dietrich Bonhoeffer, *Life Together*

> I am not proud of the following but it does have a happy ending and I learned a valuable lesson. I was cleaning my home one day when the Holy Spirit said to call Rosanne. Her daughter was in youth group with mine, but we were not really in the same circle. Her husband was on the Elder Board, and they were generational Free Methodists. Honestly, I did not know what to say to her and so I went on cleaning my house. Next day was a repeat, I quenched the call of the Holy Spirit which vexes me to this day. On the third day, repeat, but this time I responded, I will call. I do not know what to say, I may have egg on my face, but I will be obedient. And so, I called. Rosanne had been in a terrible ordeal. It is not my story to share and so I will not divulge the details. The long and short of it was that she was going through a horrendous ordeal alone. She could not talk with her husband, nor her family, nor anyone at church. She wept bitterly and I vowed to stand by her side until the Lord raised her from this dark valley. It took two years of continual intercession before the Lord. Then another young person in the youth group had troubles

and I was involved in her deliverance. I arrived at the evening church service to witness Rosanne tenderly reaching out to Sharon, the mother of the young person in trouble. I raised my prayers of thanksgiving to my Lord with a heart of overwhelming joy because the Lord had healed Rosanne's heart and the situation was resolved, and she was now gently reaching out to another traumatized mother. Faith in action. Intercession in action.

In a day when instant gratification and the deification of self is highly prized, the person of faith can offer no better gift than to intercede on behalf of another human. It is humbling to consider that in this one simple act of intercession your plea on behalf of another can be lifted up to the heavens, heard, and answered. Intercession has a ripple effect, for not only does our intercession reach the heavenlies, but it also wars against all the enemies of our soul who desire us to get bogged down in the quagmire of self and the flesh. Intercession is then a victory for mankind created in the Divine Image of God.

The Test of Ministry

"Every day brings the Christian many hours on which he will be alone in an unchristian environment. These are the times of testing."

"Has fellowship served to make the individual free, strong, and mature, or has it made him weak and dependent? Has it taken him by the hand for a while in order that he may learn again to walk by himself, or has it made him uneasy and unsure?"

"When tested, did your solitary devotions lead you to the unreal, where you awake in terror when the week begins? Were you transported to spiritual ecstasy that vanishes when you return to your everyday life?"

"Blessed is he who is alone in the strength of the fellowship and blessed is he who keeps the fellowship in the strength of aloneness." Dietrich Bonhoeffer, Life Together

> Three years after David's death, I awoke on a beautiful Montana morning, on July first. As was my custom, I listened to what the Lord would have for me. The words of the Holy Spirit were as follows, "Begin an online community and go in front of the camera." I had been a published photojournalist since I was in Junior High School. National Geographic asked if I could do photography for an expedition. My first knee-jerk reaction was, I do excellent work behind the lens of a camera, but I am not in front of camera material. This was to be my test, where the rubber meets the road in my faith walk.
>
> One thing I am is obedient, whatever the cost. So, I swallowed my "feelings" and did as the Lord instructed. The first three months were agonizing. I felt like my throat was being strangled, my knees

quaked, my palms sweated, and my stomach was in knots. It was quite miserable, but I persevered. Suddenly! I will never forget the day, three months later, I discovered that I enjoyed this new journey the Lord was leading me on. As for the community, I learned what it means real-time to be in leadership. I did not ask for it, nor was it something I desired, but it

was the Lord's instruction. Being the leader of a community was a learning experience. In these days communities ebb and flow. As a leader, one pours their heart and soul into this calling. I learned of things that I had never experienced before, such as betrayal, intrigue and just how powerful the tongue is-- for good or for evil.

Then it suddenly dawned on me, as if the clouds of heaven parted, and I could see the Light on why the Lord had taken David. I had always been a very strong woman of faith. The one thing that had never occurred to me is that I had never been truly broken.

In the early days of David's death, I got on the floor and beseeched God to take me to join David in the grave, even though I knew David was with Jesus in heaven, though his bones lay in the dust awaiting the resurrection. I did not want to live any longer. I knew distinctly that his was not my calling, but I asked, borderline demanded (which I never advise), Him to call me home. Maybe you have felt that way a time or two?

In retrospect, Jesus healed my broken heart and broken body-- because He had a plan for my life. He also has a plan for your life. For me, His plan was to put me on the Global Stage. To minister to many of you. To accomplish this task, I needed to be totally broken and healed. I could not minister to your hurts from an academic or intellectual perspective. I needed to feel your pain, know your struggles. Praise Jesus!

Furthermore, I was no longer alone. I am blessed that each of you is the silver lining in this dark drama. You have become fellow workers in the harvest field, confidants, and dear friends. My Father in heaven and His Son Jesus accomplished this miracle.

What is the purpose of a season of aloneness and solitude? It is that place, where undistracted, you commune with God, clearly hear His Word, receive comfort, and listen carefully to the plans that He has laid out for your life. You will then receive this cascade of living water of blessings. Powerful waters of strength, courage, bravery, boldness, unwavering in your path...not in your own strength, but in His strength.

Once your season of solitude has concluded, you are restored to the community for service. Each of us will have our seasons of solitude but they will not sink us into the depths of despair. Rather, we will learn to secretly long for and enjoy those quiet moments where we can abandon the world and its cares to listen to timeless lessons from our Abba Father.

We have arrived at the place where the dialogue between the man of faith and the man of culture comes to an end. Modern man has transformed the language of faith into the vulgar cultural vernacular, consequently, we find ourselves lonely, forsaken, misunderstood, and ridiculed by the devotees of the new perverted religion of man.

The moment of estrangement strikes. My dear friends, your ordeal as the person of faith begins, and you are on the brink of being compelled to withdraw from society-at-large. Fear not! For just as the Ancient of Days withdraws or hides His face at times when we are in the Divine Image of God so must we. Just as with Moses and Jesus, you retreat to your solitary oasis fortress. Your abode of loneliness, and yet we are not alone. Yes, the loneliness of our generation is distinct in the entirety of history. We find ourselves lonely by voluntarily withdrawing from Godless virtual constructs and the parallel dimensions with their social isolation and social distancing.

My brethren in the faith, this is your destiny. You find yourself within the historical context of the man and woman who keep a rendezvous with your eternity. It will be each of you, who in spite of everything, will continue tenaciously to bring the message of faith, the Good News of Jesus Christ, to this godless world.

May God bless you, each one. May your fruit for the Kingdom be abundant! Be blessed.

CHAPTER 11

He Is Faithful To Forgive: Repercussions Of The Covid Shots

Dr. Sherri Tenpenny

In 1 John 1:9 we read: "If we confess our sins, He is faithful and just to forgive us our sins, and to cleanse us from all unrighteousness."

In Ed Dowd's book, "Cause Unknown," (which everyone should own and share), he has documented, in hard numbers, the exponential increase in sudden deaths and disability claims. He is soon to release the next round of irrefutable numbers: the number of people now experiencing chronic ill-health due to the jabs. In a recent interview, Ed said on his Twitter feed:

We have chronicled the dead, the disabled & now the chronically sick. The 'vaccines' are devastating our economy. Next week we will tie all this together and put an annual $

Dollar figure on this damage and the tragedy.

What's actually causing all this carnage?

We need to tell the truth about this question: We don't know what's in those shots. While there are things we DO know, there are dozens or more nefarious chemicals etc. we DON'T know or have yet to be identified.

We debate back and forth:

It's the mRNA – no it's not.

It's the spike proteins – no it's not.

It's ONLY the graphene oxide – no, graphene oxide isn't even in the shots.

Our DNA is irreversibly changed or damaged by the spike protein (by direct insertion) and/or the mRNA (by transfection) – no, there's no proof (and the papers that discuss it are not believed.)

It's the hydrogel – it's the EMF/5G – it's the lipid nanoparticles – It's the PEG and a ton of unknown, yet-to-be-released chemicals – it's nanotechnology – now, it's the opsins.

I personally think it's ALL OF IT – at different times, in different combinations, in different lot numbers. Actually, this database proves it.

Spiritual Importance

Why did people get the shots?

FEAR (mostly).

Convenience (I want to travel, etc.).

Coercion (I have to keep my job, etc.).

Virtue signaling (It was the RIGHT thing to do - I protected YOU).

Other - the catch-all of reasons/excuses to justify your choice.

From the very beginning, I was troubled and completely perplexed as to why Christians would get this shot. Instead of turning to God, taking their FEAR to Him in prayer, asking Him to remove the demon, the spirit of FEAR, from their body/mind/soul, they chose to be injected with pharmakea's evil, experimental 'medicine' in a vain attempt to remove their fears.

And now that they are realizing this was not such a good idea, they expect the Lord to say, "Oh, it's ok. No worries," giving their CHOICE a wink, a nod, and a pat on the head.

What does the Bible say about defiling the temple?

Here are two verses that are pretty clear:

1 Corinthians 3:16-17 - Do you not know that your body is God's temple and that God's Spirit dwells in you? If anyone destroys God's temple, God will destroy him. For God's temple is holy, and you are that temple.

Romans 12:1-2 - I appeal to you therefore, brothers, by the mercies of God, to present your bodies as a living sacrifice, holy and acceptable to God, which is your spiritual worship. Do not be conformed to this world, but be transformed by the renewal of your mind, that by testing you may discern what is the will of God, what is good and acceptable and perfect.

So, if any Christian messed up and took the shot, bottom line? They sinned. They chose the things of the world. And yes, they violated their Holy temple.

What should a person do, especially if they are a Christian, if s/he chose the shot for reasons #1, 2, 3, 4, or 5 (listed above.)

Repent.

The dictionary definition of repentance is described as:

The act of reviewing one's actions and feeling contrition, sincere regret, or remorse for past wrongs, accompanied by a commitment to take actions that show and prove a change for the better.

In this case, it means admitting you made an unfortunate choice. Admit that you volunteered to roll of up your sleeve and be injected, more than once. Stop blaming your spouse, your parents, your siblings, your adult children, your neighbors, your colleagues, your boss, and anyone else on your list.

Repentance starts with accepting responsibility for your choice. Perhaps you didn't know the consequences in 2021 when the shots first came out, but now you do. Take your decision to the Lord in prayer. Ask for forgiveness.

Stand on today's verse, 1 John 1:9:

If we confess our sins, He is faithful and just to forgive us our sins, and to cleanse us from all unrighteousness.

But also, be aware of these two verses that sandwich the verse of ultimate forgiveness:

1 John 1:8 - If we say that we have no sin, we deceive ourselves, and the truth is not in us.

1 John 1:10 - If we say that we have not sinned, we make him a liar, and His word is not in us.

The Bible says >300 times FEAR NOT. If God bothered to repeat Himself that many times, it must be important. And the Enemy knows the power of fear. He has used FEAR to trick those not grounded in faith. The coercion and lies were so great, many of His Children were coerced into violating their Temple.

Consequences?

Are you – or others you know who took the jabs - experiencing life-altering side effects? Are you in need of long term disability payments? Are you suffering from a chronic illness you did not have before the jabs? Stop denying the connections.

Do you have myocarditis, heart disorders, strokes, blood clots, or neurological conditions since the shots?

Are you, or your family members and neighbors, experiencing infertility or miscarriages? Has anyone had a baby die unexpectedly and/or "without cause" during the third trimester, referred to as 'late term fetal demise.' Did the mother take the jab?

What if your genetics have been disrupted? Have you or has anyone you know had a baby recently with birth defects and/or neurological damage?

What if you developed a new, aggressive cancer, often referred to as "turbo cancer" because of how rapidly it occurred and how rapidly it can lead to demise?

What if your cancer was in remission… and now it has aggressively reoccurred?

What if your cardiac condition was completely controlled, but it suddenly out of control?

What if you have a new autoimmune disease that 'came out of nowhere' within weeks to months after a covid booster?

What if after getting the shots you are simply not yourself anymore and no one can figure out what's wrong with you or how to help you?

Or, coincidentally and thankfully, what if you are experiencing no adverse events whatsoever after the jabs?

No matter your personal result, the temple of the Holy Spirit was violated by an experimental bioweapon designed to harm, even kill you.

Now the Good News

The Lord is standing by, with open arms, waiting to forgive you for your choice? He loves you so much perhaps He will talk to you about your healing. Even though "With God all things are possible." Luke 1:37 (ESV), I say 'perhaps' because your physical healing is between you and the Lord and not guaranteed.

However, spiritual healing and forgiveness for all of eternity is ABSOLUTELY guaranteed, if you sincerely repent, go forth, and choose differently. However, if your infirmities are not resolved remember this: (Isaiah 41:10).

FEAR NOT, for I am with you. Do not anxiously look about you, for I am your God. I will strengthen you, surely I will help you. Surely, I will uphold you with My righteous right hand.

A Prayer For You

Dear Father, thank You for meeting me where I am along my journey through this life. Please cast out any residual FEAR that remains in my mind, body, or spirit. Fill me with Your love, Your Glory, and the assurance that You have forgiven the choices I made that were not in the best interest of my relationship with You.

I take responsibility for any sin I have committed that defiled my Temple, the place where Your Holy Spirit dwells. By Your righteousness, I am grateful that I am forgiven.

By faith, I receive Your loving forgiveness that will impact my life, my family, and my world. Grant me the spirit of wisdom. Teach me to ask for Your guidance over every decision I make. Going forward, may I always ask, before I do. I am forever grateful that I can always come home to You. In Jesus' precious name, Amen.

EPILOGUE

This collaboration between several medical professionals, pastors, researchers, and biblical scholars, has been a labor of love motivated by our collective desire that the body of Jesus the Christ be educated with the best information available related to current events. Having the truth emboldens people for action.

Mark Sutherland gave a history of recent events in the United Kingdom and pointed to obvious connections between what is happening in Europe and what we see happening in the United States. Clearly, the globalist planners are adamant about their desire to enslave the entire earth's population. The solution begins by trusting in Jesus for the salvation of your soul. Then, we are adequately equipped to address the crimes being committed in our midst. The weapons of our warfare are mighty for the destruction of the globalist empire.

Carl Teichrib encourages us to recognize the "empire building" that is reemerging from the distant past. The longing by unregenerate man to create an earthly utopia where people become their own gods never left us, even after the destruction and dispersion of the masses living and building together on the plains of Shinar under Nimrod's direction. This drive for *oneness* appears often in the literature of the organizations leading the charge for a global "revolution" of change. Of course, those who would elect themselves to manage this new global community, do not care about freedom, liberty, or self-rule by the people for the people. Freedom as defined by those who fancy themselves our master is really only freedom with the chains, they are forging to keep us within their desired boundaries. Our response? It must be grassroots where each individual Christian becomes engaged with the people of their community, daring to stand firm in their faith and unflinchingly stating that Jesus the Christ is the only way to true freedom for us and our world, for true freedom is freedom from the bondage of sin and death. Without that freedom, every effort of mankind to forge oneness in blissful utopia is doomed. The solution is to educate yourself concerning this world's system, and speak truth in love, standing firm in your faith.

Dr. Lee Merritt exposes the heretofore unknown practices for identifying and treating what are commonly called "viruses;" evaluating the frightening consequences of the recent covid scamdemic, consequences by the way, which are emerging today. What we have witnessed could have easily been avoided by a medical industry focused on truth in treatment. Alas, that was not the focus at all. Rather, the medical industry fell in line as if mesmerized by a Pied Piper, or an

assortment of Pied Pipers known as the World Health

Organization, the Food and Drug Administration, the Center for Disease Control, and the myriad satellite organizations which take their orders and carry them out faithfully.

The solution is taking responsibility for our own health. There are several known actions that will work together to improve health and put up a strong wall against the many toxins and poisons that characterize life today.

Randy Conway walks us through the puzzling maze created by a federal and state bureaucracy that seems to end in dead ends everywhere. History is a wonderful teacher and Randy brings history forward in a way that will surely surprise many and shock some. How is it possible that Americans have become so deaf and blind to what has happened to us?

The solution to the current situation is presented in great detail. He provides a powerful remedy that brings people back to their God-given freedoms. The responsibility is on the reader to follow up on the information that Randy provides.

Dr. Ana Maria Mihalcea shares the truth behind the C19 so-called vaccines. Her research and collaboration with other researchers reveal the alarming reality of the purposeful geo and bioengineering behind the C19 shots. Her solutions are to take responsibility for (1) knowing information about what pharmaceutical companies are creating as vaccines, and (2) take decisive steps to counteract, (3) speak out about what is being done to mankind.

Derek Gilbert brings biblical history and geography to life

through his research and analysis. Middle East geopolitics without a biblical/historical context does not provide any hope of a soon coming solution. To this mix Derek masterfully adds a biblical eschatology build upon solid exegesis to show us that the Christian's Great Hope remains the same – the return of the Lord Jesus Christ to His city, Jerusalem. Until that day occurs, we are to occupy until He comes. Thus, the solution is to keep our minds and hearts focused on the Lord Jesus and His assignment for each of us, while simultaneously staying alert to developments within the world but especially in the Middle East between Israel and her neighbors.

Pastor Caspar McCloud takes readers through a broad and deep rehearsal of past, recent, and current events all aimed at bringing readers up to date on the various and evil machinations of the world's elites and the organizations that have stepped to the forefront of our current war over freedom and liberty.

Expertly weaving Scripture with examples from around the world, Pastor Caspar shows the inconsistencies and outright lies of those who are bent on the evil of depopulation and the destruction of mankind.

His solution points people to the rock-steady truth of the Lord Jesus. We have the true truth that the entire world needs to hear. When we are in tune with what God has for us in these troubling times, He will use us as beacons of light to a world in the grips of fear.

Mike Spaulding reminds us that we are living in the days of chaos but, that is not the end of the story. Regardless of how dark it gets; God will bring victory to His creation.

It is not a matter of holding on but of standing up and speaking out. The solution to our troubling times is to walk in the power of God's Holy Spirit and fear no evil.

Celeste Solum recounts her personal journey in a heart-touching way. The Faith Lessons she learned are shared with readers as a way to encourage and strengthen those who might find themselves on a similar path. Also remember brothers and sisters, you are God's beloved and His lovingkindness is from everlasting to everlasting.

Dr. Sherri Tenpenny offers hope and the ultimate solution – seek the forgiveness that God offers too all. If you made the mistake of taking the jab thinking it would protect you from what the government and media convinced you would likely kill you, then repent and seek God. Admit that you trusted the fables of man more than you did Him. There is still time, don't put it off for another day.

Made in the USA
Columbia, SC
19 October 2023